REASONABLE BELIEF

REASONABLE BELIEF

A Survey of the Christian Faith

A. T. HANSON AND
R. P. C. HANSON

Oxford New York Toronto Melbourne
OXFORD UNIVERSITY PRESS · 1980

Oxford University Press, Walton, Street, Oxford OX2 6DP

OXFORD LONDON GLASGOW NEW YORK TORONTO MELBOURNE WELLINGTON
KUALA LUMPUR SINGAPORE HONG KONG TOKYO DELHI BOMBAY
CALCUTTA MADRAS KARACHI NAIROBI DAR ES SALAAM CAPE TOWN

© *A. T. Hanson and R. P. C. Hanson* 1981

British Library Cataloguing in Publication Data
Hanson, Anthony Tyrell
  Reasonable belief.
  1. Theology, Doctrinal
  I. Title II. Hanson, Richard Patrick Crosland
230 BT77.3 80-40481
ISBN 0-19-213235-0
ISBN 0-19-213238-5 Pbk

Printed in Hong Kong by Sun Fung Printing Co.

Contents

Introduction

This volume is a survey of the Christian faith by two Anglican theologians who have spent most of their lives studying and teaching theology. It is written in the conviction that such a book is needed at the present time and that no other book precisely fills that need. Readers may recall three works written within the last forty years which might be thought to have the same intention as this one, *Doctrines of the Creed* by O. C. Quick (1938, repr. 1949, 1963, 1968), *The Christian Faith*, by C. B. Moss (1943), and *Principles of Christian Theology* by J. Macquarrie (1966). Of these the first was written in a markedly different atmosphere, reflecting different pressures and circumstances, from those of today; the second, marked by a certain glibness and cut-and-dried confidence, can scarcely be called a work of critical theology, popular though it (perhaps unfortunately) is with theological students and clergy; the third, which is still in print and enjoying a wide readership because of its undoubted merits, is a work of systematic theology which therefore has a different aim and treats its subject in a different perspective and proportion from this work.

Our book is not a work of systematic theology. That is to say, it does not articulate first its philosophical assumptions and logically deduce all its theology in the light of this articulation. It does not commit itself to either a philosophy of Being or a Process philosophy or an Existentialist philosophy; instead it treats each part of Christian doctrine historically, starting from the Bible and often describing some part of the history of the particular doctrine in Christian tradition, and attempts ultimately to suggest the most satisfactory way in which the reader can approach and understand the doctrine today. This has been for over a hundred years a characteristically Anglican way of dealing with the subject of Christian doctrine. It has its limitations and is open to the criticism that it is not a thorough or logical way of treating the subject, and it does not easily appeal to those whose theological education has been primarily philosophical rather than historical. But it has the virtue of paying serious attention to the basic documents of Christian faith and tradition; it avoids the temptation of allowing speculation or dogmatic preoccupation to evade the witness of historical fact; and it places each doctrine in a proper historical perspective. At the same time, the authors have tried to avoid the pitfall of credulity or fundamentalism. We have used Scripture as our basic document indeed, but we have tried all through the work to use it only with a conscious and critical awareness of its proper role.

It is perhaps needless to say that this book is written from the standpoint of faith. It is not an objective and scientific account of Christianity as a purely human phenomenon. The audience which it envisages includes all intelligent Christians, clerical and lay, men and women. But the faith professed by the authors is not, as the reader will quickly see, an uncritical faith. It is a faith which, while it recognizes that obedience or commitment which is part of faith, tries to do justice honestly to contemporary scholarship and thought generally, re-examining and reassessing the traditional faith in the light of the intellectual needs and demands of the late twentieth century, as we discern them. We believe that this kind of reassessment is the peculiar task of theology in this age, as a corresponding reassessment has constantly faced theologians in all periods of Christian history.

Though we frequently refer to creeds and other traditional formulae, we have not built this book round any particular creed or confession. We have written about what must appear to any intelligent person to be the main and central doctrines of Christianity, and treated them in that proportion which seemed to us proper for contemporary theology to give them. Thus the Christological portion of the book is by far the largest, and the section devoted to Church, Ministry, and Sacraments may disappoint some readers by its brevity. But this appeared to us to be the right amount of space to devote to these respective subjects when regard is paid to their importance and relevance to Christian thought today. Similarly we have devoted a whole section to Christianity and History, including in it our treatment of The Last Things, because it seemed to us that this is the proper category in which such a subject should be placed if it is to be understood against the background of contemporary thought.

We write as Anglicans, but not, if we may adapt a phrase of the famous John Pentland Mahaffy, in the offensive sense of that term. We do not attempt to suggest that there is a peculiarly Anglican form of every doctrine dealt with here, and consequently to defend that form against all criticism. On the contrary, we have felt ourselves free to criticize on occasion Anglican doctrine, custom, and practice. But our presentation is inevitably coloured by Anglican experience and Anglican tradition. One of the authors is an Anglican priest and the other an Anglican bishop, and neither can jump out of his skin. Even if, however, our primary thought in writing was to appeal to an

Anglican audience, we believe that our outlook is comprehensive enough to appeal to Christians of other traditions, just as the book *Christian Doctrine* (1942, repr. 1976) of Dr. J. S. Whale was found useful by readers of many denominations although its author is a member of the United Reformed Church. It may cause readers some surprise that though we occasionally refer to the XXXIX Articles we have made no attempt to take them as a consistent guide. All properly educated Anglican theologians have been to some extent formed by the thought of these Articles, but their significance in Anglican thought today is, it must frankly be admitted, historical rather than normative.

Two omissions in this book may strike the reader as curious. We have said nothing about Christian ethics. This is partly because we do not think that we are competent to write on the subject; partly because ethics can be distinguished from doctrine clearly enough to justify such an omission; and partly because the book is quite long enough already without trying to include this wide and important field of thought. There is also virtually no mention of Mariology. This is quite simply because we are not convinced that this subject is an integral and indispensable part of the Christian faith. Perhaps there is something lacking in our intellects or imaginations or aesthetic sense; all we can say is that to this chord our hearts do not respond.

There are no footnotes on this book. We believe that its readers will find this omission as refreshing as the authors (who have spent their lives writing and reading books full of footnotes) found it in the process of writing. Instead we have from time to time given references to books to consult on the various subjects dealt with. The fact that we mention a book does not mean that we necessarily agree with its contents either in whole or in part, but only that it is relevant, and the books which we mention vary in length and weight and even occasionally in language. We wish to help both the advanced student and the reader who has neither taste nor opportunity for intense study.

It should perhaps be explained that this book is a collaboration not only between two Anglican theologians but between two identical twin brothers who are collaborating for the first time. The reader will be clever if by internal evidence he can determine where in the book one brother ends and the other takes up the theme, and fortunate if he can read the book with the same ease and pleasure as the authors experienced in combining to write it.

Finally we wish to claim that we have written this book as those who see themselves continuing the theological tradition of the late Very Reverend Alan Richardson DD, sometime Dean of York and Professor of Theology in the University of Nottingham, and we would like the book to be regarded as a tribute to his memory.

A. T. HANSON
R. P. C. HANSON

I · GOD

1 Our Knowledge of God

a. Religious Experience

Ever since biologists in the last century labelled our species as *homo sapiens*, the custom has grown up among philosophers and writers of attaching some other Latin word to *homo* in order to emphasize some salient feature of man. Thus technologists have called him *homo faber*, he is distinguished from the rest of the animals by his ability to make things with his hands, and so on. Perhaps we could add one more to the list by suggesting that one could very well call him *homo religiosus* or *homo orans*, in the sense that religious activity and the practice of prayer is a universal characteristic of man in distinction to the rest of the animal creation. This feature is not only found in primitive man, or man in agricultural society, but is also true of Westernized industrialized man: everyone prays at some time; religion is not to be equated with going to church.

It is true indeed that one widely influential tradition in the West, the depth psychology originated (or at least made famous) by Sigmund Freud, denies the validity of man's religious experience and claims to be able to account for the phenomena of religious experience in terms which explain it as something wholly confined to man's unconscious mind, without the necessity of assuming the existence of any being outside man. In very general terms, Freud explains away the ideas or intuitions which we think we have of God along two lines: (a) the actual concept of God is in fact a projection of the father-image, and is caused by the impact on us during our very earliest years of the figure of our father; and (b) in more general terms, man, finding himself face to face with a potentially hostile world in which he knows all sorts of misfortunes and evils may happen to him, consoles and fortifies himself with belief in a benevolent God, who will probably shield him from disaster in this world, and certainly reward him with bliss hereafter. This Freud calls 'wishful thinking'.

Christians would be foolish to ignore Freud; indeed some of them have benefited greatly from his insights in the realm of the psycho-

1

logy of the unconscious. But his views on religion must not be regarded as either constituting the most valuable part of his teaching, or as possessing any sort of 'scientific' authority. Freud believed that he was being scientific in putting them forward, but the subsequent development of the study of this area of psychology has not justified his claim, and no unbiassed psychologist today would say that it has. We may well point out that Freud's experience of religion was confined to the Judaeo-Christian tradition, which emphasizes the fatherhood and personal nature of God. It is not by any means certain that, had Freud been able to conduct his research in a culture which had a different concept of God (as has for instance Hinduism or Buddhism), he would have come to the same conclusions. In any case, supposing it be true (as sometimes in the West may be the case) that the concept of God in a child's mind is closely associated with its idea of its father, this does not prove anything about the reality of God one way or the other. To take the analogy of a child's concept of authority: the earliest form in which authority and law are presented to a child is normally the authority of its parents. That authority may be very unsatisfactory; the child may even be given the idea that obeying the law means behaving in a way which the rest of society would regard as most undesirable and unlawful. But we do not on that account normally conclude that the entire concept of authority and law is quite invalid, the mere invention of subjective imaginings. So also with the concept of God: Freud may have correctly described the way in which the concept of God is formed in the mind of a child in certain social circumstances. He has done nothing to disprove the reality of God, nor has he shown why God should not use this image of the father as a mode of communicating with the child.

Freud's claim that belief in a benevolent God is wishful thinking will not stand up to close scrutiny either: it does not explain why so many people in the history of the Judaeo-Christian tradition at least have found that their belief in God brought them not happiness but misery. Consider Jeremiah in the seventh century BC: he believed in God's call to him to utter God's words to Israel, but he frequently protests that this has brought him nothing but contempt and suffering. And here the promise of happiness hereafter does not apply, for Jeremiah had no thought of a happy life after death. If Freud is right, Jeremiah ought to have given up belief in God early on in his life, but in fact, despite the misery which he incurred by carrying out what he believed to be God's will, Jeremiah never abandoned his mission throughout his career. Or consider a character like Søren Kierkegaard in the nineteenth century: his belief in

God, far from bringing him happiness, compelled him to pursue a career of isolation and conflict. In our own day we can point to Dietrich Bonhoeffer. If belief in God were only wishful thinking, enabling him to face the vicissitudes of life with greater fortitude, why did he deliberately return to Germany from America in 1939, when he knew that he could have honourably remained in America and that 'bonds and imprisonment' awaited him in Germany? Belief in God does not always seem to make for an easy life. Freud himself admits that religious belief, though he calls it an obsession, is a harmless obsession and indeed where a person is deeply religious there is usually an absence of neurotic symptoms.

Besides, the 'wishful thinking' argument can cut both ways. Why should not atheism also be an example of wishful thinking? We can all imagine examples of people who, if God really exists, have every reason to be alarmed. The man or woman who has wasted his life, been a parasite on others, or spent his time doing positive harm, the drug pusher, the professional criminal, the confidence trickster — these people obviously do not want to believe that they will ever be called to account for how they have spent their lives. For them belief that there is no God is just as much wishful thinking as belief in God is to any besotted devotee. The truth is that Freud had no understanding of religious experience from the inside, and his attempted explanation of it is too much influenced by out-of-date nineteenth century rationalist presuppositions. Too many people assume that his views on religion have some sort of scientific basis. They have not.

We have no good reason therefore for discounting the validity of religious experience on purely psychological grounds. So universal a phenomenon cannot be so easily dismissed. If historical confirmation of this is required, surely the history of Christianity in the USSR during the last sixty years provides this amply: Marxism in its Russian form assumes that religion is a diseased frame of mind, and that it will disappear when social circumstances no longer support it. The rulers of Russia have not been content with this tenet (perhaps they don't believe it?), for they have persecuted and harried all forms of religion with unprecedented severity and are still doing so. But religion has survived and is now undoubtedly on the increase in Russia. Even an agnostic might well conclude that there must be some reality in religious experience if it can survive and increase in such unfavourable conditions.

This does not mean however that any and every religious experience is of equal value and significance as far as Christianity is concerned. The deliverances of religious experience must be

3

criticized by reason and understood in the light of revelation. To take a very simple example, Tertullian in one of his works tells us of a vision which a Montanist prophetess received: she saw a soul, and it was of pale pink colour. Tertullian accepts this as authentic, because by the time he wrote this work he was a Montanist himself and regarded their prophets as divinely inspired. But we certainly are under no obligation to accept this nonsense just because it can be described as religious experience.

We shall be dealing later on with the topic of revelation and shall be arguing that we cannot do without this concept in Christianity. But we must point out at this stage that revelation itself is to a large extent based on religious experience. We cannot understand Jesus Christ as the final revelation of God unless we can see him against God's revelation of himself to Israel as recorded in the Old Testament. But the mode of revelation in the Old Testament necessarily includes a large measure of religious experience. Not only is God known through such events as his rescue of Israel from Egypt or his banishment of Israel to Babylon, but he is also known through the utterances of prophets about his word to their contemporary situations. Such utterances are always mediated through the religious consciousness of prophets, very often expressed in the form of visions, such as Amos's series of visions and Isaiah's great vision of the theophany in the temple. Not only this, but God is also revealed through the hymns of psalmists, whose religious experiences are so vividly and authentically expressed in the Psalter that generation after generation of Christians as well as Jews have been able to make them their own and use them as an expression of their own experience of God. In other words, God's revelation of himself to Israel is very often witnessed to primarily in the faith of Israel, or at least the faith of prophets, writers, and seers in Israel's history. What this revelation signifies is something that we must examine later, but we cannot possibly avoid the conclusion that it is largely dependent on the validity of Israel's religious experience.

There is a great variety of religious experience, but for most people private prayer is the most basic and familiar form of it. We are not here concerned with mysticism as such, that is the approach to God which transcends the subject-object relationship, though we do give it some attention when we come to define the relation of Christianity to other religions. Nor do we intend to concern ourselves with the question of intercessory prayer. In the New Testament very little indeed is said about mystical prayer and on the whole the writers, taking their cue from Jesus himself, seem to be most concerned with intercessory prayer. But there is one element that runs all through the New Testament and that is an emphasis on obedience. Obedience is closely linked with faith. God desires man's obedience; it was the obedience of Christ that constituted the substance of his offering. We suggest therefore that for Christians prayer might well be looked on as being primarily an act of obedience. Indeed one could well argue that there is only one form of religious experience that is absolutely obligatory on all Christians at all times, and that is the act of trying to obey God's will. When someone declares, 'I do not know how to find God; where am I to begin?', the right advice is 'Sit down and in quiet try to make yourself open to God; try to listen to him; try to subject yourself to his will, even if you do not believe that he exists'. Raymond Pannikar, in his book *The Unknown Christ of Hinduism*, has drawn an interesting parallel between Hindu thought and Hebrew thought which is relevant in this context: Hinduism, he says, has never regarded reason as a satisfactory way of knowing God, so the Indian answer to unbelief is not 'go on thinking' but 'purify your life'. In a similar way Hebrew thought has always associated knowing God with obeying God. Indeed Professor J. Weingreen has maintained with much probability that in the Hebrew Bible the verb which is used for 'to know God', yd^{ς}, should rightly be translated 'to acknowledge God'. It follows then that private prayer, that primary channel for our knowledge of God, is as much a matter of the will as of the intellect, and that, at this level at least, God cannot make himself known to us unless we will to know him.

In this respect Kant was right. Anyone who has any acquaintance with Kant's philosophy will know that, having excluded to his own satisfaction any possibility of our knowing of God's existence by arguments drawn from the nature of the outside world, he introduced another way by which we can know of his existence; in effect through our moral experience, that is, our experience of taking moral decisions. Because we find the notion of duty universally acknowledged as binding, we must, if we are to make sense of this fact, acknowledge the existence of a good God who rewards those with immortality hereafter who have done their duty. However much we may condemn Kant's own religion as a cold and rationalistic moralism, we should admit that he was right in placing experience of God basically in the area of moral experience. The two are not identical, but they belong to the same area of experience. Thus, if anyone says to us that experience of God means nothing to him and demands that we tell him what sort of thing it is, we can refer him to his own moral experience and tell him that experience of God is of the same kind, though encountered in a personal mode. A man may deny that he has had any experience of God, but he cannot, unless he is very obtuse or out of his mind, deny that he knows what moral experience is.

Finally, one warning is necessary: we must not be afraid of subjectivity. It is perhaps just this fear that produced the sterile 'death of God' theology of the sixties. Partly through a positivistic strain in Karl Barth's thought, and partly perhaps through the influence of Logical Positivism, the 'death of God' theologians based their whole system on denial of the validity of religious experience. This was primarily because religious experience is by its very nature subjective: my religious experience cannot be communicated to you in the way that my intellectual ratiocination can. It was therefore dismissed as having no authority and being incapable of playing any part in a rational scheme of theology. But the realm of subjectivity is also the realm of the personal, and Christianity, with its emphasis on the personal nature of God and its claim that God is supremely revealed in an historical person, cannot possibly afford to dispense with the personal dimension. We in the West are still very much under the spell of the Victorian view of science; according to this view nothing can be regarded as certain or true that cannot be subjected to objective tests, preferably those which physical science uses, i.e. tests of measuring and weighing. Ideally, therefore, we ought as theologians or students of religion to occupy ourselves with devising means by which the truth of religious experience can be tested by scientific methods. Indeed this way of thinking about reality goes back farther than the last century. It has its roots in the Enlightenment of the seventeenth and eighteenth centuries. Western man has been progressively cutting himself off from the realm of the subjective for the last 250 years. This is one of the reasons why religion in the West seems to be in decline.

But this passion for the objective is in fact already beginning itself to show signs of declining among us. In the first place physical science, that paragon of Victorian objectivity, has begun to betray the cause. There is reason to believe that at the most microscopic level the presence of the observer makes a difference to what is observed; in other words the subjective element has unexpectedly intruded itself. Moreover the old Victorian notion of the physical universe operating according to iron 'laws of nature' that can be objectively observed and charted can no longer be regarded as valid. What the Victorians believed were objective laws turn out to be no more than statistical averages. In addition even the most objective observations presuppose the existence of a mind observing; but the actual operation of a person observing cannot itself be wholly subsumed under objective laws. An unavoidable element of subject-ivity must enter into every attempt to give a total account of the universe, or of any element in the universe where mind plays a part. And thirdly, the whole realm of art, including poetry and drama, necessarily presupposes the validity of subjective experience. The very conception of 'scientific' painting, 'scientific' poetry, or even 'scientific' architecture, or 'scientific' history, is a contradiction in terms. If we maintain the inadmissibility of subjective experience as evidence, we must reconcile ourselves to doing without the artist.

Perhaps the traditional African experience of God may come to our aid here. Possibly because African culture has never known a literate, philosophical, schematizing period, as have both Western and Indian culture, the African does not have our Western horror of the subjective element in experience. Educated Africans, as well as uneducated peasants, believe in the validity of information received in dreams. For them the barrier between the conscious and un-conscious is not so absolute as it is among us. In their religion the ties that exist between the present generation and past generations are real and objective. As the African Church begins to make its indigenous contribution to Christian thought, it may be that their theologians will help us Westerners to assess more accurately the place that subjective experience should play in our knowledge of God.

b. Natural Knowledge of God

There are two reasons why until recently the suggestion that man could learn something about God by the use of his reason apart from revelation was unpopular in the Western world. The first reason was the influence of Karl Barth's theology. Karl Barth reacted againt the prevailing theology of the nineteenth century, which stressed the place of religious experience and the omnicompetence of human thought. He accused it of substituting a man-made system for God's revelation of himself and of making man rather than God the true subject of theology. Falling back on one tradition of the Reformers, and also quite consciously echoing Kierkegaard, he declared that all attempts to discover truth about God apart from his revelation in Jesus Christ were vain and only likely to lead to error. Whenever Christianity makes a special alliance with philosophy, as it did for example in the thirteenth century, it comes off the loser and ends by teaching a doctrine of God which is untrue to the God of the Bible. Barth devotes a long section of his *Church Dogmatics* to demolishing any idea that natural theology can be reconciled with biblical theology. Indeed his doctrine of God is so christocentric that he not

7

only disallows any real knowledge of God in non-Christian religions, but also claims that the knowledge of God to be had in the Old Testament itself is to be tested and screened by God known in Jesus Christ.

This reaction against natural theology launched by Barth was one of the elements in Barthian thought which was accepted and furthered by Rudolf Bultmann. Although he did what Barth said should not be done – adapted to Christianity a contemporary form of philosophy – the philosophy he embraced fitted in very well with Barth's rejection of natural theology. The Existentialism which Bultmann applied to his interpretation of the New Testament is a form of philosophy which is by its very nature antagonistic to theological or cosmological speculation, putting great emphasis on the importance of facing and coping with the actual predicament or life-situation in which man finds himself, and encouraging man to adapt himself psychologically to the unknown elements in his environment rather than to spend his time in profitless speculation about them. Bultmann does indeed bring God into this philosophical approach, for he claims that God can be apprehended by means of the challenge which Jesus of Nazareth presents to each individual. But Bultmann is totally opposed to any attempt to philosophize about the God who is thus apprehended. Christians must not attempt to orientate their cosmology to their knowledge of God, since the way in which we know the world and the way in which we know God constitute two different dimensions which must not be confused.

At the same time as Barth, and after him Bultmann, were warning Christian theologians not to have anything to do with a theory of a natural knowledge of God, the trend of philosophy in the Anglo-Saxon world was from its side strongly emphasizing the difficulty of any knowledge of God at all. This is the second of the two reasons to which we referred above. Kant, it will be remembered, in his *Critique of Pure Reason*, denied that the human mind could learn anything about God from a contemplation of the phenomena of sense. In the ensuing century under the influence of Hegel this Kantian prohibition was swept aside, and the strong tide of Idealist thought which prevailed during the nineteenth century seemed to provide a very favourable situation for theologians. Consequently right up to and including William Temple, theologians could assume a more or less Idealistic philosophy as one that would be accepted by most thinking people. But at the beginning of the twentieth century the Idealist tide began to ebb, and before the century was half over Idealism as a philosophy had almost disappeared from Britain and

America. Its place was taken not by Existentialism as on the continent, but by a form of logical philosophy which harked back beyond Kant to David Hume. Its earliest form, Logical Positivism, was soon abandoned by most philosophers, but Logical Analysis remains the prevailing influence in British universities, and in many philosophical schools on the American continent too. This form of thought tends to demand empirical verification for any statement that is to be regarded as true or even meaningful, and thus to dismiss not only all theological statements, but all metaphysical statements as well, as being strictly meaningless. It is true that Wittgenstein, who is one of the most influential thinkers in modern Western philosophy, never adopted exactly this view. He always maintained that 'the mystical' was there, but he added that philosophy could not say anything about it. In his latest phase, he may well have allowed that theological language had a system and a purpose of its own, but he never indicated whether it was possible to say that there was any connection between theological language and reality.

We should perhaps at this point give more attention to the problem of religious language; how we are to speak (and therefore think) about God. A moment's reflection will convince us that we cannot use words about God in exactly the same sense in which we use words about anything else. Words were invented in order to describe things in the universe; but God transcends the universe. We must not think of God as we would of anything else; we must not regard him as just one more object of thought, even the greatest. We would not wish, for example, to say, 'there are all sorts of things in the universe, trees and animals and stars and people — and God'. God is not to be classed with anything else. He is in a class of his own.

This has been recognized from very ancient times, perhaps nowhere more clearly than in India, where classical Hindu philosophy insisted that one can only say what God is not. One cannot say what he is. Our thinking process is simply unable to comprehend God, because he transcends all categories of thought. This negative approach to God suits traditional Hinduism very well, but might seem rather unsuitable for Christianity. Christians want to be able to make a number of very definite statements about God: he acts in history; he revealed himself in Jesus Christ, etc. However, this negative approach (often called apophatic theology) has played a big part in classical Christian theology. Augustine adapted it from the form of Platonism that was dominant in his day, and it was greatly encouraged by the work of Pseudo-Dionysius the Areopagite, a Syrian monk of about AD 500 who wrote a whole system of theology

9

based on the apophatic approach. This work was very influential with Thomas Aquinas; he has a careful discussion about how far we can use human language about God, and denies that words can be used of God univocally, i.e. literally and directly.

Those who use the apophatic approach often recommend some way of knowing God that transcends or bypasses the intellect. This is what the Indian religious tradition does, and this is what the mystics tend to do. Augustine did not commit himself completely to a supra-intellectual approach to God, though his stress on the will and imagination as essential elements in our understanding of God has remained as a permanent legacy to Christian theology. Thomas Aquinas holds that one can use human language about God if one makes use of analogy. And this is, roughly speaking, how modern theologians have met the challenge of the logical empiricist of today.

This is essentially what Tillich does when he maintains that we can only use symbolic language when we speak about God. God himself, he says, must be described as 'the ultimate ground of being' or 'ultimate being'. This is not to be understood symbolically, but literally. However every other assertion we make about God must be expressed in symbolic language, since God is the limit or terminus of our intellectual reasoning. Reason can indicate that there is a mystery there (compare Wittgenstein's phrase 'the mystical') but it cannot tell us anything about the mystery. By 'symbolic language' Tillich does not mean 'fanciful language' or 'primitive language' or mere rhetoric. He means that we can only apprehend and convey significance about God if we speak of him in language that is not direct but symbolic. But the symbol is not empty; it does convey meaning.

But the school of Logical Analysis to which we referred above has recently presented a new challenge to those who wish to speak meaningfully about God. They do not now demand exactly that every statement must be capable of being verified by sense perception, but they do demand the possibility of 'empirical verification' for every statement which is not to be called meaningless. You may not be able to verify your statement about God by sense perception (impossible for God anyway, who is by definition spiritual), but you must be able to say what difference your God-statements make. How can they be verified, or at least how could they be falsified?

The late I. T. Ramsey in his book *Religious Language* (published in 1957) undertook to answer this challenge. His method is in fact to show that there are situations in ordinary life in which we make statements that cannot be verified or falsified by the standards required by the Logical Analyst philosophers, but which in fact no ordinary person would regard as meaningless. The two most obvious areas in which this occurs are the areas of moral action and the area of personal action. In both these areas, he claims, we cannot prove our assertions by the language of science or of sense-experience, but can only use language in such a way as to help our hearers to experience a disclosure of meaning (very much akin to Tillich's 'symbolic' language). For example, I might say, 'It is my duty to subscribe to a charitable cause'. This statement is not just an account of my psychological condition. Nor is it an admission that I am subject to the pressures of society ('I must do what society demands, otherwise I will be punished'). It cannot be verified empirically. But the statement is far from meaningless. We all know what it means. Again, take the statement: 'I decided to take the train to Salisbury'. If you ask why I took the train to Salisbury, it is not sufficient to explain the attraction Salisbury had for me, or to emphasize the comfort and ease with which one can travel by British Rail, nor even to make the suggestion that I had a Salisbury-complex which compelled me to go there (if that were really the case my saying 'I decided' is an illusion). The ultimate reason is that I freely decided to go. The truth of this cannot be verified, for the personal centre is not amenable to scientific or empirical investigation. And yet we all know what is meant by the statement. It is very far from meaningless.

If then there are these two vast areas in our everyday lives, moral action and personal action, that are not amenable to the sort of verification which the Logical Analysts require, it is not at all surprising or nonsensical that there should be yet another area where this sort of criterion does not apply, the area of religious experience. God, says I. T. Ramsey, is not someone whose existence and activity can be proved or demonstrated in the way that the empiricists demand – but then neither are moral imperatives nor the personal centre capable of such proof. But we may apprehend God by 'disclosure' in a way analogous to how we apprehend duty and accept the existence of other selves. He defines religion as a combination of discernment and commitment, and insists that all disclosures of God in our experience are also challenges to action. He does not deny that there is an empirical element in religious experience, just as there is in moral experience; but 'the empirical anchorage of the Christian faith is not in the kind of situation with which any scientific language, as such, could adequately deal'. Perhaps since he published that book more than twenty years ago the belief that the possibility of only empirical verification can render a statement meaningful has tended to wane among philosophers. But Ramsey's book remains as a remarkable answer to a philosophical challenge.

In fact the concept of a natural knowledge of God being accessible to man cannot be so quickly disposed of. In the first place there can be no doubt that the writers of the New Testament assume that man can know something of God unaided by revelation. This is presupposed in the first chapter of Romans and Karl Barth's elaborate attempts to explain it away are not convincing. It is true that New Testament writers underline the ignorance, darkness, and error which characterized the paganism of their time: e.g. in Ephesians 2: 1-3, 12. But they do not give us the impression that they regarded pagan man as having no knowledge at all of God: cf. Acts 17: 22-9. In any case, if men apart from Christ had no knowledge of God, it would be very difficult indeed, if not impossible, to preach to them about God. Anyone who has any experience of preaching Christianity to non-Christians will know that one must begin by assuming that they have some knowledge of God. Hence a total rejection of natural theology is incompatible alike with the assumptions of the Bible and the presuppositions of missionary preaching.

As well as this, it is not the case that all modern theologians have abandoned the concept of a natural knowledge of God, or the hope of an accommodation between theology and philosophy. Paul Tillich, for instance, actually had the courage to construct his own metaphysic in order to fit in with his theology. He took his materials partly from Schelling (a German philosopher of the first half of the nineteenth century) and partly from Heidegger (who is generally regarded as the representative *par excellence* of modern Existentialism). Tillich, we have seen, defined God as the ground of being and he claimed that reason, though it cannot explain or articulate the ground of being, can indicate that it is there as the limit which reason encounters. Tillich also elaborated a Logos doctrine (that is a doctrine of the divine reason); the Logos within man, he says, is able to recognize the Logos within the universe. Paul Tillich's philosophical theology does not appeal to everyone, but he cannot be ignored, and his numerous disciples are an indication that a theory of a natural knowledge of God apart from revelation has never entirely disappeared from the theological scene.

Another liaison between philosophy and theology has recently been formed in what might appear at first sight to be the most unpropitious environment, liberal Marxism. (This is more fully discussed under V, 11 (b) below, pp. 199-200.)

There is also a school of Neo-Thomist philosophers who believe that they can modify the original Thomist synthesis of philosophy and religion so as to allow for the fact that today our understanding of the universe must be conceived in dynamic rather than static terms. They would certainly still maintain that the existence of God can be known apart from revelation. Their most distinguished representative on the American continent is B. Lonergan and in Britain E. L. Mascall.

But since the Logical Analytical movement in Western philosophy began, the philosophy of science itself has not stood still. Indeed in some ways it could be plausibly maintained that the development of physical science itself has outmoded the expectations which the original Logical Positivists based on it. What attracted them about science was that it seemed to be a closed system, in which every hypothesis could in theory at least be verified by sense-experience, whose arguments were of a demonstrative type. It is not surprising then that some modern theologians accuse the Logical Analysis philosophers of basing their approach to philosophy on an outmoded, atomistic understanding of science. Ever since the discoveries of Einstein at least, physicists have been insisting that the physical universe is a dynamic process, in which everything is interacting with everything else. The old notion of a universe operating according to unbreakable physical laws has gone. In its place is a much more open-ended model, in which one level of existence merges imperceptibly into the level above it, and the electron, the ultimate unit of matter, cannot be exactly described by any one model. This development in the understanding of the physical universe produced in the twenties of this century two outstanding philosophies, those of Alexander and Whitehead, who based their metaphysical systems on the picture of reality presented by science. Alexander spoke of space-time as the matrix of all reality, and Whitehead envisaged reality as consisting of one dynamic process, in which both mind and God played an essential part. From the work of these philosophers has arisen a definite school of theologians who deliberately attempt a synthesis of Process philosophy and Christian theology. These Process theologians have a considerable following in America; their leaders are Charles Hartshorne, John Cobb, and Norman Pittenger.

Another attempt to marry Christian theology to scientific thought was made by the distinguished Jesuit palaeontologist Teilhard de Chardin. During most of his lifetime the papacy, greatly alarmed by what was called the Modernist movement in the Roman Catholic Church, had sternly forbidden that any concessions should be made on the part of Catholic theologians to modern thought in any form. Among other theories, the Darwinian hypothesis that man had evolved from the primates was declared to be quite incompatible with orthodoxy. But Teilhard de Chardin was convinced that the evolutionary hypothesis was correct; and he proceeded to work out an elaborate and impressive system in which Christ was seen as the end or goal of evolution and God was both the movement within evolution that made it work and the force at the very centre of matter that explained why the electron should behave as it does. His system included what was in effect a proof for the existence of God drawn from the observed phenomena of evolution. Teilhard was never allowed to publish his work during his lifetime, but since his death in 1955 his works have been published and have influenced many educated people. Scientists seem to react to him in one of two ways, either contemptuous rejection or ecstatic acclamation, neither perhaps a very good mood in which to assess his value coolly. But he has posed some disturbing questions to scientists and has certainly shown that modern science is not a system of thought from which God is necessarily excluded.

The traditional proofs for the existence of God are the Ontological Proof, propounded by Anselm at the end of the eleventh century, and the *Quinque Viae* of Thomas Aquinas, the five proofs of God's existence drawn from a consideration of the characteristics of the universe. The Ontological Proof has often been refuted, notably by Kant; but it always seems to reappear, and only recently there has been a lively discussion among philosophers as to whether it is valid or not. In essence it seems to be a proof based on the rationality of the universe. As Hartshorne comments: 'All meaning implicitly asserts God'. If you believe that the meaning which our reason finds in the universe belongs there, and is not just a projection by our minds, then you must assume an ultimate meaning for the whole universe, and this implies a divine mind behind it, which we may call either God or the Logos. Any force there may be in the *Quinque Viae* seems to derive from the same assumption. For example one of the five proofs is the proof from the contingency of the world: everything we observe in the world is, but might have been otherwise. We cannot say of anything in the world that it must exist by the very nature of things. But a totally contingent universe could never have come into existence: ultimate reality cannot have just happened to begin. Therefore there must be an absolutely necessary being to explain how the contingent beings came into existence. That necessary being is God. All these proofs therefore may be called conditional proofs; if you are prepared to assume the rationality of the universe, they are valid. But they are not demonstrative, because it is always open to you to deny the rationality of the universe, to refuse to seek for ultimate meaning, to declare that you are quite ready to accept that the universe is meaningless, absurd, irrational.

Recently however the German theologian, W. Pannenberg, has made an attempt at elaborating what might be called a natural theology based on the implications of the concept 'meaning'. He begins by showing that the demand for verifiability by sense-experience cannot be met in all cases, even in the area of science. For example, many conclusions in the area of science are drawn by means of induction: a phenomenon is noted as occurring invariably, and the conclusion is drawn that it must occur in all instances of the phenomenon. Bees are invariably found to possess a sting; the conclusion is drawn that all bees have stings. This works admirably in practice, but it is not a demonstrative argument. In order to be demonstrative, it would be necessary to examine every single bee in the world. He then passes on to the consideration of history as a science: he points out that history also is not completely amenable to the demand for empirical verification or falsification, since it is concerned with events in the past that cannot be repeated. In fact history seems to be a discipline in which general conclusions of a non-demonstrative nature are drawn about non-controllable phenomena, events in the past. But history can hardly be dismissed as a work of the imagination or as a discipline to which scientific criteria cannot be applied. If then history is a process of forming generalizations in order to apprehend meaning in events, we must conclude that all systematic knowledge is a seeking for meaning in phenomena by means of applying hypotheses. In the broadest sense this applies to scientific knowledge also. Pannenberg even argues that the very ability of men to communicate their thinking to each other implies their acceptance of a 'universe of discourse', a common meaning in which all thinking people share. I could not communicate my thoughts to you if my words did not convey sufficient meaning common to us both, and if my reasoning processes were not sufficiently similar to yours. In the end he concludes that all meaning in human communication depends on the implicit assumption of one overall meaning to the universe. That overall meaning implies the mind of God. This meaning we cannot hope fully to apprehend, because the universe is a still-evolving process; but we must assume that it exists. We may quote Pannenberg himself here: 'no unity of meaning and no perception of meaning is autonomous in itself. Every specialized meaning depends on a final all-embracing totality of meaning in which all individual meanings are linked to form a semantic whole'. We have had to sum up a 500-page work in a few hundred words. But perhaps we have made it clear that theology nowadays is by no means invariably ruled out of court by the philosophers, and that a natural knowledge of God is something which some competent philosophers and scientists are quite ready to admit.

c. God as Creator

Christian theologians have traditionally held that God created the world *ex nihilo*, out of nothing. Whether this can be accurately described as a biblical doctrine is doubtful. Certainly the account of the creation in Genesis 1: 1–2 does not relate a creation *ex nihilo*: 'the deep' already existed. The Hebrew writer must have imagined God bringing light and order to the waters of chaos. However by about AD 170 we find Christian theologians claiming that God created the world out of nothing. This claim was made necessary by the fact that the only two alternative theories of the origin of the world were unacceptable. If God did not create the world out of nothing, then either he created it out of already existing materials, or he created it out of himself. The first of these two alternatives was accepted by both Plato and Aristotle: for them matter was eternal and coexistent with God, and creation meant the ordering of pre-existent matter. Christian thought rightly rejected this because it introduced a most undesirable dualism into the world. Matter inevitably became opposed to God and (in some Platonic traditions at least) the source of evil and non-being. But the Judaeo-Christian tradition has always held that the creation is in itself good because it has been created by a good God. The second alternative, that God created the world out of himself, seems to imply a Hindu-type monism; the world in that case must be in some sense part of God. But here again the Judaeo-Christian tradition has always insisted on the otherness of God: the ontological bridge between God and his creation cannot be crossed (except in the doctrine of the incarnation, but that is to anticipate). This second view was held by many Gnostic teachers. They regarded created being as an emanation from God; the Greek word was *aporrhoia*. The earliest theologians of the Church had no objection to using this word for the relation of the Son or Logos to God, because he was on the side of divinity, and before Origen no Christian theologian hesitated to regard the Trinity as an evolution within God which has not existed from eternity. But they would not use the word for the created order.

We might perhaps pause for a moment here to ask: is the doctrine of creation *ex nihilo* part of revelation? Only, perhaps, in a secondary sense. We shall be maintaining later that the Old Testament is a record of how the Jews came to understand God's character, and that process was certainly a process of revelation. In as far as a doctrine of creation *ex nihilo* is necessary in order to avoid a concept of God which identifies him too closely with his handiwork, or in order to avoid an intolerable dualism in the universe, that doctrine is part of revelation. But this is revelation at one remove. The doctrine of creation *ex nihilo* is not directly connected with Jesus Christ, who is the centre of revelation.

In the middle of the last century a great many educated Christians in this country were convinced that there was an unavoidable conflict between the findings of natural science and the revelation of God in the Bible over this very question of creation. This was because Christians understood the opening chapters of Genesis in a literal, historical sense. So understood, Genesis seemed to be making all sorts of statements about creation which contemporary science denied: creation took place in the space of six days; man was created whole and at once as a separate species; woman was created by being taken out of man's side, etc. Today the vast majority of educated Christians freely admit that their ancestors of a hundred years ago were mistaken in attempting to defend the literal truth of the Genesis narratives. These stories are to be understood as parables, not scientific accounts. The universe has existed for thousands of millions of years; man has evolved from the higher primates; woman has evolved *pari passu* with man. That particular battle between Christianity and science has ended in a decisive victory for science. Nevertheless we are entitled to ask today: does the doctrine of creation *ex nihilo* clash with the findings of modern science?

Strictly speaking it cannot do so, because the doctrine of creation claims to speak about how the universe began, looking at it so to speak from outside, from God's point of view. Science, whatever its conclusions, can only speak from the point of view of man, who is inside the universe. It can never hope to answer the question: why did the universe begin? But this is in fact the question which the doctrine of creation claims to answer. All the same Christians can hardly fail to be interested in the lively debate which in recent years has been taking place among astrophysicists as to the origin of the universe. The two theories have been called the 'steady state' theory and the 'big bang' theory. According to the 'steady state' theory the present evolution of the universe has been going on steadily from eternity, maintained by continuous creation of matter. According to the 'big bang' theory, the present evolution of the universe began with an explosion of the original matter some thousands of millions of years ago. Christian theologians, having burned their fingers a hundred years ago, have been very careful not to claim that either of these theories is more favourable to the doctrine of creation *ex nihilo*. Here they have surely shown their wisdom: Christians do not want to be put in a position where they are anxiously waiting for the conclusions of scientists before they can believe that God created the world! It now seems in fact that the 'big bang' theory has prevailed. But this does not mean that the 'big bang' is the scientific way of referring to what Genesis 1: 1–2 narrates.

It is however interesting to observe that some modern scientists are not averse to contemplating the possibility that the creative action of God may be a reasonable explanation of certain difficulties connected with the understanding of the evolution of the universe. In a recent lecture Sir Bernard Lovell has suggested both that there is plenty of room for divine action as an explanation of the state of affairs before the 'big bang', and that at a certain point in the formation of the earth's atmosphere the probability of the actual conjunction of elements required to explain man having emerged by chance is so remote as to be almost negligible. Too much must not be made of this. It is only the opinion of one expert, though a very distinguished one. But it does indicate that the Christian doctrine of creation is not unscientific in the sense that science disproves it or renders it improbable. At the same time we must observe that, even if Sir Bernard Lovell is right in his suggestions, we are not justified in saying that science now proves that God created the universe and directed its evolution. We have no right to expect science to prove any such thing. All we can say is that science cannot disprove such a belief, does not render it improbable, and may at certain points even find it an acceptable hypothesis.

We must also remind ourselves that in talking of creation we are, strictly speaking, using the language of myth. By 'the language of myth' we mean the sort of language which we must use when we are speaking about matters where neither science nor philosophy can guide us, because we are dealing with the borderline between the finite and the infinite. We cannot imagine a time when the universe was not. The very word 'time' here is misleading, because space-time is the very environment of the universe, and when there was no universe there was no time (the word 'when' is equally inappropriate here). Hence it may be wise not to try to say anything very definite about that ancient source of perplexity to theologians, the relation of the creation to time. Hebrew thought apparently conceived eternity not as timelessness but as time indefinitely prolonged. Only when the Jews encountered Greek culture did they meet the Platonic concept of eternity, a state wholly removed from time, a timeless 'now'. This Platonic idea of eternity enabled later theologians to speak of God as experiencing all time, past, present and future, in a timeless moment. The usual image is of the man standing on a mountain who can see two parties coming to meet each other as they make their way round the mountain; he can see their immediate future because he stands above them. We do not wish, probably, to call the universe coeternal with God, though Thomas Aquinas said that, as far as his own understanding of God's relation to the universe was concerned, he would have no objection to allowing this. Only the biblical revelation prevented him from believing it. We should probably therefore be wise if we said with Augustine that the universe was created with time rather than in time. And we can freely affirm that the Christian doctrine that God created the world out of nothing is in essence a myth, though a necessary myth if we are to safeguard the Christian apprehension of God and his relation to the universe.

It would be a mistake to imagine that the doctrine of creation *ex nihilo* refers to one event in the past only. It would be more accurate to say that the doctrine not only expresses God's original relation to the universe but also his constant relation to the universe. The New Testament claims not only that the world was created through the Son or Word, but also that he is the force by which the universe holds together; see 1 Corinthians 8:6; Colossians 1:17; Hebrews 1:2–3; John 1:1–4. We will be discussing the Son's rôle in creation later on, but these passages indicate that God's creative work is not regarded as concluded with the original creation of the world.

Perhaps this word 'myth' needs a little more explanation. We should be reconciled to using it once we realize that in this realm it is no use looking to science for an explanation. Sir Bernard Lovell, in his book *The Centre of Immensities*, says at one point (p. 114) that it is virtually impossible to describe in scientific terms the state of the physical universe just before the 'big bang', the rapid expansion that set in train the events which finally produced a state of affairs on the planet earth conducive to the emergence of life and ultimately of human mind. As far as scientific deductions are concerned, the astrophysicist must say that just before the expansion the physical universe must be assigned infinite density and zero radius. So startlingly paradoxical a statement simply means that at this point (and this is not the point of creation; physical matter already existed) scientific categories fail us. Sir Bernard even suggests (p. 122) that a scientific explanation may be inherently impossible, and he concludes with the very reasonable statement: 'there is a problem of a beginning — a creation — of matter and of man's existence in this particular universe . . . The rediscovery of the validity of non-scientific modes of thought and investigation will establish once more the faith of the people in science itself' (pp. 158-9). So if theologians assert that God created the universe out of nothing, the astrophysicist, though he will certainly not admit that this can be proved scientifically, will have nothing to say on scientific grounds against it. He must regard it as one possible explanation.

But are the philosophers so easily satisfied? Not necessarily. Some philosophers have objected to the concept of creation by God as irrational or contradictory: the doctrine makes it impossible to believe in the true reality of the universe; God cannot create without diminishing his own being; God must be different after creating to what he was before creating, and this discredits his eternity; God either creates a universe that exists independently of him, in which case we have dualism; or it remains entirely dependent on him, in which case it is not really a universe. These are some of the objections to the concept of creation that have been made by philosophers.

This is not a work of philosophy, so we cannot deal with all these objections in detail. It may be more helpful briefly to outline one modern philosophical account of creation, which treats the concept not only as unobjectionable but as actually being the only satisfactory way of accounting for God's relation to the universe. It is taken from R. C. Neville's book *God the Creator* (Chicago, 1968). Neville begins from the Platonic-Augustinian viewpoint that God in himself is completely beyond all categories and not to be described or comprehended in any definite terms, positive or negative (this is incidentally the viewpoint of Greek Orthodox theology to this day). This means that we must not say that God is the most perfect example, or the supreme manifestation, of being, because that would put him in the same class with the objects that go to make up the universe (which we shall call 'the many'). On the other hand, when we consider the many, we do not see in themselves any reason why they should be as they are. The details of the universe exist, but we cannot find in them any reason why they should be, or why they should be what they are (this is the philosophical equivalent to Sir Bernard Lovell's assertion that science cannot tell us what the very earliest matter was, how it came to be, or why it came to be). In other words, 'the many' are contingent. They exist, but we cannot see why they should exist, or why they should exist as the particular things which they are. Now, says Neville, only a creator can have made everything to be what it is and not something else. This is because the reason for their being what they are could not be found in the things themselves: each thing is what it is and not something else; but it could not be this unless there were other things for it (so to speak) not to be. Imagine an object x; we could not distinguish or recognize it, and it could not exist as x, unless there were other objects, y, z, etc. with which to contrast it, and against which it can assert its individuality. Now, still considering x, all the other things, y, z, etc. cannot be the reason why x is x. They might be the reason why x is not y or not z, but we cannot expect to find the reason why x is x in anything that is bound up with x in the same universe in which everything is itself and not some other thing.

Now we see the point of Neville's description of God as beyond all categories of thought and wholly transcendent in himself. Only in him can we find the reason why things are as they are, because only he is sufficiently independent of the universe not to be caught up in its nexus of being this and not that. To say that God is the reason why things are as they are is the same as saying that he created them to be what they are. Of course this account of creation is not inconsistent with what science tells us about the actual evolution of the universe. We do not need to hold that God created everything perfect without allowing any scope for evolution. It would be quite sufficient as far as Neville's theory is concerned to say that God created the universe before the great expansion. Its subsequent evolution is part of what he originally put into it.

This philosophical account of creation out of nothing is not necessarily the only possible one. But it may perhaps be sufficient to indicate that the concept of a *creatio ex nihilo* is not necessarily a lost cause with the philosophers.

2 Revelation and Faith

We are going to consider God's revealing himself, first in the events recorded in the Old Testament, then in the career of Jesus Christ. But we must first consider the general subject of revelation. Is it possible for God to reveal himself? Does the New Testament maintain that he has revealed himself in Christ?

We will deal with the second question first. It has recently been maintained that the New Testament does not speak in terms of revelation and that Christianity should not be presented as a religion of revelation. The original Christian message, so the argument runs, was one of salvation in Jesus Christ. The notion of revelation was only imported when the theologians of the Church began to interpret this message in terms of intellectualist Greek thought. Now it is true that Jesus himself did not proclaim a revelation; he proclaimed the kingdom, and he did not suggest that his life or teaching constituted a new revelation of God. But, as Pannenberg has pointed out, the Jews had always regarded the coming kingdom of God as the time when God would be fully revealed, so the coming of the kingdom itself implied a revelation. Again, revelation is by its very nature something which is more likely to be recognized through mature reflection than at the actual time of the revelatory events; so the fact that Jesus did not speak in terms of a revelation does not imply that he could not have constituted a revelation in himself.

When we turn to the three great theologians of the New Testament we find that all of them, Paul, John, and the author of Hebrews imply that they believe in a revelation, though they use very different terms to describe it. Paul speaks of the mystery of God (see 1 Cor. 2:7;4:1, Col. 2:2 and cf. Rom. 16:25; Eph. 1:9 – Colossians and Ephesians are probably slightly later than Paul). By this he meant the whole event of Christ understood as the saving action of God. But it needed faith to understand and recognize God's action; it therefore constituted a revelation. Moreover Paul often speaks of 'knowing' God or Christ, and this too implies that God has revealed himself newly and uniquely in Christ. John likewise constantly presents Christ as manifesting in himself God's nature and intention: John 1:18 alone implies a profound doctrine of revelation. Finally the author of Hebrews begins his work by declaring that God, who 'spoke of old to our fathers by the prophets . . . in these last days has spoken to us by a Son' (a verse to which we must revert presently). This must imply a doctrine of revelation, even possibly of progressive revelation.

Thus if we are to take the message of the New Testament seriously, we must be prepared to accept some sort of a doctrine of revelation. So we turn back to our first question: is it possible for God to reveal himself? In a general sense we have answered this question already, for we have defended the validity of religious experience, whereby some men and women at least at some times in some circumstances have come to know God. We have defended the possibility of assuming the existence of God on philosophical grounds; and we have shown that we cannot legitimately be precluded from talking rationally about God by purely logical arguments. We must therefore repeat that knowledge of God is available to all men at all times. But such knowledge must be called 'revelation', that is, it must be intended by God and be the gift of his grace.

This is because we cannot possibly admit that God is the sort of object which one can come to know whether God likes it or not. Our knowledge of God is not like scientific knowledge, which, in theory at least, means coming to learn something about some object of experience by our own efforts, without any consideration of whether the object wishes to be known or not. Our knowledge of God is more like our knowledge of other persons; we cannot know other people at any sort of depth at all unless they permit us to know them. So it is with God. This general knowledge of God, therefore, available to everyone, must nevertheless be described as revelation, because it is the consequence of God's goodwill towards mankind. He wills to make himself known to men.

There is another important feature of our knowledge of God. Just as God is not an object that we can compel to reveal itself to us, so he is also someone about whom we cannot be neutral or objective. Our knowledge of God is by faith: in other words there is an element of commitment in it. We noticed this element when we were considering Ian Ramsey's account of how we can know God. If, by whatever means, I come to know God, I cannot just treat that knowledge as I might, for example, treat the discovery of a new planet: 'Ah, so they have found a new planet! Interesting! I might take up astronomy when I retire'. Not so with God: if you once know him you cannot ignore him. You must obey him, or else forever thereafter carry a guilty conscience. This means that there is an element of will in our knowledge of God. Just as we could not know God at all unless he had willed us to know him, so we cannot know him unless we wish to know him (the analogy with knowing persons still holds good here). Men can always find reasons for not believing in God.

23

When we speak of a special revelation, as contrasted with this general revelation that we have just been considering, we do not want to suggest that a special revelation implies a special mode of knowing God. A special revelation means perceiving God (by the same methods as we have detailed above) in a special series of events, a particular set of circumstances, in one distinct national history and one distinct religious tradition, and above all in one particular human life. We shall go on presently to explain in greater detail how that special revelation took place and what its content was. But it is first necessary to realize that we only call it a special revelation because it is mediated by one particular set of events out of all the events in the world. This does indeed imply that God wills to make himself known in the course of, and by means of, a certain relatively short period in history confined to one particular part of the world. But God is free to do this. Just because he is not to be identified either with the world, or with some general principle regulating the world; just because he has made it out of nothing, and because that defines his relationship to it, he is free to express himself by means of some particular element in it (a human life), and during one particular period of the world's history (roughly 2000 BC–AD 30).

This element of particularity, of what Tillich calls 'concreteness', is underlined and safeguarded by the eschatological strain in the Christian message. To many thoughtful Christians throughout the ages the eschatological element in Christianity has been a stumbling block. They would have preferred to think of God as expressed in eternal principles, or moral ideals, or spiritual truths. They found it difficult to accommodate Jesus' proclamation that the end was about to come, and the early Church's conviction that the end had in some sense arrived. But it is this very emphasis on Jesus as the end, the last word, that preserves the specific nature of the revelation. If God has made himself known in one particular period in history, it must have an end, otherwise we would have the totally unchristian conception of a God who is only partially known, and who may therefore at some time in the future show himself to be quite different to that which we had previously believed him to be. In other words, the eschatological element in the Christian message preserves what the Bible calls the truth of God, that is his faithfulness, his reliability, his unchanging character. God, we must maintain, does reveal himself generally and has revealed himself specially. We must now consider how this special revelation has come about.

a. Revelation in the Old Testament

'God, who spoke of old in varying degrees and by various methods to our ancestors by the prophets, has in these last days spoken to us in the mode of Son'. This paraphrase of Hebrews 1:1–2 forms an admirable introduction to the topic of God's revelation of himself to Israel as recorded in the pages of the Hebrew Bible – for that is what we mean when we use the shorthand phrase 'God's revelation in the Old Testament'. We do not mean that the Hebrew Bible itself constitutes the revelation, for that would identify God's revelation with statements made in books. The Bible gives us the indispensable record of the revelation. The revelation itself was made to persons and was received and recorded because of their experience and faith. The great difference in this respect between the Old Testament and the New is beautifully brought out in these two verses from Hebrews, although of course the author of Hebrews had no idea of the New Testament as a book. But he does clearly contrast the variety, almost the sporadic, heterogeneous character of the revelation in Israel's history, with the unity and concentration of the revelation in the new dispensation, where all is focussed on the one figure of Jesus Christ. We could expand this contrast further, pointing out that the revelation recorded in the Old Testament spans a period of about a thousand years, compared with the brief thirty years of Jesus' life. The Old Testament revelation is much less consciously recorded than the New; the writers of the Old Testament had all sorts of different aims in view in writing their various works, whereas the New Testament writers nearly all shared the same desire to witness to Jesus Christ. The Old Testament revelation is unfinished; most of the writers are still looking forward to God's decisive revelation. The New Testament is written in the belief that the divine revelation has taken place – and so on.

How was God revealed in Israel's history? The answer to this question will involve us in analysing the various books of the Old Testament according to their bearing on revelation, but we must constantly remember that, when we talk of God's revelation, we do not primarily mean the written words, but the actual experience of the writers which they recorded. With this caution, we proceed to analyse the revelation in the Old Testament as follows.

i. Revelation through salvation history: this phrase 'salvation history' is one which has been used in various senses. We use it to mean Israel's apprehension of God as saviour through the way he has dealt with Israel in history. It is a process, not a mere series of casual incidents, because Israel always thought of God as being in charge of its history and as leading them on through history to an appointed goal. By 'Israel' we must mean those who speak on behalf of Israel in the pages of the Old Testament, but there was also a communal consciousness in the people of being the covenant people of God, a consciousness which survived the traumatic experience of the rise of Christianity and is still very much alive among Jews today. Also of course this consciousness of being the people of God passed over to the Christian Church. All history begins in legend, and Israel's history begins with Abraham, a figure about which history can tell us nothing whatever. He is about as historical as Krishna. Even when we reach the Exodus period, when Israel received its call to be the people of God, we are still very much in the region of legend. This is not to suggest that the Exodus is a fairy-tale, or that Moses never existed, but to emphasize that, if we say as we must that salvation history begins with the Exodus and the covenant made on Mount Sinai, we are not thereby claiming some special historical status for these events. All we have are traditions written down three or four hundred years after the events; what emerges from these traditions is a consciousness on Israel's part that God had called the people, made the covenant with them through Moses, given them the elements of a law, and pledged himself to look after them.

Israel emerges into the full light of history during the period of the judges: Deborah's song in Judges 5 is a contemporary comment on an historical event. From then on in the various historical records of Israel we learn how the writers of these records saw God as related to his people. Even the narrative of David's life in 2 Samuel and 1 Kings, by the very reticence of its references to God's hand in the events it records, tells us something about how it regards the God of Israel. The various political disasters which overtook Israel subsequently, culminating in the exile in Babylon in the sixth century BC and the slow and partial return under the Persian domination, are all commented on by historians and prophets in Israel so as to provide us with a picture of how God is understood as manifesting his character in history. After the return from exile the tension relaxes and in any case the evidence becomes far more scanty. But with the Antiochean persecution in the second century BC and the emergence of the apocalyptic literature (most of which is not in the canonical Bible), tension begins to rise again. Through all this Israel's God is known by what he is understood as doing in history. This does not at all mean that he marks his guidance of history by means of superhuman miracles (though some do form part of the record). It is rather that he is known as a God whose judgment and redemption are manifested by means of Israel's completely secular historical career.

ii. The prophetic revelation: whether we look at Israel of old from the literary or from the historical point of view, one of the most striking features of its history is the emergence of the canonical prophets. From Amos and Hosea in the middle of the eighth century BC till the anonymous prophet of the exile whom we call Second Isaiah, an astonishing series of prophets appeared, who claimed to speak directly in the name of God. The really great prophets are Amos, Hosea, Isaiah, Jeremiah, and the Second Isaiah, though they are reinforced by a number of secondary but remarkable characters such as Micah, Habakkuk and Ezekiel. What is unique about these prophets is that they do not on the whole rely greatly on religious tradition, but utter God's verdict immediately on the historical situation in which they find themselves and that they frankly and fearlessly condemn Israel by the standards of God's own character. 'There is no faithfulness or kindness', says Hosea (4: 1), 'and no knowledge of God in the land'. Faithfulness and kindness (a feeble translation; 'integrity and love' would be better) are required of Israel because they are basic characteristics of God. Equally remarkable in these prophets is their own deeply personal relation to God. Hosea uses the husband-wife relation as an existential analogy for the relation to God both of the individual Israelite and of Israel as a whole. Jeremiah, particularly in that part of his work known as his 'confessions', exhibits an amazing boldness and intimacy in his approach to God. At one point (Jeremiah 20: 7) he even accuses God of seducing him! Deeply impressive also is the total commitment of the prophets to the God whose message they uttered. Despite his violent protests at what God asked him to do, Jeremiah never abandoned his vocation. The Second Isaiah is magnificently confident that, contrary to external appearances, God will carry out his plan of bringing Israel back from exile. These prophets do not, as later Judaism did, appeal to a written code as the standard to which Israel should conform. There is not much talk about the law, the Torah. What they appeal to is God's known character: they face their hearers with God's immediate presence and demand. This is essentially an appeal for faith and obedience. God is reflected in the prophets as a personal, caring, saving, almost a suffering God.

iii. The revelation through Psalmists and Sages: the Psalter is Israel's hymn-book. It witnesses to the religious experience of individual Israelites that later on was used by the community and made the vehicle for their experience, their hopes and fears. Here too God's character emerges, most of all perhaps in the psalms which rejoice in God's goodness and in the presence of God, e.g. Psalms 62, 63, 84. The Book of Proverbs would at first sight seem to reflect God's revelation less clearly than do the Psalms: a good deal of its material

27

consists of proverbial sayings many of which can be paralleled in the literature of other cultures. But its concept of the divine wisdom is important because of the influence it had on some New Testament writers, and in Proverbs 8:22–end we have the attempt by some thinkers in Israel to produce a counterpart to the Logos philosophy of Greek culture or to the Isis cult of the Ptolemaic empire.

iv. Revelation through story: it is now clear that important elements in the Old Testament must be regarded as not having been originally intended as history at all. They are stories. This type of literature comes from all periods in Israel's history: the story of Joseph and his brothers in Genesis is one such. God does not figure prominently in the narrative, though his overruling providence is there in the background. Another such work is the book of Jonah: here a story is told with vivid detail and economy of narrative; an important lesson for post-exilic Israel is to be learned from it. We could put the book of Ruth in the same category; and, latest of all books in the Old Testament, the book of Daniel must be classified as story, not history in any sense as far as the narrative sections are concerned. This is perhaps the most indirect of all the modes of expressing God's revelation, but contains some vitally important elements. If we had to choose one book in the Old Testament that told us most about God in the shortest space, it would be the book of Jonah. The vividly narrated stories of persecution and faithfulness in Daniel tell us something of how God gains his ends in human history.

v. Revelation through the Protestants: this does not have any reference to what happened in Europe in the sixteenth century AD; it is a way of referring to those works in the Old Testament which can be called books of protest. There are really only two: Job and Ecclesiastes. The essence of these books is that they are concerned to refute some current orthodoxy. The author of Job protests that God does not reward the righteous and punish the wicked in this life, as the book of Deuteronomy, for instance, teaches. And Ecclesiastes (better denominated by its Hebrew title Qoheleth) sets forth a view of life that runs counter to almost everything else in the Bible, a sort of mild theistic cynicism. But both books have their value: Job's magnificent poetry, illuminated by sparkling images and illustrations on every page, brings us face to face with the inscrutability and otherness of God. Qoheleth acts as a purgative.

We must not draw a hard and fast line between the Old Testament canonical scriptures and the Apocrypha. The tradition of the Old Testament was continued in the Apocrypha. Some of the books in the Apocrypha are as valuable to us as far as knowledge of God is concerned as are some of the canonical books. Ecclesiasticus for instance (better called the Wisdom of Jesus ben Sira) is a most useful witness to the continuance of the wisdom tradition, and this could equally be said of the book of Wisdom, despite the fact that it was written in Greek, not Hebrew, and may have been composed as late as the first century BC. Likewise I Maccabees at least gives us our primary account of what is now realized to have been a major crisis in the history of Israel, the Antiochean persecution and the Hasmonean revolt.

What emerges from these five various modes in which the record of revelation is given us is basically the character of God. He is revealed as personal, holy, loving, caring, above all a saviour, of infinite power, patience, and righteousness, a living God, not an abstract concept, nor a moral principle, nor an ineffable absolute. It is true that this revelation is neither wholly self-consistent, nor steadily progressive, nor systematically ordered. By the very circumstances of its origin it must be in some sense a developing revelation, because it begins in the infancy of the people wrapped in the mist of legend. Israel learned about God through the centuries, and many instances could be quoted of the Old Testament correcting itself. The very earliest pictures of God are naïve, limited, unduly anthropomorphic. But this does not imply that we can follow the simple rule 'the later the clearer'. God's revelation of himself seemed to reach a climax with the Second Isaiah: what comes after that, right up to the coming of Christianity, though by no means negligible, does not reach the same lofty point of insight. This is why in some ways Christianity seemed to be a 'back to the prophets' movement. This revelation of God as recorded in the Old Testament is absolutely unique: there was nothing like it in any other culture of which we know.

This reference to Christianity as appearing like a 'back to the prophets' movement raises one question which we must face here. Why do we call them prophets? Was it because they predicted events in the future? What is the relation between Old Testament prophecy and New Testament fulfilment? We can answer this question most conveniently if we remember that what emerges from the Old Testament is the character of God. Now the prophets form one of the most important means by which that character came to be known: the greatest prophets knew God intimately, within the necessary limits of their culture and history. What each did in his own day was not to predict events which should happen centuries after their time, but to proclaim God's message for the situation in their own circumstances. Through that message God's character became more clearly known. Because each prophet declared how God reacted to the circumstances of his day, Israel could have learned (and some did learn) how God reacts to any circumstances, how he deals with men, what his methods are. When therefore God acted supremely, normatively, and decisively in Jesus Christ his action naturally fitted in with what the prophets had said about him. God's character is consistent, he does not act arbitrarily; so it was completely natural that his action in Christ should be seen to be in line with his action earlier in Israel's history.

We might illustrate this from one of the most famous 'prophecies' in the Old Testament, the picture of the suffering servant of the Lord in Second Isaiah (Isaiah chapters 40–55). It is by no means clear to whom exactly the prophet is referring in his four 'Servant Songs'; many modern scholars believe he is referring to himself, and the last and greatest of the Songs (52:13–53:12) is the account of the prophet's death written by one of his disciples. What the prophet is doing in these passages is to give us a picture of someone who is an obedient servant of God, called to witness to God's way of salvation by means of his own suffering and death. Indeed by the time we have read the last Song we seem to realize that obedient suffering and death is in a mysterious way God's means of redemption. When therefore in Jesus Christ God manifested and brought into operation his supreme and universal method of redemption, it was completely appropriate that the pattern of the suffering servant of the Second Isaiah should be reproduced. This is prophecy in the sense that the prophets understood the mind of God, not prophecy regarded as miraculously inspired prediction.

We have described the content of the Old Testament revelation as consisting in the character of God. The record of the revelation is, of course, the Old Testament itself. It must be clearly stated, however, that the means by which the revelation was received was the faith of Israel. There is no other way by which it could have been received. We do not believe in sacred books inscribed by the pen of angels and sent down direct from heaven. God manifests himself, grants an understanding of his doings to men and women in the circumstances of their lives. Only because they had faith were they able to record what they had learned of God. There is no avoiding this: we cannot adopt any Barthian bypassing of human religious experience, with all its imperfections, errors, and ambiguities. Of course when we say 'the faith' of Israel, we mean primarily the faith of individual Israelites. Very often these Israelites are completely anonymous, for example the author of Job, a literary genius if ever there was one; or the author of Jonah, a man (or, just conceivably, woman) of amazing religious insight. Sometimes these individual Israelites, far from representing the communal outlook, were in sharp disagreement with their contemporaries; such were Amos, Jeremiah, Ezekiel, and the great Second Isaiah himself. Even one of the very latest writers in the tradition, the author of Wisdom, seems to have suffered harassment from apostate Jews in Alexandria. Thus, if we maintain as we must that God's revelation of his character is in fact recorded in the Old Testament, we cannot possibly deny our overwhelming debt as Christians to the faith of individual Israelites, the record of which is handed on to us by the faithfulness of Israel as a whole through the thousand years that preceded the rise of Christianity.

We have been making an assessment of the development of God's revelation of himself through the Old Testament period, claiming that it reached a peak with the Second Isaiah, and so on. But this implies that we are using some criterion by which we judge what is good and what is better. That criterion can only be Jesus Christ. In this respect Karl Barth's contention (referred to on p. 7, 8 above) is quite correct. For Christians the ultimate criterion of God's revelation must always be Jesus Christ. We shall indeed discover later on that there is something circular about this, since we shall be arguing that we can only recognize Jesus as God's revelation because we know God's revelation in the Old Testament. But that will be considered in its proper place. In the meantime we must ask what right have we to use this criterion on the Old Testament? Should we not rather do as Nietzsche claimed Christians ought to do, accept the Jews' estimate of the Old Testament, seeing that they wrote it?

It is quite true that an orthodox Jew today would give a very different account of the Hebrew Bible (he would not, of course, regard it as the Old Testament). He would say that the centre and *raison d'être* of the Hebrew Bible is the Torah, the law of Moses; and that the rest of the Bible is to be understood in the light of the Torah and exists for the sake of the Torah. Thus he would give a less important place to the prophets. He would regard them as primarily men who wished to recall Israel to the observance of the Torah. And he would find in Psalms and Proverbs all sorts of references to the Torah that would not necessarily occur to us. He would feel himself on very strong ground even when he reached the book of Maccabees (which he would not regard as forming part of the Bible at all), since the great issue on which the Jews encountered the opposition of the Seleucid monarch Antiochus IV was their determination to observe the Torah.

We must certainly concede that large parts of the Old Testament are concerned with detailed observation of the Torah: four out of the five books of the Pentateuch are largely made up of law-code. Most (but not all) of the books written after the Exile, such as Haggai, Zechariah, Malachi, Chronicles, Ezra-Nehemiah, are written by men who regard Torah-observance as very important, indeed as the main duty of Israel. This is because it was only really after the Exile that the Jews' religion developed into a religion centred round a law written in a sacred book. And only after the Antiochean persecution (169 BC) did the notion arise that the devout Jew was bound to find an answer to every moral predicament in some part of the law as interpreted by oral tradition (the *Halakah*). In very early times the Torah as known after the Exile hardly existed at all. David knew of nothing remotely like the Torah of later Judaism. The pre-exilic prophets, as we have noted, are not in fact ardent devotees of a written law. One profoundly significant book, Job, pays absolutely no attention to the Law whatever. Thus one's assessment of what is important in the Old Testament cannot be based on any interpretation that arises naturally and intrinsically out of the Old Testament itself. The Old Testament is not a self-interpreting book. This is also true of the New Testament, and therefore of the Bible as a whole.

We Christians ought to judge the Torah in the same way as Jesus judged it. As we shall be seeing in the next section, he judged the Torah according to what he believed to be God's purpose in giving it. He did not regard it as something sacred and venerable in itself, only in relation to God's purpose in issuing it through Moses (of course Jesus viewed the actual circumstances of the giving of the Law on Sinai as his contemporaries did; he knew nothing of biblical criticism). Consequently, though Jesus did not repudiate the Law, he tended in effect to bypass it and to go back to God himself. We should try to apply this approach to our estimate of the Torah in the Old Testament. The Torah gives a picture (by and large) of the sort of person that God wished the Israelite to be. As such it is to be respected, but not used as the be-all and end-all of the Bible, and certainly not allowed to eclipse the immensely important insights of the great prophets. The Torah as it stands is a very miscellaneous body of precepts; some of it (such as the institution of circumcision and a great deal of the dietary commandments) goes back to primitive ritual, taboo, and apotropaic magic. We cannot help admiring the grave moral earnestness of some of the Old Testament writers who most strongly commend the Torah, for example the author or authors of Deuteronomy. But we cannot allow the Torah to monopolize the Old Testament. Biblical criticism has done much to alter our estimate both of the New Testament and of the Old, not always making matters easier for the modern Christian. But as regards the Torah we may well regard biblical criticism as an ally and a friend. It has shown conclusively that the Torah as understood by orthodox Judaism is the creation of the post-exilic community. The Torah does not go back to Moses except in the most vague, rudimentary and uncertain form. If we may appeal back to the period of the great classical prophets, we are appealing from the period of late Judaism, when Israel's religion was based on the Torah, back to the earlier period in Israel history when the people's relation to God was based much more on faith. In reply to Nietzsche's criticism we say that orthodox Judaism's interpretation of the Old Testament is, no less than ours, based on one element, though that a prominent one, in the Old Testament tradition.

b. Faith

Faith does not of itself imply knowledge. One can have faith in anything, credible or incredible, existent or non-existent. Many people believe in astrology, the theory that the stars have an influence on human destiny, a theory which has had an attraction for the human mind since the dawn of civilization but which is devoid of any solid foundation in reason, as Augustine demonstrated in his *Confessions* more than fifteen centuries ago. Others believe firmly that the earth is flat, or that the British race is descended from the ten lost tribes of Israel, beliefs which are no less irrational than those of astrology. None of these forms of faith constitute knowledge.

Many Christian writers, however, have spoken as if faith was knowledge, not least John Wesley. They speak of the illumination brought by faith, an illumination which makes the difference between utter darkness and dazzling light. They also speak of the certainty of faith. 'Ten thousand difficulties do not make a doubt', said Newman. Others, wistful unbelievers, sometimes long for faith as for something that gives assurance. We can admire somebody's faith, even though we do not share it, because it appears somehow to impart knowledge. And some Christians have spoken as if faith were quantifiable, as if it was a virtue to have more faith rather than less faith, irrespective of what the object of faith is. Is it more meritorious not only to believe that Christ is the Son of God, but also to believe that the Holy House of Loretto was miraculously transported through the air (touching down at one or two points on the way) from Nazareth to Loretto? Should we accept readily the statement of a character in *Through the Looking-Glass* that with a little bit of practice it is possible to believe six impossible things before breakfast?

These kinds of question raise the old query about whether faith involves propositions or not. The Athanasian Creed begins with the words: 'Whosoever will be saved: before all things it is necessary that he hold the Catholic Faith: Which Faith except every one do keep whole and undefiled: without doubt he shall perish everlastingly'. It proceeds to unfold a concise and lapidary summary of the doctrines of the Trinity and incarnation, including some statements which on the face of them appear highly paradoxical, and concludes with the reiterated warning: 'This is the Catholic Faith: which except a man believe faithfully he cannot be saved'. Presumably assent to the propositions included in the creed is the preliminary gateway to salvation. At the other end of the spectrum are those, like Kierkegaard, who insist that faith means trust, personal commitment to God, and not, or not primarily, assent to propositions; it means, in Kierkegaard's famous words, 'floating on seventy thousand fathoms of water and not being afraid'.

And finally we can ask whether faith is reasonable or not. To Anselm, for instance, faith looks for reasons to justify itself, and he wrote his famous *Cur Deus Homo* because he was convinced that nothing was more reasonable than the doctrines of the incarnation and atonement, properly understood. With this attitude, which was very much that of the scholastic theologians as a whole, we may contrast Luther in the sixteenth century and writers such as Gerhard Ebeling and Karl Barth in the twentieth, for whom faith must include an element of recognizing a paradox, something that challenges or defies reason. Luther spoke of 'that whore Reason'; Kierkegaard went furthest of all, maintaining that Christianity involved accepting an absurdity, a complete sacrifice of reason. Karl Barth resolutely refused to allow that faith is required to give any reasons for believing in Christ, because this would be to dishonour Christ. Pannenberg has consequently accused him of fideism, believing by a sheer act of arbitrary will. Not unlike these, in the Catholic tradition, are theologians like Newman whose concept of faith seems to be the recognition of and belief in an infallible authority, whose deliverances, once the authority has been recognized, are to be accepted in faith, though perhaps with different degrees of assent.

There can be no doubt that the teaching of the Bible is that faith involves decision, self-commitment. The profoundest thinkers of the Old Testament, the writer of the book of Job, many of the writers of the Psalms, and above all that greatest author of all who wrote the 40th to the 55th chapter of Isaiah, the prophet who lived and spoke during the exile of the people of Israel in Babylon during the sixth century BC, are united in thinking that God can only be known or indeed approached by faith. God is master of man in such a way that man cannot exhaustively know him or grasp him as a scientist grasps a scientific theory or an engineer understands the working of a machine. 'Who has directed the spirit of the Lord, or as his counsellor has instructed him?' (Isa. 40: 13, quoted by Paul, 1 Cor. 2: 16). The only attitude proper to man before God is one of trust; this, and this alone, is how God is known. The New Testament sharpens and deepens this emphasis. Jesus, to the writers of the gospels, to Paul and the author of Hebrews, is the supreme exemplar of faith, of trust in God, and they call Christians to a similar faith, in John to a faith which believes even though it has not seen (John 20: 29), in Paul to faith which throws itself on the mercy of God, bankrupt of all other resources in view of God's overwhelming act of mercy in Christ, in Hebrews to faith which 'is the assurance of things hoped for, the conviction of things not seen' (Heb. 11: 1).

Faith therefore does not require proof before it believes; it does not wait for proof. But this is not because there is an unfortunate absence of proof in matters concerning Christian doctrine. It is not because in the absence of facts we fall back upon the comforting delusion of faith. We are not like Hardy's wistful sceptic who does not believe that on Christmas Eve the ox and the ass are given the power of speech, but who might go to the byre some Christmas Eve 'hoping it might be so'. It is the nature of God that makes faith necessary for Christians. He wants our inner authentic final selves, what Jesus called our hearts. He wants our trust and love and allegiance. We can only give these by an act of self-commitment comparable to the commitment of lovers to each other, a self-giving in response to his own self-giving in Christ. Faith therefore cannot be betting on a certainty nor a matter of purely intellectual assent to rational propositions. There must be a leap in the dark, an act of belief which falls short of recognizing mathematically, scientifically or philosophically proved truth, an acceptance which does not necessarily offend the intellect but which cannot be understood in intellectual terms alone. Only so can God be known.

But through faith God *is* known. Faith is not itself knowledge but in the case of Christian faith it provides the conditions in which knowledge can be achieved. This is not a matter of, as it were, interpreting ink-blots; you might see an ink-blot as an elephant whereas I choose to see it as a wheelbarrow. Faith is neither self-hypnotism nor purely arbitrary decision to believe because it pleases us to believe (whether we achieve such a position by the road of linguistic philosophy or the avenue of Barthian positivism is immaterial). In the first place, we find God by believing. Perhaps gradually and haltingly at first but with increasing confidence and depth as we continue, we experience God, we know him as someone independent of ourselves though known through our human faculties. This is not of course scientific or mathematical knowledge or knowledge conveyed directly through the senses, but it is an authentic kind of knowledge, comparable to the knowledge with which we know what is a right decision, or the knowledge with which we know and can trust another person's character; one might provisionally call it moral knowledge. And, like all knowledge, it illuminates the world for us. It can indeed transfigure the world so that it becomes almost a different place for us. And it can give assurance and confidence, as our knowledge of what is right or our knowledge of the characters of those whom we love can give assurance and security. This is not an unbreakable infallible certainty, any more than our knowledge of what is the right decision to make involves infallible certainty. As a matter of fact, even the most demonstrable form of scientific knowledge does not give infallible certainty; any scientific truth might later by the discovery of further evidence be proved false. In our ordinary conduct of our affairs in the world we do not look for infallible certainty; when we choose a partner in marriage or try somebody on a grave criminal charge or determine that we shall go on this journey and not that, buy this house and not that, even when we entrust our very lives to the reliability of an air pilot or a bus driver, we require no such assurance, because we know that we could not possibly have it. It is irrational to demand a higher security in the affairs of God; indeed the search for infallibility, be it of the Church or of the Bible or of the individual's inner experience, is a chase after a will-o'-the-wisp and may well argue an inner insecurity which is incompatible with faith. It is the peculiar fallacy of the twentieth century to confine truth to that which is mathematically and scientifically verifiable and to abandon all other kinds of conviction to the realm of whimsy or imagination or deceit. And the demand among the pious for infallibility is a kind of mirror-image of this fallacy.

In the second place, we must note that Christian faith includes an element of moral obligation. Of course doubt too has its moral demand, and we should respect the moral integrity of those who say that they would like to believe but cannot, and of those who declare that they doubt while they believe and believe while they doubt. But it is still true that we believe not only because we want to but also because we ought to. All truth exercises a certain compulsion on us. And this means that faith cannot remain indefinitely poised between doubt and conviction. He who takes this view of faith is thinking of it in purely human terms. But faith has also its Godward side, in that it is a response to God's calling and attraction. God attracts us; he draws us to him by the magnet of love. Luther therefore was wrong in wholly divorcing love from faith in its initial stage, though he was right in rejecting the late Mediaeval idea that love of God means earning merit in God's sight, because genuine love does not operate in terms of merit. Paul's phrase in Galatians 5:6, 'faith working through love', is the best way of summing up the matter. Authentic faith recognizes God's love, and cannot hesitate in uncertainty any longer.

Similarly faith cannot be quantified, though there are one or two rather disturbing texts in Paul which suggest that it might be (1 Corinthians 12:9 and 13:2, for instance). If A believes that Christ died for his sins, and B believes that Christ died for his sins and also that the Blessed Virgin Mary was corporeally assumed into heaven, B is not necessarily a better or more faithful Christian. Lewis Carroll's quip, like most of his quips, had more than a grain of truth in it. What matters is not how much you believe, but what you believe. If Christianity is true, some part of it at least must be distinguished from falsehood and from nonsense. But further, faith is manifestly different according to what is its object. Faith in the Nicene Creed is a quite different sort of faith from faith in one's lucky star. And this is where the question of propositions is relevant. Faith may be floating on 70,000 fathoms of water, but, to extend the metaphor, the water is wet and salt and is composed of two parts of hydrogen to one of oxygen. Faith is not a sheer trust, a sheer emotion of dependence arising out of nothing. It arises out of certain convictions or observations or stimuli. We believe because we have reasons, motives, for believing. We do not have faith because we have been convinced by *proofs*; if Christianity could be proved true by scholastic philosophy or Hegelian idealism or scientific investigation or historical evidence, then, as Kierkegaard so clearly saw, it would not be Christianity; it would lose what he called its existential nature, the element of decision; it would cease to be something that involves us personally at the deepest level. But it is nonetheless true that we must and do have motives, reasons, for believing. These reasons can be based on a number of arguments drawn from history or our experience of the world, or our knowledge of ourselves, or from our own or others' specifically religious experience, or from philosophy, or from all of them. And as many writers have pointed out, such as Pascal and Newman, our reasons for belief may not be perfectly capable of being set out in rational language, but may still be good reasons. Intuition or poetic feeling or a not easily identifiable moral impulse may constitute or contribute to our reasons for making the decision of faith, or our admiration for others who believe, or even our sense of horror at the results of unbelief. But still we must and do have reasons for believing, and all the rhetoric of Barth cannot disguise this fact. The propositions involved in believing in God as revealed in Christ (and of course there are such propositions) appear both as reasons for and as implications of belief, even though belief itself does not take the form of assent to propositions. Our trust in God is not directed towards a vacuum, but to a God of a particular nature who has disclosed himself in particular ways.

This brings us to the final point about faith. We ought to see that we have the best reasons for belief, and we ought as far as possible to know what they are and to respect them. There can be – as psychology often demonstrates to us – less than reputable motives for faith. Indeed faith based on the wrong motives can scarcely be called faith. Spintho, in Shaw's play *Androcles and the Lion*, believes because he is convinced that 'martyrdom pays all scores', and he has plenty of heavy debts to be wiped out. And at the critical moment his faith fails him. This is the point at which the theologian and the pious believer are apt to quarrel. The theologian insists upon intellectual honesty, upon looking all the facts in the face and as far as possible facing all the difficulties and objections. The pious believer does not see the point of this. But each man must be honest about his reasons for believing. One may genuinely encounter more difficulties than another, just because he knows more, and we must make allowance for this. This argument, however, can be carried too far. It is not the duty of Christians to seek out carefully reasons against faith, as Van Harvey, in his *The Historian and Believer*, quaintly suggests. Anselm's motto, 'faith seeking understanding', is, if rightly understood, a sound one. If a Christian has found and experienced God and known him as true, it is entirely right and proper that he should examine with intelligence and with a good conscience the reasons which have led him to such a faith and approve them as sound or adjust them, rejecting some and allowing others. Faith and reason are not identical, but they are good partners.

3 The Status and Function of Scripture

a. Inspiration and Inerrancy

The Christian Church did not take the Hebrew Scriptures over from the Jewish people in a vacuum. By the time of our Lord there were already several well-established methods and traditions concerning the right interpretation of Scripture within the life of Judaism, and we can see the marks of all of them to a greater or less degree in the literature of the New Testament and of the early Church. There was the *pesher*-type of interpretation visible in the literature of the Dead Sea Scrolls, whereby a short passage of a prophetic book was quoted and then applied to the life of the religious community involved, and within this tradition there was already established the practice of collecting Messianic proof texts. There was the complex but rather wooden and unadventurous system of rationalizing the Torah so that it could fit the needs of the contemporary Jewish community perfected in the Rabbinic schools. And there was the flexible and fertile method of allegorizing used by Philo, that sophisticated and scholarly contemporary of Paul. This method was borrowed from the tradition of literary criticism in use among the pagan scholars of Alexandria. All these we can see reflected in the New Testament and the literature of the first three or four centuries of Christianity. Christian interpreters brought to the handling of Scripture their own peculiar emphasis and interest, of course, such as a marked shift of balance from the Torah to the prophetic writings, conceived in their broadest sense. But they used without hesitation the hermeneutical traditions and interpretations current in the Judaism of their day.

Among these traditional assumptions there were two which were common to all Jewish, and consequently to all later Christian interpreters of Scripture in antiquity. One was that the Scriptures were inspired, the other that they were inerrant. Perhaps it should here be noted that it is undesirable when arguing about the status of Scripture to appeal to Scripture in order to establish its authority. It is quite possible to find passages in Scripture asserting its own inspiration (e.g. 2 Timothy 3:16), and its inerrancy (e.g. John 10:35), but a little exercise of logical reasoning should show that to quote these as a proof that Scripture is inspired and inerrant is to assume at the outset that which has to be proved. It should be made clear also that the process of forming a canon of the New Testament (the most important part of which process occupied about two hundred years) saw also the process whereby the concepts of inspiration and inerrancy were extended to apply to the contents of the New Testament as well as to those of the Old.

By 'inspired' or 'inspiration' the ancients meant that the documents to which these terms were applied were in some way directly prompted or suggested or even written by God himself, as the well-known statement that the Holy Spirit is the author of Scripture suggests. Precisely how this operation of inspiration took place was differently conceived by different writers. Some, such as Philo, believed that the writers of Scripture were thrown into a kind of trance so that the result of their activity was almost literally what we today would call 'automatic writing'. Others, like Theophilus of Antioch or Athenagoras, used the metaphor of a pen with whom God writes or a lyre on whom God plays. Origen rejected the idea that the reason of the writers was suspended during the writing, but nonetheless believed in the inspiration of every word, almost of every letter. The fact that the vast majority of literate Christians after the first century, even the highly educated among them, read the Old Testament in a Greek translation, and the Latin readers read both Testaments in a Latin translation of the Greek, did not affect their belief in inspiration. They seldom appeal to a translator's error in order to meet a difficulty.

Inerrancy was the practical effect, in fact almost the only practical effect, of inspiration. The two concepts are closely bound up together, indeed cannot exist without each other. Inspiration implied inerrancy; the Scriptures could not be wrong because they were inspired. An early Gnostic writer, Apelles, on making the, to him, startling discovery that all the animals known to man could not possibly fit into the Ark if it was of the dimensions allotted to it in the biblical narrative, drew the inevitable conclusion: 'The story is an invention; therefore Scripture is wrong'. Inerrancy therefore meant absence of untrue or inaccurate statements. Everything in the Bible, first the Old and then the New Testament, must be true.

Even in antiquity however this concept of inerrancy had to be modified. It was simply impossible to maintain that there were no inconsistencies, no contradictions and no inaccurate statements in the Bible. It was even very difficult to maintain that there were no unworthy, incomprehensible, irrelevant, or shocking passages in the Bible. It was perfectly clear that in all the vast literature represented by the Old and New Testaments there were many such. The Rabbis had already had to face this difficulty and had invented a system of allegory or reinterpretations which, applied to any given part of the Hebrew Scriptures, purported to be able to show that it was not intended to be taken in its literal meaning. The writers of the New Testament adopted this, extending it as they attempted to show that many hitherto unsuspected predictions about Christ, the Church and Christian doctrine lay hidden in the Old Testament. The writers of the first five centuries enormously developed this technique. Not only could every difficulty and contradiction thus be cleared away, but the whole Christian dispensation could at will be read into any part of the Old and New Testaments. They turned the Bible into what might without exaggeration be called a vast crossword puzzle.

Behind this curious process lay a sentiment which can be found everywhere in the world of antiquity, among authors Jewish, pagan and Christian, a reverence for oracles. The oracle was thought to be a direct, unmediated, communication from God, or gods, or the divine, whether it took the form of utterances from well-established traditional oracular sites like Delphi, Delos, Ammon, Dodona or Cumae, or writings or pronouncements of individual peripatetic prophets or prophetesses, or the mysterious words of traditional Scripture supposed to derive either from directly inspired men and women or from records of immemorial antiquity. In the early Christian period individuals, pagan or Christian, were liable to claim divine inspiration, like Apollonius of Tyana or Simon Magus or the prophet Alexander of whom Lucian wrote in the second century, or Montanus and his female devotees. Both Jews and Christians forged and circulated *Sibylline Oracles* written in the appropriate Greek hexameter verse. And the early Christian writers found it impossible to resist the temptation to present the Scriptures of the Old and New Testaments as a complex collection of mysterious divine oracles. The status which they ascribed to Scripture was essentially oracular. Such was the inevitable result of ascribing to it inerrancy and inspiration.

But, as Milton reminds us in his *Ode to the Nativity*, oracles were superseded by the arrival of Jesus Christ. To take an oracular attitude towards God is sub-Christian; indeed it is sub-Jewish. Neither Christians nor Jews, if they are educated and thoughtful, ought to have anything to do with it. It is one form of the never-ending human search for an unmediated contact with the divine. We cannot in this life divest ourselves of our humanity. All communication with God must reach us through our human faculties, and not in spite of them nor apart from them. Grace does not abolish nature. If God speaks to men and women through documents of any sort, then these documents must be the products of human hands and minds, conditioned by the circumstances in which they were produced. There are no letters dropped from heaven, no books directly entrusted to individuals by an angel, no matter what fantasies of that sort history may have from time to time produced. To the search for oracular wisdom in the ancient world, there corresponds today the desire for infallibility, either of a book or of an individual or of a council. Both searches are equally vain, and represent the first step towards the ever-recurring sin of idolatry. The ancient doctrine of the inspiration and inerrancy of the Bible not only is impossible for intelligent people today, but represents a deviation in Christian doctrine, whatever salutary uses may have been made of it in the past by the Holy Spirit, who often turns human errors to good ends.

These doctrines have been rendered impossible for intelligent people to hold today because of the rise of historical criticism. This is the method of studying historical documents gradually developed by international scholarship since the seventeenth century, which now is accepted by all competent historians. Its fundamental axiom and insight is that all documents of the ancient, as of the modern, world are conditioned by the age and circumstances in which they were written or produced. This apparently simple truth has been developed into an elaborate and rigorous discipline which analyses sources, distinguishes influences, relates documents to their era and background, reconstructs the original situation in which they were written, extricates original texts, and generally uses the complex and demanding processes of modern historical study. This process at an early period in its development was applied to the Bible, first to the Old and then to the New Testament and rather later to the whole history of Christian doctrine. Many of its results are visible in this book. For the moment, however, it is enough to say that once historical criticism was seriously applied to the Bible the old doctrines of inspiration and inerrancy became no longer tenable. They vanished like shadows in the light of day.

b. Uniqueness and Sufficiency

Various efforts have been made to retrieve the credibility of the traditional doctrine of the inspiration and inerrancy of the Bible. It has been argued that the Bible is inspired because it is inspiring, that the authors but not what they wrote were inspired, that it was the authentic teaching and not the historical or scientific accuracy of the Bible that was inspired and inerrant. Most despairing of all is the contention that the original manuscripts as they left the hands of the authors were inspired and inerrant, but not the copies which are in our hands today, the products of centuries of copying and recopying. None of these arguments is convincing nor can stand close examination. The theory that the Bible is inspiring not only directly contradicts the view of the ancients, who were ready to argue that it is inspired in spite of being in many places uninspiring, and therefore has no right to claim any continuity with that theory, but it also is fatally subjective. What parts of the Bible are inspiring? Surely not all? And who is to decide which bits are inspiring and which not? Anyway plenty of other books are inspiring in this sense. If the authors but not their work were inspired then we should cease to apply the word 'inspired' to the text; but anyway nothing is gained in describing the authors as inspired if this quality does not attach to what they wrote. It is impossible to disentangle the authentic teaching of any given writer from the historical or scientific data which he handles. And further, there are several places where what is undoubtedly the authentic teaching of an author is such that we would recoil from calling it inerrant, as when the author of the book of Joshua records with relish the massacre of the inhabitants of Jericho by the people of Israel, or the sentiment expressed in the last verse of Psalm 137, 'Happy shall he be that takes your little ones and dashes them against the rock'. Finally, that we should be expected to believe in the inerrancy of the original manuscripts of the books of the Bible, which have long since disappeared from human ken, is no more reasonable than to expect us to believe in the aerial adventures of the Holy House of Loretto. If God has permitted later copies of the Scriptures to suffer from error, it is impossible to see what purpose he could have had in preserving the originals from error. This defence is surely the sign of a bankrupt argument.

We must candidly reject the ancient oracular view of the Bible and substitute for it the concept of the Bible as witness or testimony. The primary significance of the Bible is as evidence for the character and activity of God. The evidence is greatly varied. It takes a multitude of literary forms, history, saga, legend, law of different kinds, prophecy, proverbs, hymns, apocalyptic, gospels, Acts, letters, and many others. It covers a span of time of at least two thousand years. It comes from a great many different authors, most of whose names are unknown to us, writing in three different languages. But all this literature in one way or another witnesses to what God is like, what he has done, is doing and is likely to do. It is as witness that the Bible has been carried through Christian history, constantly copied and recopied, printed and reprinted and translated into a thousand languages. If we are to define the function and status of the Bible today we must describe it as the unique and sufficient witness to the character and activity of God.

That the Bible is unique it is not difficult to perceive. No other

collection of literature can rival the Old Testament as evidence for
God's calling and leading and dealing with his chosen people, Israel;
no other collection of documents can rival the New Testament as
early written tradition about the life and words and deeds of Jesus
Christ and the estimate of him held by his earliest disciples and the
first few generations of Christians. It must indeed be said that the
New Testament stands immovably between us and the earliest
Christian community. It is of course true that some documents, such
as the literature of the Dead Sea Covenanters, which are not in the
Old Testament, throw light upon the thought and life of Israel, and
some literature, such as the Letters of Ignatius, not included in the
New Testament, appears to be earlier and more valuable than some
of the documents of the New Testament. But as a collection of
evidence, whether taken separately or together, the Bible has no
rival as witness, witness formally and deliberately chosen by the
Jewish nation and the Christian Church to the character and activity
of God. In this sense it may be called unique. But it should be noted
that it is the subject, the matter, of the Bible which constitutes its
uniqueness, not its style nor any quality inhering uniformly in its
words nor any mysterious depth or double significance to be
detected in its language. In the matter of language, construction,
handling of sources and evaluation of the events narrated and
characters depicted, the books of the Bible are conditioned by the
periods in which they were written and their authors were the
children of their age.

With uniqueness we must couple sufficiency. It is not the function
of the Bible to supply us with infallible instruction, but only with
material sufficient for its readers to understand about their salvation.
When we ask of the Bible more than this, when we expect it to be a
magic book to answer all questions, or a carefully contrived and
concerted system of omnicompetent theology, we are asking of it
more than it can properly give, and we must not be surprised if we
can only receive a confused and uncertain response to our demands.
'Sufficiency' is a good Anglican word, to be found in the XXXIX
Articles; the adjective 'sufficient' occurs significantly in the Ordinal
of the Book of Common Prayer also. But the concept is one which
can be used by Christians of all traditions to their advantage. Instead
of expecting the Bible to display the fantastic colours of inerrancy we
should look for the soberer but more realistic hue of sufficiency.

It is in this light that we should view what is called the canon of
Scripture. The list of books which should form the Old Testament
has never been agreed upon by all Christians, and probably never
will be. The Jews of Palestine tended to reject those books like

Ecclesiasticus and Wisdom, which were manifestly written at a late period, some of them originally in Greek, whereas the Jews of Alexandria accepted them. Some of the books of the Old Testament were only accepted by the Jews after the beginning of the Christian era. The same uncertainty has attached to the Old Testament canon in its reception in the Christian Church. Jerome (*ob.* 420) and the churches stemming from the Reformation of the sixteenth century tended to be exclusive, and allow only those books which were recognized by Palestinian Judaism. But the vast majority of Christians from AD 200 to AD 1520 regarded all the traditional Christian books, 'Apocrypha' as well as the rest, as equally authoritative; the Roman Catholic Church since the sixteenth century has taken the same view, and contemporary scholarship makes little or no distinction between the two groups. Even within the New Testament, whose acceptance by the Christian Church was much more unanimous, certain problems of canonicity are raised. The story of the Woman taken in Adultery (John 7:53–8:11) and the ending of St. Mark's Gospel (Mark 16:9–20) were certainly not there in the original manuscripts and represent additions made by later tradition. Are we to regard them as 'canonical'?

The fact is that the canon of Scripture is not a *cordon sanitaire* marking the difference between writings possessed of a mysterious quality called 'inspiration' and all other literature in the world. It is a useful boundary, drawn approximately and for purposes of convenience, delineating a collection of literature the study of which is sufficient to make the reader 'wise unto salvation'. The Church guarantees that much. It does not guarantee that every document in the collection is equally authoritative nor capable of performing alone the function of the whole, nor that there is no other document which might enhance the collection were it added, nor that the collection might not serve its purpose equally well were some few of its contents removed. But if we envisage the canon as a collection of literature designed to give sufficient evidence for people to understand and embrace the Way of Life, we shall perceive the futility of making suggestions about either adding to or subtracting from its contents.

c. The Bible as a Norm

The Bible, though its status and function is that of witness, is also used in one form or another as a norm of doctrine by all Christian churches. Indeed the very fact that the Church early in its history adopted the Bible as formal evidence for its beliefs made its use as a norm inevitable. The Church did not canonize the Bible merely as a useful source of information for those who were interested in Christian origins, but as a norm for doctrine, and certainly the early Church made a strenuous and sustained attempt to use the Bible in this capacity. Early Christian believers were soaked in, conditioned by, the language and imagery of the Bible to an extent which it is difficult for us to imagine. Whatever the early theologians may actually have done, they certainly intended to use the Bible strictly as a rule of faith. And subsequent ages have in varying degree followed the early Fathers in this practice.

If, however, we today are to accept the Bible as a norm of doctrine, we must do so in a considerably more restricted and complex sense than did our forefathers in the faith. They too often seemed to think that theological propositions or even systems lay ready-made in the text of the Bible only waiting to be transposed onto the pages of textbooks, or awaiting the magic wand of allegory to appear, prefabricated, like the negative of a photographic film when it is developed. But more rigorous examination of the Bible under the influence of modern methods of historical research has made this view appear impossibly naive and simple. The biblical authors were writing for their own times and circumstances; most of them never dreamed that what they wrote would be read by millions of people over thousands of years. The immediacy and conditioned nature of much of their work demand of the modern reader a continuous effort of what we might call transposition so that its relevance to his situation can be discerned. What the Bible supplies us with is the raw material for doctrine, not the finished product itself. Irrelevant matter has to be ignored, contradictions or inconsistencies properly weighed, obsolete or archaic ways of thinking modernized, allowances for local and temporary circumstances made, and many other conditions satisfied before the Bible can be used effectively as a norm. And this applies to the least as to the greatest points involved in Christianity, from the question of whether women should wear hats in church to the doctrine of the incarnation.

At various times the Bible has been used as if it were a manual of theology, a handbook of ethics, a liturgical text, a blueprint for the form of the ministry, a guide for the spiritual life, a treatise on political and economic theory and a masterpiece of philosophy. It is none of these things, though its evidence may throw light on most or all of the subjects mentioned. If it is to be used as a norm for doctrine it must be used without any misunderstandings about its status as witness, and not as an encyclopaedia for the theologian and the believer.

In describing the Bible as evidence, witness, testimony, we do not mean to overlook one more important fact about it. The Bible is written from faith to faith. It is indeed a collection of ancient documents, but it is not just a collection of ancient documents like the *Historia Augusta* or the *History of Nennius*. During the ages the Bible has demonstrated an extraordinary power of evoking faith and kindling enthusiasm and stirring renewal and even revolution in the Church. Its appeal to the reading public never seems to grow stale. Each new generation as it makes acquaintance with the Bible experiences anew its power and its fascination. But it is the subject of the Bible that provides this attraction, and not any mysterious quality inhering in its words. The Bible is a living book because it tells of a living God, and if God is contemporary then in some sense the Bible is contemporary too.

Finally, two serious objections must be faced. In recent years it has become customary among several theologians in this country to question whether the Bible can effectively function as a norm of doctrine for two reasons, firstly because its documents are so ancient, and secondly because, in the case of the New Testament at least, the evidence is so scanty. Both of these questions must be taken seriously. We must not underestimate the vast difference which separates us from the cultures of any of the periods during which the books of the Bible were written, even the most recent of them. Even if we go back no further than the time of Jesus we sometimes seem to be like men looking at some object at the bottom of a deep mine. How remote he seems! With how vast a darkness he is encompassed! How huge an avalanche of time has fallen between us and him! The argument applies even more strongly the further back in time we trace the biblical literature. The people who wrote these pages and the men and women depicted in them had ideas about the world, about history, about themselves, and possibly about God quite different from ours. How can we have the impertinence to imagine that we really understand what they said, what they wrote, what they intended, what they did?

Such reflections should certainly preserve us from facilely reading into people and situations described in the Bible the ideas and sentiments and assumptions of our day. And this practice has been the besetting sin of Christian commentators and preachers. One cannot help observing, for instance, that the great biblical exegete of the last century, George Adam Smith, saw the prophet Isaiah as a combination of Mazzini and W. E. Gladstone, just as the German historian of the ancient world, Theodor Mommsen, tended to see much of Bismarck in Julius Caesar. But in one sense this very fault points to the possibility of bridging the chronological gulf and achieving what might be called a transcultural understanding. We tend to read the circumstances of our own day into figures and situations of the past because those figures and situations awake our sympathy and interest. We see in them something that appeals to us, that appears to represent concerns and desires and hopes and causes which have echoes in our hearts also. The imagination leaps over the centuries and in some sense, to some degree, annihilates them. Even when we have made all necessary allowance for differences of period, culture and background, we still are convinced that the past speaks to us and even comes alive for us. It would be irrational to assume that the interest and admiration and pleasure aroused in us by the *Odyssey* of Homer, by a dialogue of Plato and by a play of Aeschylus or Euripides, to take examples from a non-biblical culture and one much older than the New Testament, represent pure illusion and that these texts are really incomprehensible to us. They are not. They appeal to our hearts, they move us, they engage our attention deeply. Their antiquity does not diminish their appeal to us, any more than a superb wall-painting of a bull or an antelope in Lascaux appeals to us less because it is over twenty thousand years old. To reject the significance of a document, biblical or non-biblical, on the grounds that it derives from an antique culture which is different from ours, and on these grounds alone, is to ignore the capacity for imaginative understanding of the human mind, to assume arbitrarily that a human being in the twentieth century is someone radically different from a human being in the first century or earlier, and to leave unexplained the curiosity, the search for understanding represented by the enormous enterprise of contemporary historical research. The historical reliability of the biblical documents is a quite different question, and one with which it would not be proper to deal here.

As for the suggestion that the relatively short compass of the New Testament – two hundred odd pages of Greek not by any means all of them devoted to retailing the words and deeds of Jesus – is insufficient testimony upon which to base large-ranging doctrines like the divinity of Jesus Christ and the doctrine of the Trinity, it is sufficient to recapitulate the substance of the argument of G. W. H. Lampe in his recent book, *God as Spirit* (even though he applies it in a different context). The evidence for Christian doctrine does not consist only of the relatively meagre record of what Jesus said and did. It comprises in some sense the documents of the Old Testament and also the evidence for the impression which the whole career of Jesus, including his death and resurrection, made upon his disciples, his contemporaries and the first generation of Christians. The Church has arbitrarily (but not unreasonably) demarcated the evidence at that point. But it would be rash to say that what the Church has preserved for us is either insufficient or unimpressive. Evidence can be weighty intensively as well as extensively. If an atomic bomb falls it is not necessary to write many volumes about it in order to persuade posterity that it really did fall. One could be quite enough.

4 The Relation of Christianity to Other Religions

a. Great World Religions

One can distinguish three main stages in the development of Christian theology's relationship to the thought and practice of other religions:

i. This is the relationship that has prevailed during by far the greatest part of Christian history: other religions are regarded as a tissue of errors, darkness, and diabolical' deceit. The doctrine of demons (inherited from Judaism) proved very useful to the Fathers as a means of invalidating the religious experience, miracles, and phenomena of other religions. By the time that Christianity had prevailed all over Europe, the only other living religions the Christians knew were Judaism and Islam. Towards Judaism the attitude was one of almost unvaried hostility. Islam was regarded as just capable of being described as a Christian heresy, but almost no one in the Christian camp attempted to do justice to it. Jeremy Taylor, in the seventeenth century, marvelling at the inscrutable providence of God, laments that so many millions should have been led astray by a mad camel driver.

ii. The second stage emerged during the nineteenth century, very largely as a result of the impact of Hinduism. Here was a religion which had evolved without any influence from Christianity at all. Though there were plenty of Christians willing to put it in the category of diabolical darkness, some Europeans from the eighteenth century onwards began to show interest in it and admiration for it. Missionaries in India found themselves compelled to study it to some extent. This produced by the end of the nineteenth century Farquahar's *The Crown of Hinduism,* a book of far-reaching influence. In it he presented Hinduism as a religion which finds its true fulfilment in Christianity. He worked this out in some detail, showing an understanding of Hinduism and an admiration for it in certain aspects. But he was quite clear that it should find its fulfilment in Christianity and give way to Christianity.

This was a step forward. Obviously this approach could be applied to other religions, and indeed must have been so applied. It did at least demand a careful study of other religions with less controversial concern. Naturally this approach was vulnerable to criticism. Hendrik Kraemer pointed out quite rightly that Hinduism does not form a natural prelude to Christianity, and that Farquahar had to distort some elements in it, and suppress others, in order to make out this thesis. Moreover, S. Radhakrishnan probably delivered as effective a blow as anyone else to Farquahar's contention when he turned the situation round by claiming that Hinduism was in fact the true crown of Christianity; his arguments are no less effective, and no more, than Farquahar's. Kraemer himself, being a Barthian, underlined strongly the discontinuity between Christianity and all other religions. But this can hardly be described as a new stage in the history of the relationship, rather an interlude.

iii. The third stage is that at which we have arrived and in which we are now engaged: in it dialogue takes place between Christian theologians and representatives of other religions. No attempt is made to relate Christianity with any other religion according to any particular schema. All that is required is honesty and a willingness to listen. There is an obvious temptation at this stage to try to assimilate all religions (or as many as possible) into one world religion. But this must be resisted in the interests of intellectual honesty.

A description of the development of the relationship between Christianity and other religions does not in itself solve the problems which this relationship poses, but it is the necessary preliminary to any solution. The next step, I believe, is this: we as Christians must not deny *a priori* the validity of anybody's religious experience. The fact that we believe we know God in Christ does not justify us in ruling out of court any claims to know God by any other means. Admittedly this stance is not wholly compatible with the attitude of the writers of the New Testament: all of them would have claimed that the only other religion which they knew, Graeco-Roman-Oriental syncretistic paganism, was sheer error and led away from God (Judaism was for them not another religion but the true mother of Christianity). There are other tendencies detectable, but it is no use pretending that an open attitude to non-Christian religious experience is characteristic of New Testament thought. Today we have to adopt such an open attitude as a result of our experience of other religions. Anyone who has discussed religion at a deep and honest level with representatives of other religions can hardly fail to be convinced that some of them do certainly know God. We have to accept this as a fact and adapt our theology in order to accommodate it. This does not mean that we have necessarily to accept the interpretation of other religious experience which representatives of other religions offer us. But we must be prepared to examine their claims. We must not be betrayed into saying: 'We know that you cannot have experienced God'.

In any case, this *a priori* ruling out of court of religious experience is exactly what Christians encounter at the hands of Freudians and others. Armed with the arguments provided by Freud (though not always consciously acknowledged), the average undergraduate today is prepared in effect to claim that he knows more about what lies behind Mother Teresa's religion than she does herself, and that he can account for it without examining it in detail. The intense interest which the American reading public shows in psychology may have served to extend the illusion further in the USA. It would be very foolish and arrogant on the part of Christians to apply to other religions arguments that seem to us so unconvincing when applied to Christianity.

There is however one form of religious experience which seems to claim our special attention here, the mystic way. Undoubtedly there is a considerable body of evidence to suggest that what can reasonably be called the mystic approach to God is common to all religions, certainly to Hinduism, Buddhism, Judaism, Christianity, and Islam. This mystic approach appears in a different context in each of these religions: it is more central in the two Indian religions, and is less easily accommodated by the three 'historical' religions. But it is to be found in all of them: all of them have produced great mystics. We should not attempt as Christians to deny this, especially in the present epoch when Christians are claiming to be able to adopt techniques of meditation and spirituality taken from Hinduism and Buddhism: cf. the work of such men as William Johnston S.J. and the French abbé who has adopted the name Abhishaktānanda. But this common element of religious experience does not in itself solve our problem. In the first place, not everyone can hope to follow the mystic way. Though there are no doubt many more people who could and ought to than there are those who do follow it, it never has been and never can be a universal religion for all. Even in those religions such as Hinduism and Buddhism where it is regarded as normative and as the highest way of life, it has not been presented as the only one or as one possible for the majority of people who live in the world. It has always had something of the atmosphere of the spiritual élite about it.

In the second place, the greatest exponents of the mystical way in the three 'historical' religions have not on the whole concluded from their experience that there is in fact only one 'real' religion, the mystical approach. They have on the whole striven to interpret their experience in terms of their own various religious traditions. It has been left to others to draw the conclusion that there is only one 'real', mystical religion. Of course this might be accounted for on cultural, geographical, or historical grounds. But we would be rash, on the basis of the testimony of the mystics in all religions, to conclude that, for example, St. John of the Cross's account of the unitive stage in the journey of the soul towards God is identical with the Hindu Yogi's account of the realization that his *atman* is identical with Brahman. It is safer to conclude from the experience of the mystics that we have here an argument for the existence of the transcendent, an argument for the claim that a reality exists which is beyond and greater than man but not merely part of nature or the whole of nature. As such it is a very formidable argument indeed, one which the Freudian cannot easily dismiss.

We come therefore to the centre of the problem: in considering the relationship of Christianity to other religions, what is it that we Christians must defend and maintain as our distinctive and inalienable insight? God known in Jesus Christ. This, we must maintain, is how God really is (and this, as we argue much later on, means God known as One in Three). This, we believe, is what he has decisively and uniquely revealed himself to be. This must be our criterion with which we approach all other religions. It does not follow that God has to be known as Jesus Christ in other religions, an obvious impossibility. After all, the writers of the New Testament themselves accepted fully the validity of the revelation of God in what we call the Old Testament. But during most of the period recorded in the Old Testament the Messiah as a religious category did not exist, and only the most fervid Christian allegorist could maintain that the name Jesus has any significance whatever in the Old Testament. We are not committed to the claim that no one can be saved who does not (consciously) know God in Jesus Christ. Indeed this question is not necessarily a question about salvation at all. It is a question about the knowledge and reality of God, about revelation, about truth. Hence we can approach other religions without the burden of being obliged to deny their religious experience, but also with the conviction that we need not deny the central pivot of our own religious tradition. We are neither tied to the dictum *extra ecclesiam nulla salus* nor delivered up to the vagaries of an eclectic religiosity. If God really has revealed himself in Christ as he really is, then, in so far as non-Christians have known God (and some of them certainly have known him and do know him), they know the God whom we know as he really is in Christ, the God of self-giving love, the righteous, holy redeemer. We are certainly not committed to claiming that God can only be known within the Christian tradition. We are committed to the belief that God known outside the Christian tradition is still the God identified and revealed in Jesus Christ.

It follows that Christians are justified in seeing traces of God-in-Christ in other religions. This is very different from any tidy schema whereby other religions lead up to Christianity. But it is legitimate to look for indications of the Christian understanding of God in other religions. We can perhaps take Hinduism as an example of how this approach to other religions works out. One might certainly recognize in certain elements of the *bhakti* tradition in Hinduism an apprehension of the self-giving love of God as we know it in Christ. It has even been suggested, not without reason, that some features of the Radha-Krishna cult have something in common with the Pauline account of the scandal of the cross. And we may be sure that the Bengali theologian, Brahmabandau Upādhyāya, who lived in the early years of this century, was right in pointing out that the Hindu concept of God known as *Sacchidānanda* offers an excellent analogy to, and means of expressing, the Christian doctrine of the Trinity.

But this does not mean that we Christians merely plunder other religions, spoiling the Egyptians, accepting what we find congenial and rejecting the rest. Other religious traditions can illuminate and constructively criticize Christianity, and we should not attempt to prevent them doing so. Once more, examples will be taken from Hinduism. We can learn from Hinduism the dangers of over-institutionalization. Hinduism has nothing corresponding to the Vatican, or Church House, or even a bench of bishops; not even an annual authoritative Conference or a General Assembly. But it manages to survive and flourish. We can surely learn from it something about the need for variety and freedom within Christianity, even the advantage of having alternative modes of expressing the same beliefs. We can indeed learn something even from these elements which we are constrained to reject. For instance, we have considered the suggestion that we may see something analogous to the scandal of the cross in the Radha-Krishna cult. But we must, if we are honest, judge that the Radha-Krishna story is legend not history, and conclude perhaps that this is a pity. How much more convincing it would be if we could believe there was an historical content. How important therefore it is that Christianity can claim to be an historical religion. Again, Radha was induced to leave her own husband in order to become Krishna's partner. Here indeed is the element of scandal which we can appreciate, but it is in the last resort something which our moral sense condemns. We cannot unreservedly admire Radha, though we can appreciate what is implied in the story. We learn by this that our sense of moral rightness must have the last word. In the course of Christian history some theological constructions have been widely accepted which today offend our moral sense: the traditional form of the penal doctrine of the atonement, for example, or the doctrine that moral values have been arbitrarily determined by God and might just as well have been completely different. Thus we approach other religions neither as triumphalists nor as agnostics. We know what we regard as central and essential, but we are ready to learn. Above all, we are ready to listen.

The last point is obvious enough, but must be articulated all the same: we cannot as Christians expect to have the same relation to every other religion. The facts of history and culture make this perfectly clear. In the first place we must always have a special and unique relation to Judaism, the matrix of Christianity, with which we have much more in common than we have with any other religion (we discuss this more fully later on). The same is true to a lesser degree of Islam. It is not accurate or helpful to describe Islam as a Christian deviation. The relation of Islam to Christianity is more akin to the relation of Christianity to Judaism. But even that comparison provides a very imperfect analogy. We are justified in speaking of these three religions as having special links with each other and forming a class on their own. Anyway history has seen to it that these three have come into much closer relations with each other than with any other religions.

Our relation to Hinduism and Buddhism is quite different. Even here, however, we cannot say that Christianity is related in the same way to both. The very fact that Buddhists do not normally use the term 'God' makes a very great difference. It would seem at first sight that it would be easier to relate Christianity to Hinduism than to Buddhism because of this very difference, but in fact this does not appear to be the way in which things are working out. At the level of experience it seems, Christians and Buddhists can find something in common. Perhaps this is because Buddhism, like Christianity, is exiled from its homeland and has flourished in a great variety of cultures. This can hardly be said of Hinduism. When we turn to other religions again, such as African traditional religion, or Taoism, we find that we must be related in very different ways. It would be as rash to imagine that one can find one formula by which Christianity can be related to all other religions as it would be to attempt to construct a synthetic world-religion out of all the great world-religions. But perhaps this will be sufficient to show that, at the contemporary stage of the development of Christianity, Christians can approach the representatives of other religions with openness and honesty without in the process being compelled to abandon their own central convictions.

b. Relation of Christianity to Judaism

'His blood be on us and on our children!' These terrible words (Matt. 27:25) are attributed by the evangelist to the Jewish crowd as it clamours for the death of Jesus before Pilate. It is in the last degree unlikely that any crowd at that point uttered so elaborate and so unnecessarily compromising a cry. No doubt the evangelist was not looking further than the fall of Jerusalem in AD 70. But it reflects adequately the attitude which the early Christians took against the Jews even at a point when Christian thought had not developed far. It was to remain the leitmotiv of what the Christians thought about the Jews for well over a thousand years, almost to our own day. The Jews were regarded as the murderers of Christ; Melito of Sardis calls them 'slayers of God' as early as about 170. It was not just the generation of Caiaphas and of Judas who incurred this odium; Matthew's words 'and on our children' enabled the Christians from the early Middle Ages onwards to extend the alleged guilt of the Jews indefinitely in time so that any Jew or Jews at any time or place could be regarded as inheriting responsibility for the death of Jesus.

This odium was intensified by the refusal of the Jews to disappear from history. According to the Christian scheme of things, that is exactly what they ought to have done. They had crucified Jesus; they had not long afterwards started an unsuccessful rebellion against the Roman government. Their city of Jerusalem had been captured and their temple destroyed. Two further Jewish revolts within the next hundred years had been equally futile. They ought now to cease to be a people, to leave the stage of history. Manifestly God had given judgment against them and had no further use for them.

But the Jews obstinately refused either to turn Christian or to cease to exist. Persecuted, driven out of many countries, regarded as dangerous and unassimilable aliens, herded into ghettos and branded as outcasts with few political rights, they still resolutely continued to survive. Christian spite and bigotry of the vilest sort were exercised against them all through the Middle Ages. From time to time they were subjected to local massacres, most recently in Tsarist Russia, where these occasions were called 'pogroms'; it perhaps should be noticed that usually both mediaeval kings and mediaeval clergy tried to protect the Jews against pogroms, the former because the Jews were useful as financiers, the latter because some faint sparks of decency and compassion may have lingered in their breasts.

Now in the twentieth century civilized societies do not persecute Jews, but grant them toleration and equal rights with Christians. This claim is, admittedly a precarious one, because less than fifty years ago the German government was persecuting Jews with a pathological ferocity unparalleled in the history of anti-Semitism, and because the government of the USSR, utterly disregarding the meaningless platitudes about toleration of religion enshrined in its constitution, is at this moment persecuting Jews and disseminating anti-Semitic propaganda with an efficiency which Tsarist anti-Semitic statesmen and Jew-baiting mobs might have envied, and at any moment it might encourage or tolerate a Marxist version of pogroms. But in Western democratic countries, and in most other countries, Jews are tolerated. In these circumstances, what should the attitude of Christians to Judaism be?

Relieved indifference will not do. Judaism may have no particularly close bonds with Christianity, but Christians can never forget that their religion sprang out of Judaism, its mother, aptly symbolized in that greatest of all Jewesses, the Blessed Virgin Mary. Jews and Christians are half-brothers in the faith. We use their Bible, though they do not use ours. Jesus was wholly and undeniably a Jew. He never uttered an anti-Semitic saying in his life: on the contrary, on the cross he said; 'Father, forgive them, for they know not what they do.' In fact, the granting of some territory in Palestine to the Jews after the First World War as a national home by the British Government was clearly motivated by a certain sense on the part of the British people of possessing, as Christians, a brotherly, or perhaps cousinly, relation to Jews. The Jews themselves, by the use of methods of ruthless terrorism with which we are all too familiar today, enlarged this national home into a modern sovereign state. We are certainly not called upon to follow some Christians of today in seeing this state of Israel, where the cost of living is among the highest in the world, as the fulfilment of the eschatological promises of God. But we must ask ourselves, what positive attitude can Christians now have to Jews?

Manifestly the alleged cry of the Jewish crowd at the trial of Jesus must be disowned. If any Jews were responsible for the death of Jesus, the moment for retribution is long, long past, and retribution was clearly against the mind of Jesus himself. To extend the responsibility to later generations of Jews was never justified, and if the Jews liked to turn the tables and suggest that the blood of the millions of Jews killed by Christians was on us and on our children we could hardly blame them. We must recognize that God has a divine purpose for the Jewish people as a people. It is perhaps more difficult for Christians than for anyone else to see what that purpose is, but the survival of the Jews through the ages strongly suggests that God has a purpose for them. Christians should be content to wait for that purpose to become clear to them, and meanwhile should do their best to promote mutual understanding between Jews and Christians, in things religious as well as in social matters, and to be particularly vigilant in supporting the Jewish people against those governments, such as that of Russia, which still discriminate against and harass Jews because of their religion. This attitude of constructive sympathy towards Jews, as distinct from mere indifferent toleration, does not necessarily involve an uncritical attitude towards the state of Israel. This particular state appears in Christian eyes to resemble an ordinary national sovereign state in a condition of ordinary twentieth-century nationalism rather than the kingdom of God on earth.

Judaism as a religion today depends on the assumption that the Torah as we have it in the Hebrew Bible is very much as it was when Moses delivered it to Israel on Sinai. But this assumption is completely denied, indeed disproved, by modern critical study of the Bible. It is very doubtful if anything but the vaguest outline of the Torah as we have it in the Bible goes back to Moses' time. The great bulk of it grew during the centuries between Joshua and Ezra; a certain proportion of it, especially the purely ceremonial or dietary laws, can be traced back to an origin in very early tabu, apotropaic ritual, or primitive magic. The great majority of Jews do not know this, and the great majority of Jewish rabbis, though they know of the existence of this critical approach, will not accept it. It is very much as if the critical approach to the Bible had never been acknowledged by Christian scholars, and as if we all still held the old-fashioned 'verbal inerrancy' approach to Scripture.

The question is, how long can educated and intelligent Jews continue to refuse to listen to the biblical critics? It may be that they will continue to do so indefinitely, in which case Judaism will gradually become a religion which consists entirely of routine observance, ritual, diet, and worship, and will cease to have any appeal to the educated. If, however, the findings of biblical criticism slowly begin to be accepted by educated Jews, then we may see something like a movement of convergence with Christianity. Not that they will be led directly to acknowledge Christ, but that they will begin to appreciate the great prophets for what they are in themselves, and not merely as witnesses to the Torah. This might well incline them to revalue their religious tradition as a whole, in the course of which they must encounter their greatest prophet between Malachi and Maimonides, Jesus of Nazareth.

II · CHRIST

5 Doctrine of the Incarnation

a. The Historical Jesus

It is necessary in our day to distinguish between the historical Jesus and the Jesus of faith. This is because New Testament study has now made it clear that the only records of the life of Jesus which we have, the four Gospels, are written from the point of view of those who believe in the risen Jesus, encountered in the fellowship of the Church through the Spirit, and that to a greater or lesser degree they have all superimposed upon the figure of the historical Jesus some of the characteristics of the risen Lord. Till the rise of biblical criticism in the eighteenth and nineteenth centuries, all Christians assumed that the Jesus of history and the Jesus of faith were identical, or rather that the Jesus of faith *was* the Jesus of history. This would be a possible hypothesis, except for the fact that the four Gospels do not present a harmonious picture of Jesus. We cannot therefore say, as some have in the past, 'You must choose between the consistently presented figure of Jesus as he is found in the Gospels and a purely speculative reconstruction of the critics.' In the Gospels Jesus is not consistently represented, but appears as more or less evolved with the features of the risen Lord. Roughly speaking, Mark's Gospel represents him as nearest to mere humanity (though by no means as an ordinary man), then comes Luke, who has taken some steps towards a more divine, superhuman figure. Matthew is definitely farther from giving us a figure of mere humanity than the other Synoptists (the disciples are more respectful; Jesus says he could summon legions of angels to help him, etc.). But when we turn to the Fourth Gospel we find a Jesus who has undergone almost a transformation compared with the figures in the Synoptic Gospels; he is aware of his substantial unity with his Father; he is well informed about the future; he openly declares himself to be Messiah; he is always in command of the situation, especially at his arrest, trial, and execution. He remembers his pre-existent state. It is no exaggeration to say that the Jesus of the Fourth Gospel is simply not compatible with the Jesus of Mark: they cannot both be true to the historical Jesus.

Scholars have not unnaturally concluded that neither is true and have attempted to rediscover the historical Jesus for themselves. In the nineteenth century, when this attempt was first made, it was often motivated by a rather arrogant confidence that the theological superstructure imposed on the Jesus of history by the early Church could easily be demolished, and a clear historical figure would emerge. This has not happened. On the contrary, the more that scholars have attempted to remove what they thought was the early Church's accretion which adhered to the historical figure, the nearer they have come to finding themselves with no historical figure left underneath. It has proved to be not a process of scraping the dirt off an ancient statue that has been buried for ages, but rather a process of peeling the skins off an onion: there does not seem to be any core. Some scholars have accepted this conclusion (Rudolf Bultmann for instance) and have declared that we can know almost nothing about the Jesus of history. The last fifteen years or so however have witnessed a reaction against this extreme position, and it is now possible to offer a plausible reconstruction of Jesus' teaching and intentions, though certainly not one that will be accepted by a consensus of scholars. There is no consensus among scholars about the characteristics of the historical Jesus.

This work is based on the belief both that some reasonable knowledge about the Jesus of history is essential as a basis for any adequate doctrine of the person of Christ, and that such knowledge can be had. The reconstruction that follows can be defended on reasonable grounds of scholarship, though the nature of this work does not give us space in which to offer that defence. We must however warn the reader in advance that the story of Jesus' birth from a virgin will form no part of this reconstruction. This is because we do not regard it as sufficiently based on historical evidence. Later on, in our discussion of Christology, we will discuss its significance in the New Testament account of Christ.

Jesus appears in Galilee preaching that the kingdom of God is about to come. He has some connection with the movement inaugurated by John the Baptist, for he has received John's baptism. But it seems likely that he only began his preaching ministry after John was imprisoned. Jesus always seems to elude our categories, and it is not easy to say whether we should call him a rabbi or not. Certainly he was hailed as 'Rabbi' by his contemporaries, and he had a group of disciples as rabbis had. But he does not seem to have himself received training at the feet of some older rabbi, as all accredited rabbis were expected to do, and his methods of teaching are very unrabbinic in the sense that he never appeals to traditional authority and never mentions other rabbis of the past to support his teaching. G. Vermes has made the interesting suggestion that the right category for Jesus is 'charismatic', which would put him somewhere between the position of a rabbi and of a mystic. The fact that he came from Galilee would give him a slight aura of unorthodoxy in the eyes of the strict Pharisaic party.

The kingdom really means the kingly rule of God, not an area ruled over; so where Jesus announces the kingdom he means that God is about to intervene personally in history and manifest his rule. Men and women are called upon to prepare themselves for the kingdom, and much of Jesus' teaching (notably the Sermon on the Mount) is a description of the sort of character that will feel at home in the kingdom. Jesus' message therefore was eschatological, in the sense that he declared that the end was coming, that end of this present era to which pious Jews had been looking forward ever since the secularization and corruption of the Hasmonean kingdom had convinced them that there could be no solution to Israel's problems in the sphere of power politics. But was his message also apocalyptic? Did he think that the end would be catastrophic, that all human history would cease, and that the only alternatives in the near future were either heaven or hell? This is the conclusion to which the famous Albert Schweitzer came seventy years ago, and he has been very influential among New Testament scholars. But recently, as in the case of Bultmann's scepticism about the historical Jesus, a reaction has set in. Jesus' teaching does not on the whole suggest that he regarded human history as virtually at an end, otherwise why should he give teaching about how to live in the kingdom, love for one's neighbour, etc.? On the other hand it is very difficult indeed to decide what exactly Jesus did believe about the future. Much of the material on this subject attributed to him, especially Mark chapter 13, must be regarded as of doubtful authenticity. All we can say with confidence is that his death and subsequent vindication were to inaugurate the kingdom, and that perhaps he envisaged a total consummation (what the New Testament calls the *Parousia*) at some time after that. But we should notice that the message of the kingdom itself implies a doctrine of salvation: God's action in history was to be an act of salvation (and therefore also inevitably of judgment). Jesus' message was not merely one of moral renewal.

Because the kingdom was so near, Israel's only hope lay in repentance, faith, and an appeal to God's mercy. This had the radical consequence that in effect there was now no difference between the righteous and the unrighteous; all are equally under judgment and all are equally in need of God's mercy and the wise man is the man who realizes his need for forgiveness. Such parables as the Pharisee and the Publican in the Temple, and the Prodigal Son, bring out this element in Jesus' teaching. This also explains why he deliberately associated with the outcast, the publicans, the prostitutes. Such people had no illusions about their own righteousness and therefore were nearer the kingdom than those who believed that they were in good standing with God. But Jesus was not merely one who uttered a call to repentance, like John the Baptist. He constantly said that if you approach God in penitence you will find that he is merciful. Indeed his stress on the love and mercy of God is an all-important element in his message. God sends his rain on all alike, cares even for the sparrows, comes to seek the strayed, as in the parable of the Lost Sheep. Thus faith on man's part and mercy on God's are absolutely basic to his teaching, the essential elements in Paul's gospel also.

Any teacher in Palestine at that time would have to declare his attitude to the Torah. The Pharisees, who were the dominant and liveliest party as far as the practice of religion was concerned, held that total obedience to the Torah was what God required of Israel in response to God's choice of Israel as his own people. They had elaborated the *Halakah*, a system of casuistry by which the ordinary devout Jew was enabled to apply the Torah to all the circumstances of daily life. Now Jesus was certainly nearer the Pharisees than he was to the Sadducees. He believed in life after death, for example, as the Pharisees did and the Sadducees did not. But he as certainly did not accept the Pharisaic approach to the Torah. He undertook what W. D. Davies has called 'a radicalization of the Torah', he called men back from a study of the detailed prescriptions of the law to a consideration of God's purpose in giving the law. Thus he approved the famous 'great commandment', that is 'thou shalt love the Lord thy God and thy neighbour as thyself'. That is the purpose of the Torah, and as long as that is fulfilled the detailed requirements are not so important. Similarly he called men back from the permission given in the law for a man to divorce his wife to a consideration of what God originally intended by the institution of marriage, and even goes so far as to imply that a command in the written law (the permission to divorce one's wife) should be ignored. The whole tenor of Jesus' teaching, then, was to lay less stress on detailed Torah obedience, and to bring men and women to a direct encounter with God unmediated by the niceties of the *Halakah*. It was in the circumstances an extremely radical message, for the underlying implication was that Israel was not bound for ever to the Torah. It was this no doubt more than anything else that brought Jesus to the cross.

We should not ignore one other very striking feature of Jesus' teaching; his use of parables. He evidently preferred to teach this way, and it is in fact an extraordinarily effective technique. It means that he joins hands with the greatest of the prophets, who used striking and memorable stories and illustrations: Isaiah's story of the Lord's vineyard (5: 1–7); Amos' series of rapid vignettes in Amos 3: 3–8; Hosea's brilliant sketch of an unfaithful wife (1, 2); Jeremiah's picture of Judah as a wild ass in heat (2: 24); Ezekiel's vivid and uncensored account of Judah the orphan girl (16); the Second Isaiah's astonishingly bold comparison of God to a warrior setting out to battle (42: 13). Jesus stands in this tradition. His use of parables implies a most remarkable originality, an ability to appeal to elements in man other than the purely rational, a suggestion that God is to be found by means of the everyday; almost a sacramental approach to life.

What did Jesus teach about himself? This is the topic about which there is least agreement among scholars today. It seems to us very difficult to deny that he did in some sense see himself as Messiah, but so unexpected a Messiah that in fact his disciples only recognized him as such belatedly and imperfectly. He certainly did not proclaim himself Messiah. But much of his teaching has a messianic background (e.g. the parables which describe a marriage feast), and it is hard to imagine how someone in his position could avoid the challenge of messiahship. Did he claim to be Son of Man? Certainly he did, but what did the title mean on his lips? Did it imply a heavenly figure as described in Daniel, who was to be expected at the consummation of history? This does not seem likely. It seems more probable that for Jesus the title Son of Man was a modest or an ambiguous way of referring to himself, though it probably also carried an overtone of representative mankind. It probably does mean that Jesus saw himself as in some sense representing Israel before God. What about his sense of sonship? Certainly Jesus had a very vivid, intimate, and direct sense of relationship to God, whom he addressed as 'Abba'. This means 'Father'. It *almost* means 'Daddy', but such a translation does not quite represent the exact meaning. We have to be content to say that he experienced a unique filial relationship to God. He encouraged his disciples to approach God in confident faith and themselves to pray 'Our Father'. He did not call himself Son of God, though such a title would not have been absolutely unimaginable in his lifetime in the sense that Israel was God's Son. We would add one more descriptive name, the servant of the Lord. There is some evidence that Jesus did see himself as God's servant in a repre sentative sense. This would mean that he identified himself with the suffering servant of the Psalms (Mark 15:34) and perhaps with the servant of the latter half of the prophecy of Isaiah. This is a view which would be rejected by most scholars today (though defended by J. Jeremias). But it is hard otherwise to account for the unanimous witness of the evangelists that Jesus foresaw his own violent death; and now the *Hodayoth* or Hymns of the Qumran documents show us that the leader of the Qumran sect could use the language of the suffering servant about himself, even though it has no messianic overtones. It is possible also that Jesus saw his death as possessing an atoning significance; he is represented as using the figure of 'the cup' on two occasions when speaking of his destiny of suffering (Mark 10:38f; 14:36). This figure of the cup has an Old Testament background in which it is associated with a destiny of suffering which God decrees for nations and individuals. The purpose of the suffering in Jesus' case must be redemptive. There is no hint that it could be punitive.

When we put together all that we can be confident about concerning Jesus' own intentions, we get the picture of an absolutely unique vocation. Bultmann, who denies that Jesus saw himself either as Messiah, or as Son of Man, or as servant of the Lord, still describes Jesus as God's last word to Israel. The full impact of his career is astonishing: he passes through his ministry speaking with sublime authority, proclaiming the advent of the end time, announcing Israel's last crisis, and all is integrally connected with his own person, death, and subsequent vindication. The Gospel writers are entirely true to history when they represent Jesus' presence as having elicited from those who knew him the question: who is this?

We know in fact very few of the actual deeds of his career. He certainly exorcised the insane and cured the diseased. The Gospel writers on the whole do not employ Jesus' miracles in the way later theologians used them in order to prove his divinity. Jesus himself seems to have regarded his healings and exorcisms as an important element in his campaign against Satan, a campaign which reached its climax on the cross. It seems likely that the loud cry which the Synoptics say that Jesus uttered just before he died on the cross is intended to be taken as a cry of triumph. John interprets it with the words 'It is finished' (19:30). The Synoptics represent Jesus' miracles as signs of the approaching kingdom: God's power is already at work. John understands them rather as indications of who Jesus really is, indications which only faith can rightly decipher. About the more spectacular miracles, the walking on the water, the changing of water into wine, the raising of Lazarus, modern scholars tend to be agnostic or sceptical. Some miracles are probably parables turned by frequent narrative into miracles (e.g. the cursing of the fig-tree), and some few may be completely legendary, e.g. the miracle of the coin in the fish's mouth in Matthew 17: 27.

Two other of Jesus' activities are important: he called disciples; he expected them to follow him personally, to death if need be; and he probably designated twelve of them specially. The number suggests that they were to be the nucleus of the new Israel. And secondly, he instituted the eucharist. Those scholars are probably right who say that the eucharist was not a totally new departure. It had its origin in fellowship-meals with his disciples of which the accounts of the various feedings of the multitude are examples. It is impossible to believe that the Last Supper itself had no connection with the Passover feast. It was perhaps the anticipation of the messianic feast when the kingdom should have come. At any rate this is how the early Church seems to have understood it.

So he goes up to his last Passover celebration, aware that he was courting death, believing that such a death might well be God's will for him. He is arrested by the treachery of Judas, arraigned before the Jewish authorities, and handed over by them to Pilate for execution on a political charge. The details of Jesus' trial (or trials) are obscure and inconsistent, but this much seems clear. He does not attempt to defend himself. He is scourged and crucified and dies after about three hours. He is buried in a tomb near Jerusalem. On the third day the tomb is found to be empty and a number of Jesus' disciples are convinced that he has appeared to them alive. This much must be said if we are to give a complete account of Jesus' career. The problems and significance of his resurrection we discuss more fully in the section concerned with Christology.

Those who have any acquaintance with traditional accounts of Jesus' life will notice one remarkable omission in the account given above. Nothing is said about Jesus claiming to be God. This is quite deliberate. On the basis of the evidence available we must conclude that Jesus did not teach that he was God, did not claim to be God, did not believe that he was God. Anybody who believes that Jesus *did* claim to be God can only do so on the basis of one book in the New Testament, the Fourth Gospel. Jesus is never represented as claiming to be God in so many words in the Fourth Gospel, but he does claim unique union with the Father, he does claim to remember his pre-incarnate state, and he does not repudiate the charge when the Jews accuse him that 'You, being a man, make yourself God' (John 10: 33). We must honestly state that we cannot accept such passages in the Fourth Gospel as giving us authentic historical information about Jesus. Not that we regard the Fourth Gospel as totally devoid of historical information, but those places where John seems to be farthest from giving us a picture of the historical Jesus and most desirous of supplying his own theological interpretation are precisely the passages in which Jesus makes such claims as these. In any case we must ask ourselves whether this sort of claim was really possible for a sane man in the culture and historical position in which Jesus was born and brought up. Not, surely, for someone who was completely human. But was Jesus completely human? That is the central question. We hope to show in the ensuing pages that it is quite reasonable to hold on the one hand that Jesus was completely human and that he did not claim to be God, and on the other that he was the unique and supreme revelation of God the Word, and that in him God manifested himself, active for man's salvation, as never before or since in the history of the world.

b. The Revelation of God in Jesus Christ

At the end of section I,2,(a) we said that God's character had been revealed during Israel's history: he was personal, loving, a saviour, holy, righteous. But till the rise of Christianity God was only revealed as such to the Jews. There was really no opportunity for a revelation to a wider community until Israel should encounter a culture that could provide it with the intellectual tools to express its knowledge of God. There had been very little also in Israel's religious tradition to suggest that God should be made known to the Gentile world, perhaps an odd hint in the Psalms, a definite prediction in Second Isaiah (though this is denied by some scholars); only in the astonishing book of Jonah is God represented as taking any real interest in the Gentiles.

But from 333 BC onwards Israel was brought into compulsory contact with Greek culture. They lived under Greek overlords for the next 200 years. They could not hope to escape the influence of the Greeks. The Greeks had in a comparatively short space of time achieved amazing heights in drama, in poetry, in history writing, in oratory, in technology, and above all in philosophy. The Greeks were nothing if not rationalists, and Greek education tended to make its recipients demand a rational explanation for everything they believed. Culturally speaking, the Greeks were infinitely better equipped than the Jews; only in one area, religion as a living monotheism, were the Jews their superiors. At first the Greeks were inclined to view the Jewish religion with friendly interest. They knew that the Jews were fanatical monotheists, that they observed high moral standards (higher than those of contemporary Hellenism), that they had scriptures written in a barbarous tongue which they claimed pre-dated Homer and anticipated Plato. Up to the middle of the second century BC there might have been a reasonable compromise between Judaism and Hellenism. The living God of the Old Testament tradition might have been made known to the Greeks.

But in 168 BC Antiochus IV Epiphanes, the Greek monarch who ruled Palestine at the time, instigated by a powerful 'liberal' party within the Jewish state itself, launched his disastrous attempt to Hellenize the Jews by force. Persecution ensued. Many Jews apostasized, but a large minority resisted, first by accepting martyrdom, then by guerrilla warfare. Antiochus IV himself soon passed from the scene, and his successors, coping with the rising power of Rome, had no time for religious persecution. But the damage had been done. The guerrilla fighters turned into regular warriors, and within twenty years the Hasmonean family that had led the original revolt were installed as independent monarchs in Jerusalem. The devout Jews who had resisted the Hellenizing movement now proceeded to ensure as far as they could that there would be no more compromise between Judaism and Hellenism. Total obedience to the Torah was commended. Those elements in Judaism which acted as a repellent to Gentiles, circumcision and the dietary laws, were given fresh emphasis. Rules of ritual purity were invented and enforced that made it increasingly difficult for a devout Jew to have social relations with Gentiles. The Samaritans, half-Jews who claimed to be bearers of the authentic Jewish tradition, were finally excommunicated. All this programme of segregation was in the hands of the Pharisaic party, the most influential group in Judaism. It looked as if the God of Israel had been effectively cut off from anybody who was not a Jew.

Then came Jesus. Looking at the origin of Christianity from the outside, one might fairly say that the most striking immediate consequence of Jesus' career was that the God of Israel was made known to the Gentiles. Others had tried to do this before, of course. Philo of Alexandria, a learned Jew who died about AD 50, had written a number of works designed to commend Judaism to the Greeks. His method was to allegorize the law of Moses, so that what looked on the surface like an articulated law-code was made to appear as a vast repository of philosophy, psychology, and ethics, all drawn from Platonic or Stoic sources. But Philo thereby left out the one important thing, the living God, who calls, judges, saves, acts, in history. The only effective way of conveying him was to include him within a framework of salvation history, to relate how he had dealt with Israel throughout Israel's history. Could one have the living God and salvation history without the Torah? Jesus showed that one could. But in order to make this break with the purely Jewish tradition he had in some sense to maintain that the end of history had come. This is the profoundest significance of his eschatology for us today. He came announcing the imminent end. When the smoke had cleared it could have been perceived that the end of Judaism as the exclusive preserve of God's revelation, the beginning of his revelation to the entire world, had taken place.

Not that Jesus had any explicit intention of revealing the God of Israel to the Gentiles. His intention was to proclaim the coming of the kingdom and to enable it to come in fulness through his own death and subsequent vindication. In doing this he constituted in fact a new and full revelation of God's own innermost nature, both by what he taught and by what he was. We have seen how Israel of old had known the love or mercy of God as one of his leading characteristics. Jesus in effect reorientated the Jewish understanding of God, so that God's love, which had hitherto been thought of as one of God's characteristics among others, was now seen to be the central normative characteristic. It was not just that God could show mercy, but rather, as Paul put it in Romans 9: 16, he was recognized as the God of mercy. His love was a self-giving, sacrificial love. This is why the events surrounding the death of Jesus are given such prominence in all four Gospels: the death of Jesus is the climactic manifestation of God's character, self-giving love.

This essential point is implicitly made by the evangelists, but it is explicitly stated by the two greatest theologians of the New Testament, Paul and John (we call the author of the Fourth Gospel 'John' without prejudice to the question of whether he was John the apostle). Paul in a passage such as Corinthians 1: 18–25 describes the cross of Jesus Christ as 'the foolishness of God and the weakness of God', and goes on to make it clear that for him the actual crucifixion was the point at which God's revelation of himself was most specific, most effective, most manifest. This is for Paul the central mystery or paradox of the Christian message. John teaches the same lesson in a different language: for him the cross is the supreme manifestation of God's glory, and 'glory' here means 'innermost nature'. At several points in his Gospel he uses the verb 'glorify' to refer to the crucifixion, almost as if it was a synonym for 'crucify' (see John 7: 39; 12: 16, 23–28; 13: 31f; cf. also 3: 14; 8: 28; 12: 32–34 for a similar use of a word meaning 'exalt'). Reverting to Paul, it seems likely that what he is trying to say in that famous passage in Philippians 2: 6–8 is that 'being equal to God', i.e. divine status, does not consist in possessing unique privilege, but in self-giving, and that this was demonstrated in the life and death of Jesus Christ.

As we shall be seeing later, theologians have argued profoundly about the relation of the divinity to the humanity in Jesus Christ. Sometimes they have suggested that he was divine despite his humanity. More often they have given us a picture of a Christ in whom divinity and humanity exist side by side. The New Testament, it seems, has a more profound and more radical message than this: the divinity is manifested *by means of* the humanity. What this means for our doctrine of the person of Christ we must work out in the next section, but here it must be enough to say that through Jesus Christ God has shown that his clearest mode of self-revelation lies in a life of complete human obedience, crowned by suffering and death. There is no other means by which God, being who he is, could have revealed himself more truly, just because he is the God whose very nature is self-giving love. This is exactly what the author of Hebrews means when he says that God, who revealed himself of old through the prophets, has now spoken to us 'in the mode of a Son'. The Greek is literally 'in Son', son-wise, not 'in a son', as if God could have several sons, nor 'in his Son', for in Hebrews the pre-existent Christ is never called God's Son. The mode of Son, with all it implies for human obedience, is the chosen way of God's revelation.

When we understand this, we can see how God's obedient servants in the earlier period of revelation fit into the picture. God's character became known through those who obeyed him: not only through the legendary Abraham, but through three-dimensional historical figures such as Amos, Hosea, Isaiah, and above all Jeremiah and the anonymous prophet of the exile, who obeyed God's call to proclaim his message, sometimes against their inclination and often at great cost to themselves. Now also we can understand in true perspective the meaning of the resurrection of Jesus Christ. It was not just the happy ending to an otherwise tragic story; it was the necessary vindication of God. It was God's 'Yes' to Jesus' offering. It was God's declaration once and for all that those who obey him are not put to shame, that God honours their faith, that he wills to be known by means of their lives. It is God's owning of Jesus Christ (and implicitly all his predecessors in Old Testament times) as his chosen mode of revelation. It is the assurance that obedience to God in all circumstances is not fruitless, that God's power, manifested in human weakness, really is powerful, that he is not a frustrated, powerless God, but that his ways of bringing about his purposes are ultimately effective.

Once we see Jesus Christ as the supreme revelation of God, we find that we have a criterion by which we can judge and appreciate the Old Testament revelation. This has been proved down the ages to be an essential ingredient in the Christian understanding of the Bible. The Church has always been tempted to treat the Old Testament as being on a level with the New as far as revelation is concerned. Whenever it has given way to this temptation it has found sooner or later that sub-Christian elements from the Old Testament take over its theology, and it ends up by preaching a God who is not even the God of the highest point of revelation in the Old Testament, but an early, primitive tribal deity. For long periods in its history the Church was saved from this danger by an arbitrary but convenient use of allegory on the Old Testament, so that any Old Testament passage when allegorically interpreted could be made to yield a Christian message. But in certain periods and in certain areas the allegorical method has been rejected without any other means of rightly orientating the Old to the New being put in its place. Thus at the Reformation, when there was a widespread revolt against mediaeval methods of exegesis, we find Church of England apologists justifying the total subordination of the Church to the Crown by the example of the pious king Josiah in the seventh century BC. A hundred years later we find Scottish Covenanters justifying taking up arms against their enemies by casting themselves in the role of the Israelites and their opponents in that of the Amalekites. And in our own day we find sectarian movements who glory in their lack of education often preaching a gospel which has more in common with the crudest ideas of Israel a thousand years before Christ than with the message of the New Testament. To treat the Old Testament as possessing equal authenticity with the New is to court disaster.

All this can be avoided if we use the revelation in Jesus Christ as the screen through which we pass everything that the Old Testament tells us about God. Using this criterion, we can freely admit that in the earlier period of Israel's history their apprehension of God was limited and sometimes mistaken: they could represent him as demanding the death of all the Amalekites for an offence committed generations earlier (1 Sam. 15); as capable of inciting those with whom he was offended to commit sin (1 Sam. 26: 19; 2 Sam. 24: 1), as killing someone for an entirely involuntary error (2 Sam. 6: 7). Even in a much later period long after Israel had returned from exile, the Chronicler could represent God as blasting King Uzziah with a terrible disease as a punishment for a purely ritual offence (2 Chr. 26: 16–21). But it is not only from sub-Christian conceptions of God in the Old Testament that we are delivered by a true understanding of Jesus Christ as the normative revelation of God. Such an understanding can also deliver us from sub-Christian ideas generated by Christian theologians in the course of the centuries, from the doctrine, for instance, that God was delighted to punish his innocent Son as a substitute for mankind, or from the suggestion that God deliberately deceived the devil by means of clothing the divinity of Christ in the garments of humanity. We may even occasionally, and in fear and trembling, appeal to Christ against the New Testament itself. One could well claim, for example, that the suggestion in 1 Timothy 2: 11–15 that woman is more prone to temptation than man is not compatible with the spirit and intention of Jesus' life. The revelation of God in Jesus Christ is therefore both the culmination and climax of his revelation of himself to Israel and the essential means by which we judge the revelation recorded in the Old Testament itself.

In section I,2,(a) we mentioned that our doctrine of revelation might seem to involve a circular argument: we claim that we can apprehend God's revelation in Jesus Christ because we can recognize in him the salient features of the God whom we came to know through the revelation recorded in the Old Testament. We then turn round and claim to use the revelation in Jesus Christ as a criterion for deciding what elements in the Old Testament picture of God are more true and what are less true. This is in fact a circular argument, but it is worth while pointing out that we use similar sorts of arguments in purely secular contexts and expect them to carry conviction. For example, palaeontologists writing about the emergence of the species *homo sapiens* from certain higher primates millions of years ago do not hesitate to use the word 'progress' of that evolution. They can trace how the species emerged from hominids and collaterals such as Neanderthal Man, till we meet *homo sapiens* about 40,000 BC. After that he gradually progresses through a more sophisticated use of stone tools, manifesting as early as 20,000 BC a remarkable artistic talent, until some time more recently than 10,000 BC he makes the immense leap forward of inventing stock-breeding, agriculture, pottery, and weaving, and so on till the final developments take place that bring him to the very verge of historical times, the discovery of metallurgy and the invention of writing. So as to avoid invidious comparisons with modern man, let us take as the climax of this progressive development the educated Athenian of the fourth century BC. He was the heir already to a brilliant tradition of poetry, drama, history-writing, rhetoric and sculpture, a profound development in metaphysics, and very remarkable achievements in technology. Confining ourselves entirely to the cultural level, and not provoking any questions of spiritual development, we can surely say that Athenian man was an immense improvement on palaeolithic man, and very much better equipped culturally even than the man of

20,000 BC, who had nevertheless great artistic achievements to his credit. Thus we judge the long development of *homo sapiens* by the criterion of Athenian man. But we do not thereby put Athenian man above or outside the species *homo sapiens*. He is still man, biologically continuous with his ancestors right back to the higher primates. We recognize him by what he has in common with his predecessors, but we can still use him as a criterion of excellence for the whole development. This argument seems no less circular than that which we have used in giving our account of the relation of the revelation in Christ to the revelation recorded in the Old Testament. But it appears to be a perfectly good argument all the same.

Moreover, the essential logic of God's revelation in Jesus Christ demanded that it must be a universal revelation. This was not explicit in the mind of Jesus, but we have suggested that his attitude towards the Torah meant that sooner or later the barriers that separated Jew from Gentile must break down. In fact it happened very soon, within a very few years of Jesus' death and resurrection. This necessary development was aided by the very first and earliest ecclesiology of the early Church: the first Christians claimed to be the people of God. But this was a claim based on a theory of salvation history: God had originally called Israel, had accompanied them through all the vicissitudes of history, and now bade them open their ranks and receive the Gentiles as joint-heirs in the Messiah. God had not ceased to be active in history. On the contrary, in Jesus Christ he had just accomplished his greatest and most decisive act of salvation. He had thereby shown himself to be not the God of the Jews only but also of the Gentiles. Salvation history is not to be regarded as ended: there is still one more great act to come, the *Parousia* or ultimate consummation. But in the meantime the new Israel is to be made up of both Jews and Gentiles, living in the light of the coming of God in Jesus Christ, reproducing perhaps in some new dimension the experiences of Israel of old (cf. 1 Cor. 10: 1–11), looking forward to the end which would not be wholly strange. Thus the event of Jesus Christ had succeeded in opening the living God of Israel's experience to the whole world, without imposing the minute regulations of the Torah on everyone, and without losing the dimension of salvation history. Jesus had indeed reorientated in a radical way the Jewish understanding of God, but he did not destroy the continuity of revelation.

c. The Resurrection

In I,2,(b) we pursued the course of Jesus's career up to and including his resurrection on the third day, and in I,2,(c) we claimed that that resurrection was the vindication of God, both in the sense that by means of it God vindicated Jesus, and that God was himself vindicated. We must now assess the evidence for the resurrection of Jesus.

The earliest evidence is provided by Paul in 1 Corinthians 15: 3–8, in which he gives us a list of the appearances of the risen Jesus to his disciples. We should notice that before referring to the resurrection Paul says that Christ 'was buried'. It has often been claimed that this implies a knowledge on Paul's part of the fact of the empty tomb. It has equally been denied, on the grounds that Paul only means to emphasize the fact that Jesus really did die. Paul does not make any reference to the empty tomb elsewhere. On the whole it seems more likely that by his reference to Christ's burial Paul does betray a knowledge of the empty tomb story. There is also the consideration that a Jew would more naturally think in terms of a bodily resurrection than of an appearance after death which had no relation at all to the body. The date of 1 Corinthians is not certain. We should not be far out if we put it about AD 51. But scholars have pointed out very truly that this list of appearances is not Paul's own compilation. He says he received it, by which no doubt he means it was the official list of resurrection appearances that was taught him at the time of his conversion. This of course puts it back more than ten years earlier than the writing of 1 Corinthians, to within two or three years of the event itself. This makes it very early evidence indeed. We must assume, however, that Paul has added on to the list he received the reference to Christ's appearance to him on the Damascus road.

This very appearance to Paul constitutes something of a problem, because he does not seem to make any difference between it and the other appearances. If we are to follow the Gospel accounts, the other appearances, to the women, to Peter, etc., all took place actually on the third day or relatively soon after it. The appearance to Paul in the Damascus road must have taken place at least two years later. This might be explained by the fact that Paul refers to this event as 'like an abnormal birth', thereby suggesting that he knew it was out of time and the very last to be expected. More puzzling however is the implication contained in Paul's list that the mode of the appearance of the risen Christ to Paul was the same as the mode of his appearance to the others. If we follow the Gospel accounts of the appearances, we would conclude that they were rather more three-dimensional, rather more specifically connected with the risen body, than what we seem to discern in the Damascus road appearances. If it were not for Paul's putting all the appearances together in one

73

class, we would be inclined to describe the Gospels incidents as 'appearances' and the Damascus road incident as a 'vision'. (Indeed Luke represents Paul as using the words 'heavenly vision' about his conversion in Acts 26: 19.) The right conclusion from this peculiarity of Paul's treatment of the resurrection appearances is probably that the Gospel accounts of the risen Christ, as found in Luke, Matthew, and John, have undergone a process of elaboration whereby the corporality of the appearance of the risen Jesus is emphasized. This reaches its climax in Luke 24: 41–43, where the risen Christ actually eats a piece of cooked fish. It is likely that all the appearances were 'subjective', not in the sense that they were hallucinations, but in the sense that the risen Lord could only appear to those who believed, or were ready to believe, in him and could recognize him. Paul in his theology of the risen Christ rightly emphasizes that the resurrection of Jesus was not a resuscitation of a dead man to the previous existence which he had enjoyed (as John represents the raising of Lazarus to be). It was a rising of the Lord into the new dimension of the Spirit. And in the dimension of Spirit faith is the essential precondition of knowledge.

The next evidence in chronological order for the resurrection of Jesus occurs in Mark's Gospel, 16: 1–8. We must note very carefully that Mark does not describe a resurrection appearance, though he seems to know of one that took place in Galilee (14: 28; 16: 7). The remainder of Mark's Gospel as it appears in our Bibles, Mark 16: 9–end, is a later addition (or a series of later additions) and does not come from the time of the writing of Mark, but from early in the second century AD. Mark therefore, as we have him, describes the empty tomb but not a resurrection appearance. The decision as to whether his Gospel ever did contain an account of a resurrection appearance will depend on the decision as to whether his Gospel was originally intended to end at 16: 8, or whether Mark as we have it has actually lost its ending.

Then comes the evidence of the other three Gospels. They all describe both the empty tomb and at least two resurrection appearances. Matthew has two, Luke two, and John four, but we must note that the fourth is contained in chapter 21, which many scholars regard as an addition to the Gospel by an editor later than the John who wrote chapters 1–20. All these accounts have undergone some amount of elaboration in the process of transmission. Matthew's accounts could almost be called 'sketchy', though it is interesting that he confirms Mark's allusion to an appearance in Galilee. Luke's narrative is vivid and human; he evidently wants to dispose of the suggestion that the appearances were mere hallucinations. John's story is careful and impressive. The leading motif of the appearance in chapter 21 is a desire to rehabilitate Peter: his threefold denial is cancelled out by a threefold affirmation of love, and the very circumstances of the denial are recalled by the charcoal fire at the lakeside. Here also is some more evidence for a Galilaean appearance. Luke has, it seems, deliberately confined himself to describing appearances at Jerusalem, from whence the Church's mission is to set out. We should also observe that only Luke (and that only in Acts) recounts a forty day period during which the appearances take place, ended by an ascension. If we follow Matthew we must allow time for the disciples to travel to Galilee before the final appearance is granted. John 20 appears to suggest that resurrection appearances and ascension took place all within a week (see 20: 17, 26). But John 21 seems to have a similar tradition to Matthew's (and perhaps Mark's), as he places the latest appearance in Galilee.

We must not try to harmonize these accounts. They cannot all be completely accurate: the four evangelists obviously have diverse traditions about the appearances, and Paul for his part refers to some appearances of which the evangelists are apparently ignorant (the appearance to James and the appearance to 'five hundred brethren at once'). We must not claim that we have clear historical accounts of the resurrection appearances, though the argument commonly employed in defence of these accounts has some force in it: so unique and astounding an event, it is suggested, must have produced confusion and disarray. If the resurrection stories had all neatly dovetailed together we might well suspect that they had been doctored.

Apart from those who maintain that the resurrection accounts are straightforward history and can be harmonized, one can distinguish three attitudes among Christian scholars to the accounts of the resurrection of Jesus. We can describe them as follows:

i. 'Reductionist': according to this view, we cannot say that the resurrection was an event in any sense at all. All that happened was that at some point after the death of Jesus his disciples came to the conclusion that so great a teacher could not have simply ceased, but that he must be in some sense still alive in the hearts of his disciples. Both the story of the empty tomb and the accounts of the appearances of the risen Christ are later constructions intended to make this belief more convincing to early converts. The most distinguished defenders of this view are the late Professor Bultmann and Professor Marxsen in Germany, and Professor Lampe in England.

ii. 'Veridical visions': according to this view Jesus really did appear to his disciples and thereby convince them that he had risen from the dead. The appearances were objective in the sense that they were not hallucinations, but if someone had been present with a camera nothing would have been recorded on the plate. This view usually goes with a dismissal of the story of the empty tomb as a later construction.

iii. 'Veridical visions, but the empty tomb is historical'. This is simply (ii) but with the addition that the story of the empty tomb cannot be dismissed as legendary. This view definitely regards the resurrection of Jesus as a miracle in the sense that the first two views do not. But defenders of this view, if asked what happened to the physical body of Christ, would probably say they must be agnostic about the question. If God raised it from the tomb, he was also able to dispose of it.

Each person must make up his own mind on this question. We would point out indeed that view (i) ('Reductionist') is not held by any New Testament writer (Paul could be claimed according to one interpretation as one who holds view (ii) though we incline to believe he held view (iii)). The 'Reductionist' view runs counter to all the evidence in the New Testament and can only be held by those who are willing to dismiss it all. The essential fact is that the earliest disciples were convinced that Jesus had risen; if we accept this as evidence, it is very difficult not to accept the statement that goes with it in the New Testament, to wit that they were convinced because the risen Lord had appeared to them. It would not be unjust to say that those who hold the 'Reductionist' view do so not because of the New Testament evidence but rather because of their own presuppositions as to how God operates in history and nature.

The second view, which we have called 'Veridical visions', has much to be said in its favour. It can claim a great deal of the New Testament evidence on its side, and it preserves the essential fact that the disciples were convinced by Christ (or rather God-in-Christ) rather than by auto-suggestion. It does however encounter the evidence for the empty tomb. This may be witnessed to by Paul, is witnessed to by Mark, and is a phenomenon common to all the evangelists. Our own judgment is that the story of the empty tomb cannot be easily dismissed. It is interesting that such scholars as R. H. Fuller and G. Vermes, while not fully committing themselves to a belief in the story of the empty tomb, seem to agree that it cannot be easily dismissed.

Vermes describes the evidence for the resurrection as 'fragile and obscure'. If we accept some such description as just, this does not mean that we can refuse to accept it. It is probably true to say that nobody well-informed would believe the evidence of the resurrection simply by reading it once. We believe it because we have encountered the risen Christ in the experience of the Church. The evidence for the resurrection provides sufficient historical basis for our faith, but not full proof. When all is said and done, the main evidence for the resurrection as an actual event lies in the faith and behaviour of the earliest disciples. No other explanation seems adequate.

d. The Virgin Birth

The account of Jesus' life which we gave in I,2,(b) made no mention of the circumstances of his birth. But these circumstances are described in two of the Gospels, Luke and Matthew. The explanation for this omission is that in I,2,(b) we were giving an account of the historical Jesus, and there is grave doubt as to whether the story of the Virgin Birth of Jesus is history or legend. This doubt arises primarily from the fact that the two earliest witnesses to the life of Jesus, Paul and Mark, show no sign of knowing about it (John is another question: he may have known the story but decided that Jesus' origin from the Father from all eternity was so important that the virginal conception was comparatively trivial). Moreover the two contexts in which the two accounts of the virginal conception occur do not easily inspire belief that we are reading historical narrative. In Matthew, Joseph is informed by dreams of what he must do in a way that suggests the very stuff of legend: and in Luke the account, though beautifully and profoundly expressed, is cast in poetic rather than historical language. In addition, both the genealogies of Jesus provided for us, by Matthew and Luke respectively, trace his descent down to Joseph as his father (even though Luke 3:23 has 'the son, as people thought, of Joseph'). It is not surprising that scholars conclude that whoever provided our evangelists with these two genealogies, did not themselves know of the Virgin Birth story. In favour of the reliability of the two narratives must be put the fact that they are independent of each other. They are two witnesses to the event, not one. On the whole Pannenberg must be judged to be right when he says that the evidence for the resurrection of Jesus is much better than the evidence for the Virgin Birth.

It has sometimes been argued that if you reject the evidence for the Virgin Birth you thereby accuse Mary of having borne an illegitimate child. But this does not necessarily follow: in contemporary Jewish practice, when a man and a woman had been betrothed, consummating the union by means of intercourse was regarded as constituting the marriage, and was not thought of as sinful. It may be that it was this very sequence of events that gave rise to the story of the

Virgin Birth. In any case, if the whole story of the birth of Jesus is regarded as legendary, there is no obstacle to concluding that he was simply the first child of a normal marriage between Joseph and Mary. We have solid evidence in Mark and elsewhere that other children were born to the marriage. It is interesting however that Mark never mentions the father of Jesus.

Another objection to the view that the story of the Virgin Birth may be legendary is that, if so, Jesus must have been 'an ordinary man'. The Virgin Birth story, it is held, explains how he is both man and God: he had Mary for a mother but God for a father. But this argument, if presented in this form, leads to fatal results for our doctrine of the person of Christ. If the Virgin Birth story describes how Jesus was God and man, we must conclude that he was half God (God on the father's side) and half man (man on the mother's side). Modern biology has shown that the embryo is the product of both the male and the female. Ancient embryology mistakenly held that the female merely provided the receptacle: it was the male who created the new being. But no tradition of Christianity with the slightest claim to orthodoxy has ever held that Jesus Christ was half man and half God, a hybrid or demi-god. Such a notion is pure paganism. Hence, whether we believe in the historicity of the virginal conception of Jesus or not, we must not integrate it into our doctrine of the person of Christ. This would be dangerous on both historical and theological grounds.

In any case it is not by any means certain that Luke and Matthew, when they give us their accounts of Jesus' birth, mean to supply us with an explanation of how he was both God and man. Such an idea is really anachronistic. It is more likely that they each want to emphasize that in Jesus there was a new creation (as Paul says in 2 Cor. 5: 17). This we can readily accept, and can indeed regard Luke's account at least as an imaginative and poetically appropriate way of saying it.

Two points must be made at the end of this discussion: we are not actually arguing in this work that the story of the Virgin Birth must be legend, not history, only that it may be legend, and that therefore we should not make its historicity an essential part of our doctrine of Christ. Perhaps it is true to say that, when you understand the meaning of the incarnation, then you can appreciate the appropriateness of Jesus' birth from a virgin. But if so, it is a belief that should, so to speak, be kept within the household of faith, not treated as a foundation stone of Christian doctrine, still less proclaimed as a touchstone of Christian orthodoxy.

The other point is this: modern psychology has taught us the immense influence which the first few years of a child's life have upon his subsequent development. The environment which a child experiences during those years is all important for what sort of man he is going to be. We have to look there for the very springs of his subsequent actions. If so, Jesus must have had a very remarkable early environment indeed. We have seen how extraordinary a man he was. The Gospels certainly give us the impression that it was Mary rather than Joseph who was the formative influence in his life. We must therefore conclude on any reckoning that St. Mary was a very remarkable person indeed. Perhaps the instinct of the Church throughout its history has not been astray in according extraordinary honour to the mother of Jesus. It is a truism to say that Christians will never know (in this life at any rate) what we owe to her. Luke's beautiful sentence which he ascribes to Mary at the Annunciation can well stand both as a profound summary of Mary's true significance, and as an expression of the aspiration common to all those who seek to follow Jesus:

> Behold the handmaid of the Lord:
> be it unto me according to thy word.

e. The Doctrine of the Incarnation in the New Testament

The earliest Christian confession of faith was probably 'Jesus is Lord' (Rom. 10:9). The very first disciples regarded Jesus as the Messiah who had died and risen from the dead, whom they knew in the Spirit in worship and prayer. Through him God had brought the salvation which had been promised in the scriptures. He would shortly return at the *Parousia*. But as the Church moved out into the Gentile world, both language and thinking about Jesus had to be modified. The title 'Messiah' would not be very meaningful to Gentiles, and they would want to know what was Jesus' relation to God and to the world. Was he the centre of just one more cult? Intellectual Greeks would ask how to understand him rationally. The Church (or some thinkers in the Church) had to find a more sophisticated explanation of their experience of the risen Lord.

The first person to attempt to supply such an explanation was St. Paul. He had certainly got a good rabbinic training, and his facility in Greek shows that he must have had some education in Greek culture as well. It seems very likely indeed that before his conversion he was already familiar with the Wisdom tradition in Jewish religion, the emphasis on the divine Wisdom as a special attribute of God. This tradition probably originated in the desire among devout Jewish thinkers to find in their own religious tradition something commensurate with Greek metaphysical speculations about the divine Logos or reason pervading the universe. By Paul's day the divine Wisdom was already closely associated with the divine Word as parallel attributes of God, explaining to some extent God's relation to the universe. The two attributes receive great prominence in the Book of Wisdom, which was written in Alexandria, probably in the first century BC. We must also remember that as a Pharisee Paul would hold a very high doctrine of the Law or Torah. Certainly in rabbinic Judaism of a period somewhat later than Paul the belief was held that the Torah had been written before the world was made. Ben Sira in about 180 BC had identified the Torah with the divine Wisdom (Ecclesiasticus 24:23).

What Paul did was to transfer to Christ the status and attributes both of the divine Wisdom, and to a lesser extent of the Torah. Perhaps it would be more accurate to say that he transferred the attributes of Wisdom to Christ, and put Christ in his thought in the place that the Torah had held before his conversion. The consequence was that in his thinking Jesus Christ was closely associated with God. In a sense this had been the case from the very beginning of the Christian movement, because the earliest Christians had believed that God had acted in Christ for redemption. This belief Paul heartily endorses: 'God was in Christ reconciling the world to himself' (2 Cor. 5:19). But inevitably to this purely functional view of Christ (Christ as the instrument of God's salvation) Paul added a more *ontological* belief, in the sense that he moved towards a position in which Christ's being was more closely associated with the being of God. It is very difficult indeed not to conclude that this is what is meant by such passages as Philippians 2:5–10; 1 Corinthians 8:6; Romans 15:2–3; 2 Corinthians 8:9, and indeed the identification of Christ with the water-giving rock in the wilderness in 1 Corinthians 10:4. In other words, Paul does in fact recognize Jesus Christ as a pre-existent being closely associated with God, who entered human history as the historical Jesus, died, rose again in the Spirit, and now abides as God's elect agent to bring us back to him. Paul reached this conclusion not because he indulged in theological speculation for its own sake, but because he wanted to express the full significance of what God had done in Christ, and used the intellectual tools that were at his disposal.

This way of understanding Jesus Christ is developed in Colossians and Ephesians (which may both have been written by a disciple of Paul's after his death). In Colossians the pre-existence of Christ is made quite explicit, and his role as God's agent in the creation of the world is clearly indicated, a feature which is not so clear in Paul, though in all probability this did form part of Paul's belief. (For the doctrine in Colossians see Col. 1: 15–20). In Ephesians the relation of Christ to the universe and human history is explored (see Eph. 1: 9–10, 20–23; 2: 7; 3: 8–11). This was no doubt because the author (or authors) of these epistles was facing a situation in which some people were teaching that Christ occupied only a subordinate place in God's design. Of course the extension of the ontological role of Christ does not mean that his functional role is forgotten; see Colossians 1: 20–22; Ephesians 2: 1–6.

It is very difficult to say what Mark believes about the person of Christ. He calls him 'Son of God' and emphasizes his mysterious and supernatural character while at the same time doing full justice to his humanity. There are no signs of a doctrine of pre-existence. Luke and Matthew present a picture of a divine redeemer, while unselfconsciously assuming his humanity. Matthew is quite faithful to the human side of Mark's Jesus, though at times he tones down Mark's frank portrayal of a human Messiah. Matthew does not like the idea of Jesus being baptized by John with a baptism of repentance (Matt. 3: 12–15) and, when Mark says Jesus could not do any mighty work because of the unbelief at Nazareth, Matthew is content to say he did not do it (cf. Mark 6: 5 with Matt. 13: 58). Luke gives us some of the most vivid features of the human Jesus, his love for children, his concern for women, his practice of prayer, his compassion. Neither Matthew nor Luke seem to have held a doctrine of pre-existence.

Hebrews in its mere thirteen chapters depicts a pre-existent Jesus, agent both in God's creation and in his preservation of the universe (Heb. 1: 1–4). He also boldly applies the word *theos* (God) to Christ, a not very common phenomenon in the New Testament (see 1.8). But the author of this epistle couples with this exalted view of Christ a more complete avowal of his full humanity than we get anywhere else in the Bible: he says Christ implored God with tears to be saved from (ultimate, not physical) death, that he was heard because of his deep devotion, and that 'he learned obedience through the things he suffered'. Hebrews never tells us how he reconciles the assertion of the divinity with the avowal of the humanity, but they are both unmistakably there.

Then comes the Fourth Gospel. Here for the first time we find Jesus Christ identified with the Logos, or divine reason; and here only (1: 14) we have the immense claim that 'the Word became flesh and dwelt among us'. Moreover in the course of the Gospel we find Jesus represented as remembering events from his pre-incarnate state (cf. John 8: 58), and in 12: 41 he is identified with the Lord of Hosts who appeared in a vision to Isaiah in the temple (see Isa.

6: 1–10). But this identification of Christ with the eternal Logos does not imply that in John's Gospel the humanity of Jesus is a mere appearance, as the distinguished German scholar E. Käsemann has claimed. Jesus is represented as perfectly human in a literal sense, the perfect example of humanity. He does really pray (though he knows that his prayer is answered); he exhibits at times very strong emotion (e.g. John 11: 33–8); he has a special love for certain of his disciples. John thus gives us a full doctrine of incarnation, since he both associates Jesus Christ fully with the very being of God and insists that he really did become man.

Obviously therefore the doctrine of the incarnation did not spring fully clad from the head of the infant Church; it gradually developed. The original inspiration was the experience of the risen Christ: the risen Lord was known in the Spirit; men and women actually experienced conversion and redemption through him. It proved insufficient to say no more than 'Christ was God's agent in redemption'. The question had to be answered: 'if so, what is Christ's relation to God?'. The doctrine of Christ in the New Testament is simply the record of how the deepest thinkers in New Testament times struggled to answer this question. Among New Testament writers three stand out as thinkers (we can call them theologians) *par excellence*. They are Paul, the author of Hebrews, and John (who probably was not John the apostle). It is significant that all three propound what can be fairly described as a doctrine of incarnation, though the three doctrines are not harmonized and are not by any means identical with what later developed into the orthodox expression of the doctrine of the incarnation. One could put this differently by saying that all three found they had to say something about how God could be known in Jesus Christ before the coming of Jesus Christ. It sounds paradoxical, but it means precisely what we have already expressed in I,2,(a) and (c): if God has been supremely revealed in the historical Jesus Christ, then anyone who knew God in the period of the Old Testament must have in some sense known God in Jesus Christ, because that is how God is and always has been. The three theologians expressed this by means of a doctrine of pre-existence. We must decide later on how far we can use this expression today.

It is not surprising (still less discreditable) that the more elaborate and far-reaching expression of the significance of Jesus Christ came later. It took some time for the full significance of Jesus to be appreciated. Also, as it became more and more clear that the *Parousia* was not going to take place soon, the need to define Jesus Christ's relation to God became more urgent. Nor should we be surprised or offended that the writers of the New Testament expressed their doctrine about Jesus Christ in language that may seem elaborate or unintelligible to us. Paul said Jesus Christ 'was in the form of God' and also called him 'the only begotten Son'. Hebrews describes him as 'the reflection of God's glory and the very image of his being'. John uses this thoroughly Greek word Logos. These writers could only use the language that was available to them. Their background was Judaism influenced by Graeco-Roman culture, and their vocabulary is drawn from these sources. Granted that Christianity originated at that time in that place in the middle of that culture, it was inevitable that this sort of language should be used. The New Testament writers had to strive to make Jesus Christ intelligible to their contemporaries. They certainly seem to have succeeded.

As we review the development of the doctrine we shall find exactly the same phenomenon: the Fathers expressed the significance of Christ by utilizing the language, and hence the thought-forms of their own culture, which was more Graeco-Roman and less Judaistic than that of the writers of the New Testament. Our task is to deplore neither the ways in which the New Testament writers expressed their doctrine, nor the patristic development. It is on the contrary the task that faces the Church in every age to express the full significance of Jesus Christ in language and thought-forms intelligible to the men of contemporary culture. In so doing we cannot possibly afford to ignore the ways in which the New Testament writers expressed this significance for their own age, since they are the primary witnesses to what happened. And we would be very foolish indeed to ignore what the tradition of the later Church represented by the Fathers said, since we stand on their shoulders. We cannot go straight back to the historical Jesus, or the New Testament, paying no attention to what happened in between, since we are what our predecessors have made us. The material we have to deal with is what they have given us. But in the last analysis we must forge our own expression of who Christ is and what he means. It cannot possibly be independent of what has gone before, but it must be our expression. We cannot be bound by any particular formula or concept from the past simply because it is part of the tradition. We must study and respect the tradition, but we must be free to use the language and thought-forms appropriate to our age.

f. The Doctrine of the Incarnation in the Fathers

The history of Christology proper, that is the person and work of Christ, and the history of Trinitarian doctrine were inseparably bound together during the first three centuries of the Church's existence. The work of Irenaeus succeeded in establishing the Gospel of John firmly within the mainstream of Christian thought (where it had not been accepted before). Thenceforward no Christology had any chance of succeeding which did not in some way incorporate the thought that Christ was the Logos, the pre-existent Word of God, closely related to the being of God, though the degree of closeness might be estimated differently among different writers. There were some efforts made, indeed, during the third century to formulate a Christian doctrine of God without involving a Logos-doctrine. Their failure resulted in their being forgotten and almost lost to history, but what fragments of them survive do not suggest that they were produced by able or far-seeing minds. The Logos-doctrine went its successful way, and in developing absorbed most of the intellectual energies of those who gave their minds to Christology. It was determined that Christ was God, though how far God, in what sense God, was not universally determined. It must always be remembered that before the Nicene dogma entered, so to speak, the bloodstream of European culture, the word 'God' (*theos, deus*) had a wide variety of meanings, ranging from 'a very remarkable person' to 'the one true and living God Almighty'.

In the Gospels and in the rest of the New Testament, Jesus is unmistakably one. Nobody tries to divide him into two parts. From the time of the Fourth Gospel onward, it is frequently acknowledged that he is both God and man, 'truly God and truly man', as Irenaeus says. Little attempt is made to define further. Melito (c. 170) can accuse the Jews of murdering God; Tertullian does not hesitate to use the terms 'death of God' and 'cross of God' and 'birth of God', though he recognizes that there is what he calls an element (a 'substance') which is divine and an element which is human in Christ. He makes little or no attempt to determine their relationship. Origen, the universal developer and speculator, goes further, and, first among the Fathers, speaks confidently and often of Christ as possessing two 'natures', a human body and soul, and a divine Word (or rather the divine Word) to whom the human soul clothed with a body was inseparable, united by bonds of love and obedience. If any pre-Nicene writer attempts to depict what the historical Jesus must have been like, he usually produces a quite unreal picture heavily influenced by Stoic psychology (Clement of Alexandria) or Platonic philosophy (Origen).

The Arian controversy brought the subject of the relation of the divine and human in Christ further into the limelight. The Arians contended that the Son (who could loosely be described as the Logos also) was a mediator between God and the world; he was created by God the Father specifically to mediate; divine, but in many aspects inferior to the Father. And in order to prove the inferior status of the Logos, they pointed to the limitations of Jesus as he was depicted in the Gospels, and especially the Synoptic Gospels. He did not know everything, but was ignorant, on his own admission, of some things; he was weak, for he could become tired and needed to sleep; in the Garden of Gethsemane he had displayed fear, even cowardice. Their opponents, the supporters of the Nicene Creed, who were committed to the doctrine that the Son/Logos was God in the fullest conceivable sense, found these arguments embarrassing. They took refuge with relief in the doctrine that Christ had two natures, a divine nature and a human nature. It was the human nature which endured the limitations, not the divine; the divine nature was unaffected by the limitations of the human nature.

Athanasius found this scheme a useful one, and he bequeathed it to the Cappadocian Fathers (Basil of Caesarea, Gregory of Nazianzus and Gregory of Nyssa). It was not a necessary corollary of the Nicene doctrine, but on the contrary represented something of a drawing back from it. If Jesus was the Son of God, and the term 'Son of God' meant a distinctive entity within the God-head who was God of God, of one substance with the Father etc., then it followed that in the incarnation God had plunged and committed himself unequivocally and uncompromisingly into human existence and human affairs. It by no means followed that as incarnate God had one divine nature and another human nature carefully calculated to protect the divine nature from embarrassing contact with humanity. What caused the fourth century pro-Nicene theologians to favour the two-nature theory was not their determination to safeguard a doctrine of incarnation nor their advocacy of the divinity of Christ, but their desire to preserve the impassibility of God, the axiom that God could endure no human experiences and still remain God – a wholly Greek and not at all Jewish preoccupation. This is shown by the way in which both Athanasius and Hilary of Poitiers refuse to accept even the logical consequences of their two-nature theory. Athanasius ought to have allowed that the human nature of Christ at any rate showed ignorance and felt fear, but he would not do so. He insisted that in these instances the divine nature overcame the limitations of the human. Christ only pretended to be ignorant and only feigned fear in order to show us how to overcome our natural human fear. Similarly Hilary had an extraordinary theory that Christ felt suffering, but not the pain of suffering. And Athanasius, if he late in his career found himself compelled to admit that Christ had a human mind (as he had not envisaged earlier), made no use of it at all in his account of our salvation by Christ. It is emphatically not true that the Chalcedonian Formula, if this is the logical outcome of a two-nature theory, is the logical, inevitable outcome of the Nicene Creed.

The two-nature theory had its critics in the ancient world, of course. Apollinarius who in the second half of the. fourth century produced a brilliant but impossible reconstruction of the make-up of the historical Christ, suggested that if Christ consisted of a being with two natures, one human and one divine, the human doing the suffering, the divine the saving function, then this was not an effective scheme for bringing about our salvation. What was gained by an individual man dying on the cross? Cyril of Alexandria in the first half of the fifth century repeated and enlarged the criticism of Apollinarius. He suffered under the delusion that two Apollinarian works purporting to be written by Athanasius really were written by him, but he carefully avoided the mistakes of Apollinarius. He allowed that Christ must have had a human mind, but he refused to agree to a thorough-going two-nature theory. He was convinced that such a theory inevitably resulted in a Christ who fell into two halves, unsuccessfully united.

The two-nature theory against which Cyril constantly contended was that of the Antiochene school, represented by Theodore of Mopsuestia (c. 350–428), Nestorius of Constantinople (ob. c. 451) and Theodoret of Cyrus (c. 393–c. 466) who, it should be noted, after 431 dropped any support of Nestorius. This school taught that Christ had two natures, one human and one divine, united in a single person. The human nature did all the suffering and was a complete individual human being. The two natures were united by a union or bond which was moral, grace on the side of the divine, love and faith on the side of the human, not ontological but constitutional. Though Nestorius was condemned and exiled after the Council of Ephesus of 431, and the Antiochenes admitted in some sense that the Blessed Virgin Mary can rightly be said to have given birth to God (*theotokos*, 'God-bearer' or 'Mother of God'), the Antiochene cause was vigorously maintained by Theodoret of Cyrus who waged a pamphlet war with Cyril of Alexandria for several years. This exchange of pamphlets is illuminating in illustrating the intentions and the limitations of both the Alexandrian and the Antiochene theories.

Cyril produced the doctrine of the 'hypostatic union', i.e. that the Son/Logos and the humanity of Jesus were ontologically, constitutionally united so as to form a separate, recognizable being in whom the human nature was impersonal (*anhypostatos*), so that the

Son/Logos formed the inmost, decision-making ego (as we would term it today), even though he operated through or alongside the human mind of Jesus. Thus it was really impossible for Jesus to have faith or to experience temptation, and very difficult indeed to conceive that he could pray (? to himself). Cyril was above all anxious to ensure that in the incarnation God was actually there, not merely as a vague inspirational influence, and he only just stopped short of saying that God suffered ('he suffered impassibly', he said). This last point Theodoret, wishing above all to avoid infringing God's impassibility, made his chief accusation against Cyril; Theodoret acknowledged, as Cyril could not, that Jesus was a whole individual man, but never made clear what he meant by the word 'person' (*hypostasis, prosopon*) which was the uniting element in the two-natured Christ. Both antagonists accused each other quite unjustly of almost every heresy under the sun; neither came near to understanding the other. Among other obstacles, they appear to have been using the word 'nature' (*physis*) in quite different senses.

The Chalcedonian Formula of 451 set out to unite these two viewpoints. It allowed that Christ had two natures, one consubstantial with us and one consubstantial with God, which converged together into a single person without being confused or separated or altering each other or being capable of division, and it insisted very strongly that Christ was one. It did not directly formulate a doctrine of hypostatic union but it commended and approved works of Cyril which had advocated this doctrine, and the hypostatic union has since been regarded as official orthodoxy both in East and West. It also commended and approved the Tome of Leo, a careful and lucid statement written in lapidary Latin by Pope Leo I (ob. 461), which set out a doctrine of two natures operating distinctly and conjointly, the divine producing the miracles, the human enduring suffering and ordinary human experiences, each in some sense active in union with the other, united in a single person. The reader must be constantly reminded that 'person' to the ancients did not carry the psychological meanings which it has for us. They were not much concerned about problems of consciousness or psychological experience or subjective feeling. For them 'person' meant something much more like 'single reality', or 'existent observable fact'.

The Chalcedonian Formula was not 'the bankruptcy of Greek theology'; it was not a mere patchwork of formulae, a theological pantomime horse. It was not a presumptuous attempt to turn a divine mystery into a theorem fully understandable by the human intellect. It was a serious attempt to state, in view of the fact that a grave controversy was raging upon the subject, how Jesus Christ could be both God and man. It succeeded in some of its aims. It united some of those who held to an hypostatic union to some of those who wished to safeguard God's impassibility. It made it clear that Jesus was not a hybrid, partly divine and partly human; it established that Jesus Christ did not represent the conversion of the Godhead into flesh (to use the words of the Athanasian Creed), as Circe in the Odyssey turned the followers of Odysseus into pigs, and, inasmuch as it insisted on the separation of the natures, it rejected the idea that Jesus was a deified man. Though it did not resolve the controversy to which it addressed itself, it satisfied the majority of minds in East and West for well over a millenium and a half. This is no mean feat; the Chalcedonian Formula is no mean statement.

But today it is very difficult indeed for scholars nurtured in the discipline of historical criticism to accept the Chalcedonian Formula. The Formula is, after all, a statement about an historical figure, concerned with history in a way in which the doctrine of the Trinity is not concerned with history. It purports to give an account, to illuminate our understanding of the significance of Jesus of Nazareth. Four hundred years had elapsed since the historical career of Jesus when this Formula was drawn up. Its framers had little or no historical imagination. They were almost incapable of allowing the historical lineaments of Jesus to impress them beyond a certain limit – the propositions that he was authentically human and that he had a human mind, abstractly admitted but not historically understood. Beyond that, they were working almost wholly with the tools of Greek philosophy and Stoic psychology, which had become part of the inherited culture of their period. Their picture of a Jesus in whom humanity and divinity operate as parallel distinct natures each equally observable, each balancing or compensating for the other, the whole activated and driven by a divine omniscient subject or ego, will not fit the picture of Jesus given us by the Synoptic Gospels, or will fit it only after explanation so complex and devious as to reduce drastically the value of the Formula. We may well applaud the intentions of the authors of the Chalcedonian Formula (and it is absurd to argue that we cannot distinguish the intentions of ancient authors from their actual statements), but we cannot *ex animo* agree with their actual achievement.

g. Critics and Defenders of Chalcedon

For approximately a thousand years the compromise on the doctrine of the person of Christ represented by the Chalcedonian Formula remained unchallenged by any important force within the Christian

Church except of course for those sections, Nestorians and Mono-physites, whom Ephesus in 431 and Chalcedon in 451 had put out of communion with the rest. At the Reformation incarnation theology was not a battleground. It is true that some of the radical Reformers, notably Servetus and the two Sozzinis, rejected the orthodox doctrine of the person of Christ and questioned the doctrine of the Trinity. But this was on biblicist rather than strictly theological grounds, and their views did not command a big following among intellectuals. However the Enlightenment, that movement of thought in Europe which began in the seventeenth century and came to its climax in the eighteenth century, did certainly produce a challenge to the orthodox doctrine of the incarnation: both the Chalcedonian Formula and the doctrine of the Trinity were rejected by many intellectuals in the name of reason. At the same time the rise of biblical criticism brought objections to Chalcedonian Christo-logy from another quarter: it was argued that the doctrine of the incarnation was a later development, an arbitrary addition to the testimony of the Bible, an ecclesiastical superstructure imposed on the purely historical figure of Jesus of Nazareth. The consequence is that ever since the eighteenth century some serious Christian theologians have professed themselves dissatisfied with Chalcedonian orthodoxy as an answer to the question, 'how was Jesus both God and man?'. We must listen to their arguments, for they are neither unreasonable nor devoid of biblical foundation.

The first objection to Chalcedon might be put thus: *the Chalcedo-nian account of Jesus does not tally with the New Testament account.* The New Testament account, say the critics, is not internally harmonious, but the orthodox doctrine has borrowed far too much from the picture of Jesus given in the Fourth Gospel, and does not pay sufficient attention to the evidence of the other Gospels. The Fourth Gospel, it is generally admitted, gives us a picture of Jesus which tallies fairly well with the Chalcedonian account: we see both the natures operating, the divinity being shown in Christ's omniscience and his recollection of his pre-incarnate state; the humanity in his human obedience to the Father, his strong emotion, and his actual physical limitations. But the other Gospels show us a distinctly different picture, a more human Jesus who can confess his ignorance (Mark 13:32), who at Gethsemane is genuinely perplexed as to what God's will for him is, who is actually unable to perform miracles in certain circumstances. This figure does not easily agree with the account of the person of Christ given by the Chalcedonian fathers.

Secondly, the Chalcedonian Formula describes one who can be justly called 'the God-man'. Whether we follow the Alexandrian or the Antiochene tradition, we still are faced in the person of Jesus Christ with the person of God the Word. In other words, the humanity of Jesus of Nazareth is not self-subsistent, but is in fact attached to the person of God, so that, if one follows the orthodox doctrine one can say (with some qualification) that God walked the roads of Galilee, God dined with Mary and Martha, God wept at Lazarus' grave etc. *But this picture of the God-man is not really compatible with full humanity.* What we encounter in Jesus Christ, according to the orthodox view, is not *a* man, but a non-personal humanity, a humanity that is expressed, not in a human person, but in the divine mode of being, God the Word. It is moreover true that orthodox doctrine has nearly always taught that what God the Word assumed at the incarnation was not personal humanity, but impersonal humanity. Strictly speaking, orthodox doctrine is not that God became *a* man, but that God became man. The critics would object that impersonal humanity is a contradiction in terms. The essence of humanity is to be personal. If God in Jesus Christ assumed impersonal humanity, the incarnation was not a manifestation of God in real humanity. This claim, the critics continue, is borne out by the fact that throughout the development of Christianity, orthodoxy has always been nervous about admitting too much humanity into the concept of the incarnate Lord. The Fathers almost to a man jibbed at the suggestion that the historical Jesus could have been ignorant of anything. Early in the nineteenth century, a Protestant missionary called Marshman, a companion of the missionary pioneer William Carey, when engaged in controversy with a highly educated Hindu thinker Ram Mohan Roy, maintained that during the period of the incarnation Christ was not only omniscient, but also omnipresent. Marshman was only producing the stock apologia of orthodox theology. In other words, Chalcedonian doctrine leads to a slightly Docetic Christ, a Christ whose humanity has in it a certain element of unreality.

Attempts have been made to qualify the doctrine of an impersonal humanity. Leontius of Byzantium early in the sixth century AD suggested that we should not describe the humanity as impersonal (*anhypostatos*), but as finding its personal centre in the person of the divine Word (*enhypostatos*), and this idea has been taken up and elaborated by a modern theologian, Relton. But it cannot be said to have carried much conviction to modern theologians. In any case Relton accepts the Johannine picture of Jesus as authentic history.

The third objection concerns the relation of the humanity to the divinity in the Chalcedonian Formula. Admittedly the Formula itself does not attempt to explain how the two natures operated during the incarnation, but the Council enthusiastically accepted Leo's Tome, and Leo gives an explanation. The two natures, he said, operated in reciprocity, or perhaps alternately (*invicem*). We can recognize the divine nature in the miracles and Christ's recollection of his pre-incarnate state. We can recognize the human nature in his human limitations, his weariness, his suffering, his tears. This strikes many modern theologians as unsatisfactory: surely, if Jesus was both God and man, both the divinity and the humanity ought to be expressed in everything he did. Otherwise we seem to have a purely artificial arrangement, quite inconsistent with a real, historical figure. In short, the third objection is that *in the Chalcedonian theology the relation of the humanity to the divinity cannot be satisfactorily explained.*

There are however two distinguished modern Roman Catholic theologians, both of whom formally defend the Chalcedonian Formula as an adequate way of expressing the doctrine of the incarnation. They are Karl Rahner and Walter Kasper. We may take them together, as they have a great deal in common in their approach. The distinctive feature of these two theologians is that they fairly face all the difficulties connected with the Chalcedonian Formula. They are fully aware that the Fourth Gospel cannot be accepted as a straightforward historical record. They are aware of the atmosphere of Docetism that has usually accompanied the orthodox expression of the doctrine of the incarnation. Indeed Rahner begins his long and valuable essay on the incarnation by saying that popular doctrine has been in effect that God unrecognized walked the roads of Galilee. But he goes on to claim that in fact this is not what the orthodox doctrine means. We must therefore acclaim the honesty and openness with which Rahner and Kasper have examined, and to some extent absorbed, the criticisms which responsible theologians in modern times have brought against Chalcedon. Rahner goes so far as to say that if someone were to describe Jesus as a man completely open to God, this would not be a wrong description, as long as it is admitted that this openness to God is permanent and has metaphysical significance. One recognizes in both these theologians a genuine appreciation of the problems which Chalcedon has created for modern Christian thinkers.

And yet both of them in the end accept Chalcedon and defend it. They do it by proposing in each case an alternative formula, compatible, they claim, with all the legitimate demands of modern thought and yet consistent with the two-nature doctrine of the Chalcedonian fathers. Their two formulae are not identical, but they have this in common, they are both very complicated indeed, so complicated in fact that when one has studied them one wonders whether at the end of the day they are not saying in a roundabout way that everything is possible with God, and that we cannot hope to understand how he could become a man. In effect therefore, much as we admire the honesty and theological understanding of these two Roman Catholic theologians, we do not find that their explanations of Chalcedon throw very much light on the subject.

It may be as well to quote the relevant passages from these two theologians, so that the reader can judge for himself the truth of the comments we have made. Karl Rahner writes as follows (*Theological Investigations Vol. 1*, Eng. tr. p. 162): 'only a *divine* Person can possess as its own a freedom really distinct from itself in such a way that this freedom does not cease to be truly free even with regard to the divine Person possessing it, while it continues to qualify this very Person as its ontological subject'. Rahner is of course trying to explain how we can have one person operating with two natures in such a way that we can say that the human nature was really free. To us it seems that Rahner is using the notion of divinity to cover up a conception that does not make sense. Similarly W. Kasper writes (*Jesus the Christ*, Eng. tr. p. 239): 'Only within the idea of the hegemony of the *Logos* is the possibility of a unity in distinction "intelligible", for only God can be thought of as so "supra-essential" and "surpassingly free" that he can posit in itself with its own identity what is distinct from him, precisely by uniting it wholly with himself'. Certainly as far as words go, Kasper has offered a modern paraphrase of the orthodox doctrine of the hypostatic union between God the Word and both his natures, human and divine. We may well question, however, whether the sense is any clearer or more acceptable than it is in the Chalcedonian Formula itself. Indeed, the very attempt at paraphrase seems in certain respects to bring out the essential contradiction in the concept more clearly.

It will be plain from the way in which we have criticized the various defenders of the Chalcedonian theology that we do not believe an adequate defence for it has been worked out in modern times. We must therefore now take a look at two or three attempts in modern times to present a substitute for the orthodox doctrine of Christ's person before we state our own approach to the doctrine of the incarnation today.

h. Alternatives to Chalcedon

We shall consider three modern theologians who have presented an alternative approach to the doctrine of the incarnation. We have chosen two of them because they are profound and influential theologians whose work commands our respect and attention. The third we consider because he is English (in some ways typically English), a competent scholar, and a very recent writer on the subject who is certain to have a considerable influence.

The first is Paul Tillich. Tillich's aim is to present Christian doctrine not in traditional language, but in terms that will be comprehensible to modern educated Western man. He begins therefore by repudiating the word 'incarnation': it suggests mythology, he says, like a prince becoming a frog in a fairy tale. God cannot be transformed into a man. Tillich presents instead a doctrine of Jesus as a manifestation of the New Being. To be accurate, he says that it is Jesus as the Christ who manifests the New Being. This is no mere quibble. Tillich means that it was Jesus' vocation as Messiah that enabled him to manifest the New Being. This pinpoints what Tillich calls the concreteness of God's action in Christ. It is no general manifestation of God, or proclamation of general principles about God, but an actual individual historical life that was the medium of manifestation. What Tillich means by the New Being is simply the life of man as God intends him to live it, which means a life wholly given up to God. We must bear in mind that in Tillich's system God is defined as the ultimate ground of being, or being itself. Hence the manifestation of the New Being means the being of God manifested as far as it can be within the limits of space-time. But that in its turn implies a manifestation in a wholly human life, which is at the same time the life of God just because there is an actual (he calls it ontological) link between man and God. We must note that for Tillich the ontological link is between man and God, not, as in the Chalcedonian theology, between Jesus Christ alone and God. What orthodox theology calls the incarnation is thus in Tillich's system the manifestation of 'essential God-manhood' within the conditions of existence. Jesus Christ is both the mediator and the symbol of this New Being.

We can understand Tillich better when we realize that he has a very definite doctrine of the divine reason or Logos. The universe manifests the divine order; in this respect he takes up the old Alexandrian doctrine that the Logos can be traced in the universe. But, Tillich continues, men can apprehend this Logos because they are themselves rational and have the Logos within them. Again he reminds us very much of a theologian such as Athanasius. This link between the Logos and the New Being enables Tillich to go on to construct a doctrine of the Trinity. The New Being is a manifestation of the divine Logos, because the Logos means God in relation to his creation, and more particularly in relation to his unique creature man. We must not however imagine that Tillich follows the Greek fathers in using the miraculous as a proof of the presence of divinity in Jesus. On the contrary, as far as regards the miraculous he follows the radical school and excludes it entirely from the life of the historical Jesus. He would be classed as a holder of view (ii) about the resurrection appearances of Jesus, which we have called 'Veridical visions, but no empty tomb'.

This is a remarkable attempt to express Christian doctrine in modern terms. Tillich is no reductionist; he aspires to present a systematic theology. We have no time to consider his doctrine of salvation, but he certainly allows full scope to the saving work of Christ. Jesus as the Christ is in his system not a mere example. He has been criticized on two grounds (apart from those who reject him merely because he does not follow traditional lines). Pannenberg criticizes him on the grounds that in his system Jesus as the Christ is no more than a symbol for God. Tillich may lay himself open to this accusation: he certainly held that the New Being is manifested in other religions also, perhaps in some form in all religions. But we must remember that Tillich uses the word 'symbol' in a special sense. He teaches that reason cannot itself grasp God, the ultimate ground of being, who transcends all categories of the mind. All that reason can do is to indicate that the ultimate mystery is there. If we wish to know more about God we must use symbolic language, i.e. not language literally understood but in fact language as symbols. This is not a merely useful expedient or a poetic fancy, but an epistemological necessity. God can only be spoken about meaningfully in the language of symbol. Hence, when he says Jesus is the symbol of the New Being, he means he is the most effective and significant way of expressing and manifesting the New Being.

Perhaps a more serious criticism of Tillich's doctrine of the person of Christ is that he does not make a sufficiently clear connection between the being of God and the being of Jesus as the Christ. He wishes to present Christ as a manifestation of the self-giving love of God, but his description of God as 'the ultimate ground of being' or 'ultimate being' does not in itself seem to have any particular connection with self-giving love. How does a life of self-giving love manifest ultimate being? It is not really clear how Tillich would have answered this question. Thus, though Tillich has given us an excellent account of how Jesus as the Christ is the supreme manifestation and active expression of the love of God, he has not succeeded in making clear what love has got to do with ultimate being. Perhaps there is something of a hiatus between his theology and his metaphysics.

Next we consider the incarnation doctrine of Wolfhart Pannenberg. Pannenberg is a remarkable phenomenon: coming from a German school of radical criticism, he has nevertheless made a great name for himself as a theologian, and in his book *Jesus God and Man* has actually presented a doctrine of incarnation, a thing which Bultmann's sceptical convictions about the historical Jesus made quite out of the question for him. Pannenberg begins by repudiating the two-nature doctrine of the Chalcedonian Formula. It is bound, he says, to give us an artificially divided Christ, and he points out that the Fathers nearly all begin at what is from our point of view the wrong end. They begin with the question: how could the divine Logos become flesh? But that is beginning from above. We today, says Pannenberg, must begin from below: whatever else we know about Jesus, we know that he was a man in history. This then must be our starting point; we must ask ourselves, how can this man be also described as God?

The beginning of the answer is to be found, according to Pannenberg, in the resurrection of Christ. He regards the resurrection as a real event in history, not a series of hallucinations nor a change of mind experienced by the disciples, and describes it, as we have already observed, as an event for which the evidence is better than that for several other events related of Jesus, such as the Virgin Birth. In the resurrection, he says, we see who Jesus really is, the Son of God. It is not that he only became the Son of God at the resurrection, as some early Christians apparently held (see Rom. 1:4, not Paul's own doctrine); but that the sonship was only declared then. During the historical life this sonship was indicated by means of the close filial relationship with the Father which Jesus experienced. Pannenberg thus builds his doctrine of the incarnation on one feature in the life of the historical Jesus, though admittedly a very important one. This is probably because Pannenberg holds with many German scholars that the historical Jesus did not claim to be either the Messiah, or the Son of Man, or the servant of the Lord. He is thus left with this one historical element on which to base his doctrine of Christ.

The filial relationship of Jesus to the Father, witnessed to during the historical life and clearly proclaimed at the resurrection, is in fact a manifestation of the eternal relationship between the first and second Persons of the Trinity, the Father and the Son, or God and the divine Word. Is this in effect a revival of the doctrine of hypostatic union, the doctrine that the humanity of Christ found its centre in the person of the divine Word not in a personal humanity of its own? This can hardly be, for, as we have seen, Pannenberg repudiates the Chalcedonian Formula and insists that we must begin from the man Jesus, an historical figure. Pannenberg however uses language which sounds like traditional language: in Jesus, he says, we see the Father-Son relationship in corporeal form. In Jesus God has come, out of the other, and projected himself into human life. Of Jesus we can therefore say, *'vere deus, vere homo'*, truly God and truly man.

There seems to be a certain obscurity or ambiguity here. Pannenberg does, it is true, help out his doctrine of the incarnation by a Logos doctrine, and this of course leads on to a doctrine of the Trinity. If we compare him to Tillich, we find a stronger emphasis on the ontological link between Jesus and God: in his scheme the historical sonship is an index of the eternal relationship between God the Father and God the Son. Perhaps Pannenberg is influenced here by his fundamental belief that history, universal history, is a revelation of God. This makes it easier to understand how the historical Jesus can be an actual manifestation of God. We must surely recognize Pannenberg as an encouraging, stimulating, and profound theologian of the incarnation, full of valuable insights and suggestions, even if at the end we confess to a sense of ambiguity about how exactly he thinks Jesus was both God and man.

It is significant that both these theologians, though they repudiate the traditional account of the incarnation, retain a Logos doctrine and a doctrine of the Trinity.

Very recently several English theologians have produced accounts of the significance of Jesus which seem designed explicitly or implicitly to reject the doctrines of the incarnation and of the Trinity. M. Wiles (essays in *Christ, Faith and History*, and in *The Myth of God Incarnate* and *The Re-Making of Christian Doctrine*) and J. Hick (essay in *The Myth of God Incarnate*) and some others have suggested that it is undesirable, indeed in view of modern scholarly opinion, impossible to associate God as closely with history as these doctrines demand. A not dissimilar view has been put forward, with greater coherence, cogency and persuasiveness, by G. W. H. Lampe in his *God as Spirit*. He maintains that there is no necessity to posit a Logos or Son as mediator between God and man. All that is needed is to envisage Jesus as a man uniquely filled with the Holy Spirit. The Holy Spirit simply means the presence of God himself, which is admittedly its meaning in the Old Testament anyway. We need postulate neither a pre-existent nor a 'post-existent' Christ. He speaks of 'the Creator-Spirit's . . . age-long incarnation of himself in human personality' (p. 210), but maintains that in some sense Jesus is unique: 'Yet in fact we need no mediator. It is God himself, disclosed to us and experienced by us as inspiring and indwelling Spirit (or Wisdom or Word) who meets us through Jesus and makes us Christ-like' (p. 144). The Patristic development of a Trinitarian theology of Word/Son and Spirit merely served to put a buffer between God and man.

It would be unwise to storm angrily at such views as these. They have been put forward by competent scholars who write with entire sincerity and are responding to various pressures and needs within the world of contemporary theology. Lampe's theology is in several ways like that of the great third century theologian Origen, who accepted a doctrine of incarnation but so surrounded it with a concept of the divine Logos operating throughout all culture and thought and with the prospect of an indefinite series of existences for human souls beyond this life that it lost much of its significance, and Origen also virtually abandoned eschatology. But doctrines such as these face formidable difficulties and objections. We shall here confine ourselves to listing those which apply to Lampe's work.

In the first place, the Holy Spirit in the New Testament is not a periphrasis for God, as the term on the whole denotes when it is used in the Old Testament. The Holy Spirit is closely bound up both with the disclosure of God given in Jesus and with the End. Indeed, the Holy Spirit is an entirely eschatological phenomenon. He means God-at-the-end-of-the-world, Heaven anticipated, first instalment of the general resurrection (Rom. 1:4; 5:5; 8:11,23; John 7:39; 2 Cor. 5:1-5; 1 Cor. 2:9,10; 15:14-45; Gal. 5:16-18,25; Acts 2:16-21; Heb. 1:2; 6:4; 1 Pet. 1:5; 4:14). In the Fourth Gospel the coming of the Comforter is virtually equated with the *Parousia* (John 14:16-18, 26; 15:26-27; 16:12-24). This is very different from the Creator-Spirit who incarnates himself in human personality throughout the ages. In other words, the Holy Spirit in the New Testament is significantly different from the Holy Spirit as envisaged by Lampe.

Secondly, to maintain that we do not need a mediator is in fact to abandon so much of the New Testament as to leave it a very insufficient guide to Christian doctrine. It means abandoning eschatology and any approach at all to incarnation in its traditional sense (and with that of course the doctrine of the Trinity), and indeed the whole concept of revelation i.e. self-communication on the part of God. In fact it means refusing to see any discontinuity in God's activity in history, any possibility of God, so to speak, 'breaking in', which eschatological modes of thought convey. Instead we are shown an ubiquitously and perpetually active God, corresponding in transcendent activity to his own innate, immanent dwelling in men, educating everybody universally towards himself, the Christian religion playing the part of a focussing and concentrating manifestation of God's unceasing activity. In the end the career of Jesus Christ with Lampe (as, one suspects, with Origen), while highly desirable, is not entirely necessary. Again, this doctrine apparently necessitates regarding Jesus as a 'deified man' (Lampe uses the words on p. 19), and to this doctrine there are the gravest objections, as has been already suggested (see above, pp. 88, 95). Finally, a suspicion hangs about this account of the significance of Christ that it underestimates the gravity of sin and evil. It is not clear how we are to be redeemed by a Spirit-filled man, except by way of example. We must acknowledge that the vision which Lampe gives us is a noble one (as was that given by Origen). But it is doubtful if it can be described as Christianity.

j. An Approach to the Doctrine of the Incarnation

Having reviewed the pros and cons in the current debate concerning the doctrine of the incarnation, we must now present our own approach. We should acknowledge how much this approach owes to two modern theologians, D. M. Baillie and W. N. Pittenger, one a Scotsman and one an American. We have adopted very much their understanding of the incarnation, with modifications of our own. But before setting out our approach we must make it clear that we do not regard the traditional Chalcedonian account of the incarnation as wholly obsolete, heretical, or even seriously misleading. It will no doubt continue to be held by Christian theologians for many generations to come. Our approach is an attempt to provide an alternative for those who cannot intellectually accept Chalcedon.

It will be remembered that in II, 5, (b) we presented Jesus as the full and final revelation of God in the sense that in him we apprehend God's character more fully and decisively than anywhere else. What we have to do now is to explain what this means for what we believe about Jesus Christ himself.

Jesus was a fully human being: there was nothing superhuman about him. The miracles he performed were the work of a human being. He was *a* man, exhibiting a human personality. But though not superhuman he was certainly supernatural, in that in him God the Word was more fully present than in any other man. To adopt a dictum which we find both in Friedrich Schleiermacher and in Karl Rahner, he was the man who was completely open to God. This means that the link between God the Word and the man Jesus was one of God's good pleasure, *eudokia*, a word used in the Antiochene school to describe this union. So expressed, this might seem to mean at first sight that Jesus was 'an ordinary man', but D. M. Baillie argues with great effectiveness that to describe Jesus as 'an ordinary man' is to do an injustice to God. Baillie outlines what he calls 'the paradox of grace', by which he means a datum of our religious experience: the closer anyone is to God (the more holy and dedicated he is), the more completely is he debtor to God's grace. In other words, to be completely open to God, wholly the vehicle of his grace, far from being something ordinary, is in fact an astonishing, unique achievement of God's power. The fact that Jesus was wholly open to God's grace was not an accident: it could only happen at that time, in those circumstances, by God's will. 'God was in Christ,' says Paul, 'reconciling the world to himself' (2 Cor. 5: 19). This is what the incarnation means.

We have spoken of 'God the Word'. We mean by this exactly what Tillich meant, God in his relation to creation, and in particular in his relation to his unique creature, man. We have already observed above (see p. 68) that the greatest thinkers in the New Testament regard the cross as the supreme, unique and clearest manifestation of God. Thus complete humanity, a man completely obedient to God, is the peculiarly appropriate way of manifesting God within the conditions of space-time. The self-giving love of God is mirrored in the total surrender of the man. The man is the unique instrument and manifestation of God's being.

At the resurrection, Jesus enters the realm of the Spirit. God is now known (or knowable) to men in a new way, as Jesus Christ in the Spirit. By this we mean that ever since the resurrection the clearest way of knowing God is to know him as Jesus Christ. This is because Jesus mirrors in a human life the very nature of God, self-giving love. Being knowable in the Spirit means that he can only be known by faith and that he can be known by all men without restriction of time or place. We worship God the Word known in Jesus Christ: we do not worship Jesus, a man. We must now explain what exactly we mean by this.

First of all, we ought not to be concerned about what happened to Jesus' physical body. We have already suggested in II, 5, (c) that God disposed of it. This is as much as we can say. It seems likely that Paul was not concerned about it either; see 1 Corinthians 15: 50. This has however been a considerable problem to traditional theology: here Catholics and Protestants differed. Catholics said that the body was (mystically, sacramentally) available to be reproduced on Catholic altars when the priest uttered the words of consecration. Protestants tended to say: 'Not at all; Christ's physical body is in heaven', thereby committing themselves to the theory of a spatial heaven. (It is true that Luther attempted to have it both ways, but that need not concern us now.) Both Catholic and Protestant solutions are untenable today; we cannot make sense of the statement that the physical body which was nailed to the cross can (however mystically viewed) be said to be present in the eucharist for the consumption of the faithful. And we cannot think of heaven in spatial terms. When we speak of the Church as the body of Christ, or the body of Christ in the eucharist, we do not literally mean the physical body of Christ. In that context 'body' must have some other meaning.

We have said that Jesus rose into the realm of the Spirit. This means that through the life and resurrection of Jesus God the Word took on a new and more intimate relation to men. Previously God's Spirit had been looked on as a mere sporadic, occasional, unusual manifestation of God. It had been expected that when the end time came the spirit of God would be freely, continuously poured out. This is what has happened through Jesus. The Spirit is freely, continually available to all believers; see Acts 2: 17–18 and John 7: 39. Paul in particular very much emphasizes the newness of what has happened in Christ; see 2 Corinthians 5: 17. And this is, no doubt, why Paul elaborates his difficult and obscure theory of the Church as the body of Christ. Probably the best explanation is that given by E. Schweizer: Christ (understood as God available in the Spirit) is the area in which the Church lives and moves. He calls it 'das Raum Christi', the area of Christ.

God the Word then is known to believers in Jesus Christ in the experience of the Church. Let us try to illustrate what this means. First we only know God the Word in Jesus Christ. If it had not been for Jesus Christ, the doctrine of the divine Word or Son would not have been worked out. Likewise the doctrine of the Trinity was required to explain the incarnation and not *vice versa*. This is entirely in line with the thought of the Old Testament: God is known as the God of Abraham, of Isaac, and of Jacob. It is very significant that Jesus himself uses this argument in Mark 12: 18–27 as a proof of life after death. God has had communion with Abraham and his posterity; he has freely associated himself with them, therefore in eternity or heaven, they are still closely associated with him. This is an *a fortiori* argument: how much more then is God identified with Jesus Christ! If it were objected that Abraham, Isaac and Jacob are legendary characters, not sufficiently historical to offer our theology a firm basis, then can we not say that God is the God of the great prophets, of Amos, of Hosea, of Isaiah, of Jeremiah, of the anonymous prophet of the exile? Indeed in the case of this last prophet we approach the verge of resurrection, because it appears that this prophet (or his disciples) envisaged a vindication for him after death. You could put this another way by saying that God is a Covenant-God, the God of Moses, and David, the God of salvation-history. The fact that he is known, identified, worshipped as the God who acts through historical characters helps us to understand how we can as Christians say that supremely, decisively, permanently, God is known in Jesus Christ (these adverbs are used by early Christian writers to distinguish the incarnation from previous appearances of the divine Word in Israel's history). We could almost elaborate a name – Christology and Christians should not refer to the God whom they worship as Yahweh (still less as Jehovah!). Already before the coming of Jesus Jews had in effect ceased to use the divine Name, partly out of reverence, but also no doubt because once you realize that there is only one God you also realise that he does not need a name. If I live in a town that has only one railway station, I say 'I am going to the station', not 'I am going to Littlehampton station'. Anyway we now name him in his relation to humanity as Jesus Christ because the Word has made himself known in Jesus Christ. But the very fact that even traditional theology has never *totally* identified the divine Word with Jesus Christ is significant. We should not say that God made the universe through Jesus Christ (New Testament writers can say something very like this, e.g. 1 Cor. 8:6; but Paul had not worked out the concept of Logos), nor do we normally say 'in the name of the Father, and of Jesus Christ, and of the Holy Spirit'. Jesus Christ is the mode in which God the Word is permanently experienced by Christians. He has spoken to us, says Hebrews, 'in the mode of Son' or 'Son-wise'.

Secondly, Jesus Christ is to us Christians at least what the Torah was, and is, to believing Jews, the symbol and medium of God's revelation, the clear outline of what God wishes us to be. We use 'symbol' in a Tillichian sense. The word 'symbol' does not mean an indication of an absence which will soon be replaced by a presence ('he left his hat on his chair as a token that he would soon be back'). Symbol is the means whereby that which transcends discursive reason can be apprehended. This is probably what Paul means when he describes Christ as the image (*eikōn*) of God (2 Cor. 4:4 and Col. 1:15). Paul also calls him the image whereby we are to be transformed 'from glory to glory' (2 Cor. 3:18).

Thirdly, the cross is the permanent index of God's revelation. This is the significance of the risen Lord exhibiting the marks of the cross to his disciples. Charles Wesley wrote:

> Those dear tokens of his passion
> Still his dazzling body bears,
> Source of endless exultation
> To his ransomed worshippers.

We should not of course attempt to draw any quasi-scientific conclusions from the Gospel narratives of the resurrection appearances. But it is profoundly true to say that God is known to us as the crucified and risen Lord. We have already sufficiently emphasized the cross as the medium of revelation. God is known not just in humanity, not just in a man, not just in the Messiah, but in Jesus Christ, the perfect servant, perfectly obedient in suffering and death.

Fourthly, the presence of Christ in the eucharist may help here, indeed it must help. This is the truth that lies behind the unacceptable Catholic doctrine that the body of Christ which we receive in the eucharist is the same as that which was nailed to the cross. It is not that Christ's presence in the eucharist offers an *analogy* to his presence in the daily experience of Christians, but that his presence in the eucharist offers an illuminating *example* of his presence in the general experience of Christians. The eucharist does not provide a unique, special, *sui generis* sort of presence; it offers us a projection, a concentration, a focussing of the same presence which we can know through prayer and through the other means of grace in daily life. The eucharist itself is a projection, a focussing, a communal acknowledgement of the Christian life on the part of Christians, and the Christian life itself is our 'spiritual service' (Rom. 12: 1). In the eucharist God's true nature becomes perspicuous to faith in the mode of the self-giving. Christ is present not corporeally but sacramentally in the eucharist. In the eucharist we are offered the opportunity of meeting God the Word, God the self-giver, and this must be in the mode of the crucified and risen Jesus Christ. It does not mean that the historical personality Jesus of Nazareth is himself present at the eucharist. That would be impossible. It does mean that all that is known of God through Jesus Christ becomes accessible to us. Shall we say that through the character of Jesus Christ we encounter the self-givingness of God?

Perhaps it would be convenient at this point to meet an objection which may be brought against our description of Jesus as being completely human. 'If he is completely human', it might be said, 'how do we know that God was in him? How do we recognize the divinity in him?' Behind this objection lies a very deep-rooted belief to the effect that God can only be manifested in superhuman phenomena, and that therefore, unless Jesus had certain superhuman characteristics, we cannot recognize the divinity in him. Indeed traditional Christian apologia for the doctrine of Christ has used this argument very strongly. One of the proofs that Jesus is God in the traditional armoury is to point to his miracles and to ask whether anyone but God could do such things. But, quite apart from the question of the historical character of the more remarkable miracles, we might ask, can God only be known by means of the superhuman? We should remember that all four Gospels describe Jesus as having refused to give a sign, and a sign in that context meant a superhuman event accrediting his divine authority. Should we really want to believe in a God who proves his presence by superhuman phenomena? If a man does not want to believe, no records of miracles will persuade him, and we should not necessarily demand miracles before we choose to believe.

But the question still remains; how do you recognize the divinity in Jesus Christ? In three ways: first, as we have explained in I, 2, (a), we recognize God in Jesus because of what we know of God in Israel's history from the pages of the Old Testament. We need not elaborate this: God's character revealed in Israel's history is completed and perfected by the revelation in Jesus. Secondly, we point to the resurrection, God's vindication of Jesus, his 'Yes' to Jesus' obedience. Here, according to our account, is the element of the superhuman, and here is the supremely appropriate moment in history for it. We must boldly accept the miracle, and not try to explain it nor explain it away. By raising Jesus Christ from the dead, God has declared that he was uniquely present in him. Here Pannenberg is entirely in the right. And thirdly we experience the presence of God in Christ in the Church. We can in some sense prove for ourselves in daily living that God meets us in the mode of Jesus Christ.

We should notice that in this account of the incarnation we have been careful not to say that the risen personality of Jesus of Nazareth is available for the experience of Christians. We must believe that when Jesus the man rose from the dead, the individual personality went to reign with the saints in glory. King of saints, he prays for all men in the presence of God, enjoying closest communion with God. But he cannot personally be the mediator of God's life to men as long as we continue in this life. That mediator is God the Word, known to us in the form of Jesus Christ. The man Jesus Christ has not become God, because that is not God's intention for men. But we should observe that this can only be true 'as long as we continue in this life'. We do not wish to be dogmatic about the life to come. Since we know almost nothing about that life, we must not rule out the possibility that there, where different conditions prevail, the risen Jesus Christ could be personally the mode by which we know God the Word. Paul held that not until the *Parousia* (which for this purpose we may equate with the life to come) would we receive our resurrection bodies, which are to be like Christ's risen body. This may be his way of saying that we must not expect a knowledge of the actual personality of Jesus until we pass from this life. In the meantime we must be content to walk by faith, and that means knowing Christ as the image of God, knowing God the Word in the image of Christ.

We have freely used the concept of the Logos, the divine Word, God in his relation to his creatures. Now it could be argued that we are not justified in doing this in view of the nature of our incarnation doctrine. Was not the Logos doctrine of the patristic period only employed in order to maintain just what we deny, a God-man doctrine of Christ? Are we not trying to maintain the wallpaper intact when the wall behind it has been removed? We do not believe that this is so.

In the first place we need a Logos doctrine just as much as the traditional account of Christ does, precisely in order to safeguard the reality, uniqueness, and objectivity of the incarnation. The reason why on the whole we have tended to prefer the term 'Word' rather than 'Son' in speaking of the incarnation is because our doctrine pivots on the conception of revelation and obviously 'Word' is more appropriate in that context. But 'Son' will also serve, because what is revealed is God's character in a human life and sonship is the essence of this. The term also underlines and safeguards the self-givingness of God: the human obedience of Jesus is the correlate of the willingness of God to give himself (see Phil. 2:6-8). The danger with the term 'Son' is that it tends to imply that the actual relation of the historical Jesus to God is exactly the same as the eternal relation of the Second Person of the Trinity (God the Son) to the First. But this is exactly what we wish to avoid, since in our view it makes a genuine manifestation of God in a human life impossible. Of course the confusion is made worse if we do as all the Fathers did, and use the Virgin Birth as a means of explaining how the incarnate Son is eternally one with the Father.

Secondly, we have claimed that had it not been for Jesus we would never have known of God the Word. But at the same time it is worthwhile pointing out that at the time of the emergence of Christianity, Judaism (or one tradition in Judaism) may have been moving towards the discernment of a distinction within the Godhead. The Logos doctrine therefore, though its primary function is to safeguard and express the decisiveness and uniqueness of the event of Jesus Christ, may have been the natural development of the Jewish religion. If so, we must confess that this development was sharply terminated by the emergence of Christianity from the bosom of Judaism and the subsequent persecutions which Christians inflicted on the Jews. From the second century AD onwards Jews were more or less compelled to define their faith in terms of what they did not believe, just as certain violently Protestant sects tend to define their faith in terms of what they do not believe as compared with Roman Catholics. Anyway, if the coming of Jesus Christ is to be regarded as anything more than an incident (regrettable or otherwise) in the relations between God and man, it has to be explained in terms of pre-history as well as post-history. Some explanation must be offered of how it was that God could be from all eternity as he has now disclosed himself to be in Jesus Christ. The only way of doing this is to elaborate something like a Logos doctrine. We could even usefully perhaps attempt to guess what a purely Jewish Christianity would have made of the doctrine of the incarnation, one which austerely eschewed all Hellenistic terms. The distinguished Roman Catholic scholar Cardinal Daniélou has given us some idea of this in his book *The Theology of Jewish Christianity*: Jesus represented as an exalted angel, endless symbolism (of which the Book of Revelation is only a foretaste), legend running wild in *haggada* (embroidery of scriptural narrative), perhaps a faith unable to withstand the attraction of Gnosticism. We have already pointed out that several modern theologians who reject Chalcedon but wish to expound a doctrine of Christ that measures up to the New Testament witness to Christ, retain a Logos doctrine; Tillich, Pittenger, Pannenberg. And we can now point to a contrary example: Lampe rejects a Logos doctrine and with it a doctrine of incarnation, of mediation, or of the Trinity.

Finally we may be asked: 'have you really elaborated a doctrine of incarnation? Are you entitled to use the word?' Not certainly in its traditional sense, which is that God became man (not *a* man). But we have examined this and have concluded that it is in danger of running into meaninglessness, and is also not really a description of God active in genuine humanity. The mode of the incarnation which we have defended is after all the highest, noblest way in which God can manifest himself in humanity. When Newman wrote,

> And that a higher gift than grace
> Should flesh and blood refine,
> God's presence and his very self
> And essence all divine,

he was being very orthodox, indeed Alexandrian in view of that word 'refine'. But was he being true to the facts of Christ, to the facts of human living? What higher gift can there be than grace? If we try to imagine a higher, do we not end with something which is not really humanity? Man must be *capax Dei*, capable of receiving God. God has created us through an unimaginably lengthy process and brought us up to the status of *homo sapiens sapiens*. When he comes to redeem us in Jesus Christ, is it not something of a slight on his own handiwork if we say that he had to fashion a new mode of existence with man, indeed a mode of existence that is so unique as to be quite impossible for us to achieve? We cannot become God the Word. We can approximate (however far behind) to Jesus Christ. Our account of the incarnation, though certainly not orthodox by the standard of Chalcedon, preserves the decisive uniqueness of God's action in Christ, requires a doctrine of the Logos and hence of the Trinity, and is, we maintain, more credible to many thinking Christians today than is the traditional doctrine. We should also claim that it measures up to what the New Testament witness to Jesus requires. We do not think that 'incarnation' is an inappropriate term to apply to the doctrine which we have set forth here.

6 The Work of Christ

a. Sacrifice

'Christ our Paschal lamb has been sacrificed,' says Paul (1 Cor. 5: 7). The Epistle to the Hebrews envisages Christ as the sacrifice to end all sacrifices, at once the fulfilment and termination of the Jewish sacrificial cult. The Fourth Evangelist so distributes the events of the Passion over the last week of the earthly life of Jesus that Jesus is hanging on the cross at the precise moment when the Passover lambs are being ritually slaughtered in the Temple. Sacrifice has always been a word 'borne in the bosom of revealed religion' as far as Christianity is concerned.

The Fathers of the early Church of course accepted the concept of sacrifice as applied to Christ, but it did not figure prominently in their thought. Sacrifice as a religious act was part of the mental furniture of everybody in the ancient world, Jew, Christian, and pagan. It was universally assumed that sacrifice must form a means of man's approach to God, as it was universally assumed that the world was populated by multitudes of evil spirits, usually called daemons. In fact the chief thought of the writers of the first three centuries in connection with this subject is that the Christian is enabled by Christ's sacrifice to offer the only true sacrifice, that of a pure heart and humble mind, and linked with this the sacrifice of praise and thanksgiving (with almost invariably a reference to Malachi 1: 11). By the third century references to the eucharist as a sacrifice begin to appear (see below, pp. 237, 241).

It would, however, be misleading to say that the Fathers have any theory of sacrifice. All they have is a few disconnected ideas. Indeed, it would be wrong to say that the Fathers have any *theory* of the atonement at all, not even the *Christus Victor* one, beloved by Gustav Aulen. The textbooks of doctrine are often astray on this point. All that the Fathers contribute on the subject are a few images, such as those of ransom, of sacrifice, of victory, of a trick played by God on the devil, but they do not even approximate to a theory of why Christ had to die. Nobody produced a theological treatise on the subject during the first thousand years of the Church's existence. This is a curious fact, not often remarked upon. The reasons for this strange omission are probably threefold. First, this very domestication of the practice of sacrifice played its part. The meaning of it did not matter very much; it is likely, for instance, that modern scholars are much more interested in the various distinct significances of the different types of sacrifice detailed in the Old Testament than were the Jews of old themselves. Secondly, the patristic doctrine of the incarnation was so heavily emphasized that it left no room for the atonement. Athanasius, for instance, in his book *On the Incarnation*, when he finally reaches the question of why Christ had to die, can give no rational answer to the question at all, but only a few scattered puerile suggestions. His account of the incarnation has swallowed the concept of atonement. Thirdly, to the early Christian the Church was perhaps a kind of living contemporary atonement, forgiving sins, reconciling, healing. It was not necessary to do theology about it.

But by the time Anselm of Bec, Archbishop of Canterbury, came to write his great book *Cur Deus Homo* (Why God became Man) at the very end of the eleventh century, Christian thought permeating European culture could no longer take for granted the ancient concept of sacrifice. In his book Anselm takes very little for granted, and certainly not the idea of sacrifice. The interlocutor Boso directly questions whether it is right and rational that an innocent man should be required to die on behalf of the guilty, and Anselm proceeds to explain elaborately why this should have happened. For Anselm it is not sufficient just to quote Hebrews 9:22, 'without the shedding of blood there is no forgiveness of sins'. The age in which a sentiment like this would not startle is over.

With Anselm's book opens a new chapter in the history of atonement doctrine in which the theory was advanced that Christ by his death was in some way persuading or enabling God to forgive us, in which God had to be reconciled to man rather than man to God. This phase lasts till well into the nineteenth century. Christ satisfied God's honour or propitiated God's wrath or met the demands of justice or accepted the punishment due to us or 'offered an equivalent penitence' (Moberley) or vindicated the moral law by voluntarily accepting death. Whichever of these theories may be preferred, they all involve the offering of a sacrifice, or of some sacrificial gift or act, to the Father by the Son in order to achieve reconciliation. They all represent the atonement as primarily a movement from man (represented by Christ) to God. This is the significance which they give to the concept of sacrifice. They all suffer from one fatal defect. Inexorably, by an iron logic, they imply that the Son is more compassionate, more loving, more self-sacrificing than the Father. The Son, to put the matter crudely, does the Father's dirty work for him. Inevitably if we adopt a theory of this type we will separate the Father from the Son; we will find ourselves regarding the Son as a more approachable person than the Father. We shall envisage the Son as a sweetener of the Father; and we shall perhaps finally move towards the even more disastrous course of regarding the Blessed Virgin Mary as a sweetener of the Son. About atonement theories of this type the verdict of Christian history justifies us in pronouncing that that way madness lies.

We must envisage the atonement as a movement of God towards man, and not *vice versa*. The Fathers had been quite ready to see the motive of the incarnation as God's love; they would have agreed that God commends his own love to us in that while we were yet sinners Christ became incarnate for us, but the death of Christ as a manifestation of God's love was not a prominent theme in their thought. The first theologian to emphasize Christ's death as a manifestation of Christ's love was Abailard in the first half of the twelfth century. And finally in the nineteenth century a flood of proponents of atonement theories based on this insight appears, among whom McCleod Campbell must be given the credit of being the pioneer. In Luther's thought, however, long before the nineteenth century, sacrifice had been linked with God's love and God's activity in a new and revolutionary way. For Luther, Christ's death was indeed a sacrifice, but a sacrifice given by God to man, God's blessing, God's victory achieved for man. In Luther's thought Christ as the representative sent from God fights his *mirabile duellum* (amazing battle) on behalf of man against the tyrannical forces which oppress man; law, sin, death, devil, curse and – most surprising of all – wrath, God's wrath. Luther almost makes God into a schizo-phrenic, but he does away resolutely with the idea that we in any sense are meant to nag anxiously at God either in order to be remitted penalty or to gain merit. Luther's whole theology, indeed, is designed to remove anxiety in man's relation to God. We do not need to offer Christ because Christ has been offered by God. The only sacrifice which we can offer is the sacrifice of ourselves, our obedience, our lives, our gratitude, our worship, and even this we can only offer in Christ. With Luther the last lingering vestiges of the antique pre-Christian concept of sacrifice disappear. This repre-sents the slow age-long operation of a genuinely Christian force.

If we are to benefit from the complex and varied history of Christian doctrine about the significance of Christ's death, we must begin from the conviction that Christ's life and death represent the expression of God's forgiveness, not the removal of barriers to it. God in Christ has loved man, unexpectedly, undeservedly, inexplic-ably. God does not need man, but he wants him: 'God does not need us. Indeed, if he were not God he would be ashamed of us' (Karl

Barth). God's love has taken the initiative, expressed itself before we were prepared for it, while we were yet sinners and weak; indeed God's love overtakes us while we are busy crucifying Christ ('Father, forgive them . . .'). The master of the Unmerciful Steward takes pity on him and remits him his enormous debt. The father of the Prodigal Son goes to meet him when he is still a great way off. 'In this is love, not that we loved God, but that he loved us and sent his Son . . .' (1 John 4: 10). If we take this central insight of the New Testament seriously there can be no question of God's forgiveness being conditional or needing to be won by some action on the part of Christ. All Christ's life and career is the expression and implementation of God's unconditional, resolute and realistic love.

But this does not mean that God simply says 'Forget it, chums', and we need not bother any longer about sin and guilt. Among all the silly lines which he composed, Frederick Faber never wrote any sillier than these:

> O come to the merciful Jesus who loves you,
> O come to the God who forgives and forgets.

God is not restrained from an easy forgiveness because he has to see about satisfying his honour or propitiating his wrath or exacting due punishment or vindicating justice or the moral law, but because forgiveness is a difficult and costly business, both for the forgiver and the forgiven. Even in our ordinary experience we know that if somebody has deeply wronged somebody else, say a wife has left her husband and wishes to be taken back, it is a difficult and painful matter for both parties. Tolstoy, who was very much concerned about forgiveness, human and divine, expressed this truth profoundly both in *War and Peace* and in *Anna Karenina*. Christ's suffering and death represent, not the price God exacts, but the price God pays for forgiveness. Here in the person of his Son he faces in a concentrated form some of the most horrible effects of the sin which he is forgiving. As Christ hangs upon the Cross he is not propitiating God's wrath nor satisfying God's honour nor – most repulsive suggestion of all – accepting God's punishment, but encountering sin in innocent voluntary obedience. Christ is made sin (2 Cor. 5:21), becomes a curse (Gal. 3:13), accepts the condemnation in his flesh (Rom. 8:1–4), and this is the weakness and foolishness of God (1 Cor. 1:17–25).

If we probe further, and ask, 'What has innocent voluntary suffering to do with sin?' there can be no reasoned answer, any more than there can be a reasoned answer to the question: 'Why does moral evil exist?' A deep instinct or intuition within us affirms that the only way to overcome evil at its worst is to meet it with voluntary, innocent suffering. Regulus returns to Carthage to die at the hands of the torturer. Socrates accepts the cup of hemlock from the hand of the Athenians who have condemned him unjustly. Fr. Damian dies among the lepers whom he has rescued from disgraceful neglect. Dietrich Bonhoeffer leaves the prospect of a comfortable life as an academic in the USA to plunge into opposition in Germany to the odious tyranny of Hitler and finally to be executed by the tyrant. We can say no more.

In Christ crucified, risen, and ascended, God offers us a new being, a new humanity, a new community. It is the community of the Spirit who is God-in-Christ living and ruling in his people, establishing eschatological salvation (see below, pp. 151–3). In this community of the Spirit sin has been in principle overcome and the power is given to overcome sin in our day-to-day lives and decisions; this power is called grace, and consists of the actual indwelling of God as Holy Spirit in us. Thus far, and perhaps only thus far, can the atonement be called 'objective'. Christ is thus at once our substitute and our representative. He is our substitute because he has as an innocent man voluntarily undertaken in obedience to God to meet the effects of human sin in order to open to us this new community of the Spirit. This we could not do. He is our representative in that he is the head of the new community, and it is in union with him that we exist in it and experience God's grace and presence in it, and in that we are called to reproduce in our experience this pattern of victory through suffering which he has given to us as the peculiar sign and means of God's redemptive activity towards us. He is therefore a mediator, both as the expression and vehicle of God's forgiveness and salvation, and as exhibiting perfect human obedience to God's will in the strategy of salvation.

b. Atonement and Symbolism

Man is not all conscious intellect. He has emotions, deeply hidden urges, a whole hidden continent of the psyche which we call the unconscious. His motivation is mysterious. He is not a natural rationalist. The whole domain of art and music, which has played and always will play so large a part in man's life, reminds us that man cannot live by intellect alone. Even as long ago as 20,000 BC man was already a consummate artist, as his rock paintings hidden away in the depths of caves teach us. He needs some way of expressing that in him which is not consciously rational. The fact that doctrines of the atonement which seem to us today to be crude, violent, even immoral, have lasted so long and had so great an appeal must mean something. They must meet some need in man. Can we so present our doctrine of the atonement as to meet this need?

It is possible that we may be able to do so by the help of the distinguished psychiatrist C. G. Jung. Jung maintained, to use his own words, that Christ provided *the necessary therapeutic myth*. Jung was Freud's most distinguished disciple, but he differed from Freud in that he took a more objective view of the unconscious. Whereas Freud held that one's moral convictions and behaviour were largely the effect on the unconscious mind of one's childhood experiences, and that therefore we are largely the victims of our own projections, Jung denied that the contents of the unconscious mind should be looked on as something that we have invented, or projected for ourselves. On the contrary, the unconscious is already provided with a set of archetypal symbols, the property of the race. He claimed to be able to trace a whole series of such symbols in many different cultures and ages. Of these archetypal symbols one, perhaps the most important, is God.

We must understand that for Jung the unconscious is something over against the conscious ego, something against which the conscious ego needs to be protected. Jung believes that at the psychological level the emergence of *homo sapiens* is the emergence of the conscious ego over against the unconscious. Primitive man could cope well with his unconscious (the non-rational part of the psyche) because he had a whole array of mythological religious, ritual, and magical beliefs and practices whereby the unconscious could express itself. Ancient, and also more modern cultures have provided a similar service, largely through a common religion, public ceremonies, worship, and belief. But modern Western man, child of the Enlightenment, finds this increasingly difficult. Technological civilization has no room for anything that cannot be fully explained in rational terms. Modern Western man therefore finds himself threatened by the non-rational part of his psyche and is left without means of coping with it: hence his nervous disorders, growth of violence in Western society, upsurge of interest in the occult and in lunatic religions. Jung writes amusingly of 'the urban neurosis of atheism'. What modern Western man needs therefore is a 'therapeutic myth', i.e. an all-embracing world-outlook, a pattern of belief which will enable man to cope with the unknown, especially the unknown in himself. This myth, says Jung, must be a religious dogma. 'Dogma', he writes, 'is like a dream, reflecting the spontaneous and autonomous activity of the human psyche, the unconscious'. Dogma can therefore defend us from our unconscious selves. Jung defines it elsewhere thus: 'dogma expresses an irrational whole by means of imagery'. By 'irrational whole' Jung does not mean a nonsensical system of thought. He means that reason cannot grasp the whole of reality (a point made, as we have already noted, by Tillich). It is only irrational because it transcends reason, not because it contradicts reason.

We cannot follow Jung all the way in his theories. He certainly believes in God, but he introduces into the Godhead a principle of evil, thus providing a quaternity instead of a Trinity, and, because of this, introducing an element of irrationality into God. Jung uses the phrase 'therapeutic myth', but we would do well to drop the word 'myth', which tends to mean 'fairy-tale' to the average English-speaker, and substitute the phrase 'pattern of belief'.

But, given these modifications, there does not seem to be any reason why the doctrine of the atonement should not be a therapeutic pattern of belief for modern man, and the cross a therapeutic symbol. This would apply whatever precise doctrine of the atonement we chose to follow, whether we spoke of Christ's work in terms of an atoning sacrifice, or a struggle with the powers of evil, or an act of reparation made by God in man. Moreover our therapeutic pattern of belief is not independent of history and empirical fact. Jesus probably did see his vocation in terms of offering himself as a sacrifice on behalf of sinful Israel, and he certainly did see his life as a struggle against the powers of evil. The resurrection ultimately convinced the disciples that this act of redemption must be extended to all men. It was therefore a cosmic event. Every thinking person is aware that there is something radically wrong with the world, with society, and with himself. And every person of good will wishes to do something to put this right. Of course most people put the blame on something outside themselves, on society, the system, the government, the establishment, unscientific methods, etc. Jung calls this a process of projection. In fact healing can only begin with the self, though it must be extended from there to society. The belief that by his cross and passion Christ has overcome all that is against us can be a therapeutic pattern of belief:

> The wounded surgeon plies the steel
> That questions the distempered part;
> Beneath bleeding hands we feel
> The sharp compassion of the healer's art
> Resolving the enigma of the fever chart.
>
> (T. S. Eliot, from *East Coker* in *Four Quartets*)

As Christians we should not hesitate to claim that we have a message of salvation that speaks to the whole of man. The splendid way in which the message has been expressed in art and music down the ages should convince us of that.

However this approach needs to be handled with care. There are three conditions which we must observe if we are to accept Jung's concept of a saving pattern of belief:

i. *In accepting the message of the cross we are not arbitrarily accepting a wholesome fiction*: one could be led into a condition of intellectual desperation: 'I'll try to believe this nonsense because I think it may do me good'. Some theologians in the Roman Catholic Church of the pre-Vatican II period came perilously near to adopting this approach to intellectual converts: 'It's not so difficult to believe this stuff after all, and it will prove easier as time goes by'. Jung himself was aware of this danger, and commends the traditional emphasis on the historical Jesus as a salutary measure against arbitrary credulity. We must be able to give a reasonable account of the historical Jesus, and we must be able to show that our account both of the person and of the work of Christ is reasonably based on this.

ii. *We are not just choosing one respectable myth out of a gallery of respectable myths* ('I'll take Christianity; you try Vedantism'). Everyone, including the atheist and the agnostic, has some myth (fundamental belief) by which he lives. We can discover criteria by which patterns of belief can be evaluated. For example, what is the life-style which it produces? (Nietzsche's myth would come out very badly here). What is the actual historical basis to which it appeals? (There would be an interesting comparison here between Christianity and Buddhism.) How ancient and universal are the symbols which it employs? And so on. We must not be pushed into a position in which we seem to be putting forward a speculative system in contrast to the common-sense solution of the atheist or the agnostic. Any atheistic humanist account of things has vast questions to answer and encounters difficult problems.

iii. *Our moral sense must have the last word.* This does not mean that we can sit in judgement on God. But Immanuel Kant, for all his cold moralism, was a better theologian than Carl Jung. That is, we must not give in to irrationalism, whether put forward by Jung or by Altizer, who apparently holds that God literally died. We must not accept a pattern of belief that outrages our moral sense. Our moral sense is given us by God, and is the medium *par excellence* whereby we know God. This is a profoundly Christian intuition. We may well weigh the New Testament emphasis on obedience: obedience is nothing if not a moral act. Unless your moral sense approves what you believe about God, you have not understood God at all. If you cannot trust your moral sense, you cannot trust God either. It needs educating, of course, and must not be treated as an infallible oracle. This principle would exclude all systems which include evil in the Godhead; it would exclude the doctrine that God the Father punished Jesus Christ for our sins, and likewise the theory that standards of what is right and wrong have been arbitrarily fixed by God, and that he might just as well have fixed them the other way round (said to have been held by William of Ockham, 1300–1349). We must be able to worship God with the whole self, and not just bow down in awe before the *mysterium tremendum et fascinans*, the aweful and fascinating mystery.

c. Sin and Guilt

It is customary today to declare that modern man has little or no sense of guilt. That great American theologian, Reinhold Niebuhr, spoke of 'the easy conscience of modern man'. This observation may be true to the extent that people today do not think about sin as the people of the nineteenth century thought about it. Western European educated people generally in the nineteenth century were very uncertain about what they thought was Christian faith, but were quite confident – almost repulsively confident – about what they thought was Christian morality. It was quite clear to them what was good and what was bad. Their historians (even the very learned ones, like the constitutional historian, Stubbs and the American historian, Motley) thought it their duty to pronounce which historical figures were bad and which good, and in what proportion, and they were sure that this judgment could easily be made. When the eminent German theologian Ritschl (1822–1889) speaks of Christian moral experience (and it figures prominently in his thought) one knows very well what it means – something very like bourgeois morality. The men and women of the nineteenth century liked to talk of moral 'purity', meaning for the most part chastity according to the mores and conventions of their society.

> My strength is as the strength of ten
> Because my heart is pure,

said Tennyson's Sir Galahad, contrasting himself no doubt with the impure and unchaste heart of Sir Lancelot. Moral purity could, in the view of the men of that age, readily be attained.

We today are more sophisticated about sin and purity. We have had the experience of Marx, who pointed out how deeply the moral judgment of each one of us is influenced and conditioned by our station in society, by the economic motives which unconsciously sway us, by the class struggle into which we are unavoidably plunged. How can anyone's heart be pure if, no matter how irreproachable his conduct as an individual may be, he is perpetuating and profiting from an unjust system? We have had the added experience of Freud. A great many of our actions are motivated, consciously or unconsciously, by the sexual drive within us. Our intellects are adept at rationalizing our more disreputable desires so as to make them appear virtuous and high-minded. Perhaps the easy conscience of modern man is partly caused by his realization of how ambiguous is all our moral conduct, even that of the most respectable among us.

Again, since the nineteenth century, things have happened in history which make the doings of our ancestors of the last century look like children's games. Our century has witnessed two world wars, wars conducted on a scale much vaster than any known to history before, with all the frightful destruction and loss of life that went with them and that arose from the revolutions and upheavals which followed them. We have seen the rise of Nazism with its lethal intolerance and its scientifically conducted programme of genocide. We have seen the advent of the pitiless political creed of Communism which set up a Stalinist tyranny that made the tyranny of Ivan the Terrible seem like a Sunday School party. We have witnessed the invention, the use on two occasions, and the constant threat of the atomic bomb. We have had to live with the revival on a large scale of the use of torture by governments, a practice which the people of the nineteenth century fondly imagined to have died out along with the other barbarous relics of the Middle Ages. We are living during a new wave of kidnapping and terrorism. Evil therefore has for us a deeper and darker dimension than it ever could have had for our grandparents. Only dupes and fools any longer nurse their bright inane hopes of indefinite moral and cultural progress. We cannot measure sin with their narrow and inadequate criteria. Between us and them stands indelible experience of evil and suffering. The Jews of today describe the wholesale murder of their race by the Nazis as 'the holocaust', and several Jewish theologians maintain that after it nothing can ever be the same again for·Jewry. Well, we Christians have in another, wider and perhaps more diluted, sense, had our holocaust. Modern man's easy conscience may partly be due to his sensibilities having been dulled by horror.

But none of these considerations in the least diminishes the fact that man is a responsible being. Indeed a sense of moral responsibility is part of the essence of being human. Animals appear to have either no moral responsibility or else a much restricted one. Man has an unlimited sense of moral responsibility, and when, as sometimes happens, there appear amoral people in whom the sense of responsibility, of guilt, is lacking, we treat them as first criminals and finally lunatics. The various pretexts which people sometimes use to explain away moral responsibility are all transparently fictitious. It is futile to blame society for our wrong-doing, for society is composed of individuals (ourselves among them) who must bear responsibility each for his own sin. To say that everybody is guilty, even if it were true, it not the same as saying that nobody is guilty. To appeal to external conditioning in order to evade responsibility for our own actions is equally useless. If we are determined either psychologically or biologically or socially, then we cannot know that we are so, for our knowledge is determined by the same forces and is worthless. But there is something pathetically unreal in indulging in such fantasies. Having moral responsibility means being human; it is part of the fundamental human experience. If it is unreal, we do not exist.

We know then that we have moral freedom. We must therefore believe in the existence of moral evil, and in our guilt when we deliberately do what is wrong, even though we envisage that evil in a more complex and sophisticated way than did our great grandparents. Indeed we have perhaps learnt better than they to suspect that we can be guilty even if we are not consciously doing what is wrong. The roots of good conduct and bad conduct are deeply entwined in our inmost being. Sin is not just an unfortunate lack of education or culture, not just a rudimentary stage in an inevitable progression upwards. It is not simply the survival of the animal in us. Our wrong-doing is of course involved with our emergence from lower forms of life on the evolutionary scale, because everything to do with our nature is so involved. But this explanation does not explain away sin. As our virtues lift us beyond the animal world, so our vices depress us below it. We can become more ferocious than any lion, more lascivious than any goat. We display vices of treachery and greed and megalomania which place us in a different category from the animals. Neither can we escape responsibility for sin by persuading ourselves (as the Manichees did in the ancient world) that moral evil is part of the nature of the universe, as much a physical phenomenon as the force of gravity. Nothing in the exploration of the physical universe on the part of science gives us the slightest reason for thinking this.

The weight and fault of sin lie in the human will. Sin is not part of creation. God created everything good; sin has no permanent basis in reality, for it has not been created by God. It is a contradiction, a surd, in God's universe, against the proper order of things, a rebellion against God and a defiance of his will and his world. It is not merely – as many people today describe it – 'unethical' and 'anti-social' (though it is both); its sting lies in its disobedience to God, its tendency to make man judge of himself, its refusal to accept God's condemnation of it, its breaking of the right relationship with him. It has about it, because of its unique status of non-existence, a curious power of illusion. We rarely do what is wrong without persuading ourselves (or half-persuading ourselves) that what we are going to do is right. Our self-deceit is testimony to the fact that sin has no permanent basis in reality. One of Screwtape's clients, in C. S. Lewis' *Screwtape Letters*, remarks on reaching Hell, 'I now realize that I have spent my life doing neither what I ought nor what I wanted.' Hitler waded fathoms deep in blood in order to gain the hegemony of Europe – and lost it. But if sin arises from non-being, this is not merely to say that it is the negative of being. Non-being can be an effective force, as psychologists tell us when they say that some of their patients are threatened with non-existence, and in certain philosophies, such as some which Gnosticism, that curious type of deviation which beset Christianity in the second and third centuries, gave birth to, non-being can play quite an important part. This deepest threat to our existence, this non-being which sets itself up against God who is essential being, is a universal human phenomenon, observable in all men and women of all ages, creeds, races, colours, and countries as a possibility which they can will or not will. (For a treatment of original sin see below, pp. 128–35.)

The devil is quite a prominent character in the Bible. Judging by his appearance in the Book of Job, he seems to have begun by being a respectable member of God's administration of the world. He was 'the adversary', whose task it was to act as a sort of policeman and public prosecutor in God's court. In other circles however his character deteriorates, and by the time of 1 Chronicles 21:1 (about 350 BC?) he has definitely turned into a malevolent adversary of men, seeking to tempt them into sin. During the intertestamental period he became identified both with a fallen angel, who had led a pre-cosmic rebellion against God, and with the serpent in Genesis 3 who tempted man to his fall. He thus acquired an army of fallen angels under his command who were easily identified with demons. By the time of the New Testament there was a common Jewish belief that pagan deities were demons masquerading under the form of gods. Paul seems to have inherited this belief: see Galatians 4:8; 1 Corinthians 10:20.

The New Testament, being in a sense a product of the apocalyptic movement, which very much stressed the power of the forces of evil, has much to say about the devil. Jesus in his ministry exorcises demons; he sees his career as a campaign against Satan, see Luke 10:18 ('Satan' means 'the adversary'); in the accounts of his temptations he is represented as encountering Satan personally. John's Gospel is just as specific about the devil. The devil is represented as entering into Judas Iscariot (John 13:2,27). John the Divine in the Book of Revelation gives us an actual description of the expulsion of the devil from heaven; see Revelation 12:7–9. Paul seems to have identified the demonic forces masquerading as pagan gods with the 'elemental spirits' (Gal. 4:9), astral powers who were believed to have influence over the destinies of men.

However, all the writers of the New Testament agree that the devil and all his angels have been overthrown by Christ's victory in the cross and resurrection: see John 12:31; Romans 8:38–39; Colossians 2:13–15; Revelation 12:8–9, to take a number of merely sample passages. It seems likely also that Jesus' last cry on the cross, recorded by all three synoptic writers, is intended to be understood as a cry of triumph. At the same time, however, we are warned that, though the power of Satan has been overthrown, Christians are still open to his attacks, and must be on their guard against him; see 2 Corinthians 11:3; Ephesians 6:10–12; 1 Peter 5:8–9.

The early Christian Fathers made much use of this tradition of demonology. It was valuable to them in two ways; in the first place the theory of the extensive activity of demons could appropriately explain away the phenomena of pagan religion. The Fathers could not deny that pagan oracles gave answers (sometimes containing correct predictions), that pagan shrines sometimes could claim to have worked cures, that pagan devotees claimed to have experienced God. All this could be discounted in terms of demonic activity; demons after all were superhuman powers and could produce superhuman effects. Secondly, the devil was used as an opponent to God in a transactional account of the atonement: God, it was claimed by many Christian writers of the first five centuries, had bought back mankind from the devil by paying the price of Christ's death. Sometimes this theory was elaborated by saying that God had got a very good bargain, because he had actually deceived the devil: the devil, believing Christ to be a perfectly righteous man, had gladly accepted him in exchange for the whole of mankind, who were morally speaking damaged goods. When Satan put Jesus Christ to death on the cross he found to his frustration that he could not hold his victim, who was immortal God. Satan therefore both lost the original goods and the price he had received for them. It need hardly be said that both these uses of demonology were equally disastrous for right thinking about God.

It was Anselm of Bec, Archbishop of Canterbury from 1089 to 1109, who finally put an end to the role of the devil as a bargaining partner with God in the doctrine of the atonement. In the various versions of the doctrine of the atonement put forward by the Reformers, the devil did not play a prominent part. But the use of demonology as an explanation of the phenomena of other religions continued as popular as ever, and lasted well on into the period of missionary expansion in the nineteenth century. Only in the last fifty years has it been generally abandoned. The devil as a tempter and adversary of Christians has of course remained in popular religion to our own day.

What are we as Christian theologians to make of the devil? The idea does not easily fit into a reasonable system of theology both because it seems to lead to a dangerous dualism, and because the devil in ordinary speech has been reduced to the level of low comedy (Mephistopheles in red tights) or to a swear word. We must not conceive the devil as a conscious, personal force, marshalling an army of retainers against God, as certainly many of the writers of the intertestamental period did. This idea is too close to dualism, it is insufficiently backed by empirical evidence, and it can, if pursued too far, lead to madness.

But we could also be very foolish to dismiss the diabolical from our universe as a mere fairy-tale. There is undoubtedly a demonic element in human experience. Dostoevsky pointed this out in his novels; when man, says Dostoevsky, deliberately repudiates the authority of God and refuses to recognize any power superior to himself in the universe, he must proceed to set himself up as God. It is not just a course which he may pursue, it is an inevitable tendency. This is because man is made for God, and if he will not acknowledge the true God he must set up gods of his own. John the Divine in the Book of Revelation realizes this, for he represents the great anti-god power as instigating the Roman state as represented by the emperors to claim divine honours from its subjects (Revelation 13: 11–18). It is not surprising that some faithful Christians in Germany during the time of the Nazi regime identified Hitler with the beast in Revelation. In a sense they were right. He represented the demonic pretensions of godless man in that age and place. But it is a mistake to imagine that the image of the beast is exhausted by any one representative, whether the Emperor Domitian or Adolf Hitler. Wherever total allegiance is claimed for any human institution, the demonic element appears. Modern totalitarian regimes fulfil St. John's prophecy just as well.

Again, it is a mistake to deny or underestimate the power of evil.

There are people who have more or less deliberately given themselves over to what they know (or at least once knew) to be evil. Evil works through persons, but it also works through institutions. An evil institution, such as slavery, poisons an entire society, so that even persons of genuine commitment and good will can be unconsciously corrupted by it. All this does not prove the existence of a personal evil power, but it does suggest that evil is a force to be reckoned with, a constant source of corruption, something to be always on one's guard against.

Should the Church exorcise the devil? We should beware of conceding the devil any rights. If someone believes he is possessed by a devil it may in certain circumstances be justifiable formally to expel the supposed devil in order to allay the patient's anxiety. But what the Church is doing in exorcism (if ever it should be practised) is blessing the person not cursing the devil. It is very strange indeed, when one comes to think of it, that modern technological society has come round to a position where perhaps the only occasion when a priest is called in, as a surgeon is called in to perform an operation as the result of which immediate objectively ascertained results can be achieved, is when he is asked to exorcise a ghost! God, who has been relegated to a position of hopeless subjectivity, has suddenly become objective again.

The attitude of the Church towards the occult has always been one of hostility. This is right, though there are respectable organizations which investigate occult phenomena, such as the Society for Psychical Research. The whole subject is so obscure, so beset by fraud and delusion, and so perilous psychologically, that Christians are right to avoid it. This is not to deny that there is evidence of life after death, telepathy, even perhaps communication with the dead. But Christians have other ways of knowing of life after death and other ways of entering into communion with those who have died. They do not need, and should not use, the methods of spiritualism. There is a moral as well as a rational limit to human knowledge. There are some things that men should not try to know.

When we come in the light of this understanding of sin to consider Christ's sinlessness, we shall have to view it rather differently from the traditional way in which it has been envisaged. That Christ impressed his contemporaries – or those of them who knew him well – as sinless in some sense seems clear. Perhaps the most remarkable testimony to this fact is that no words of Christ expressing penitence for his own sin have been preserved. Perhaps the nearest utterance is the 'Why do you call me good? Nobody is good except God', of Mark 10: 18; but this can hardly be called a personal avowal of sin.

Paul and the author of Hebrews are equally insistent upon Christ's sinlessness. In the Fourth Gospel Christ is represented as almost super-human. This tendency increases markedly as the centuries go by until for the writers of the fourth and fifth centuries Christ is of such a nature that he cannot experience temptation; the temptation described by Matthew and Luke is represented by them rather as a testing of the devil by Christ than of Christ by the devil. He has become constitutionally sinless, unable either to will or to do wrong.

A hundred years ago everywhere, and still in some circles today, Christ's sinlessness was represented in terms of moral purity, stainlessness, innocence, not unlike the purity which the men of the nineteenth century demanded of their wives. In Jesus' parable of the Prodigal Son the elder brother accuses the Prodigal of having wasted his money with prostitutes (Luke 15: 30). The late nineteenth-century commentator, Plummer, is shocked at this, and indignantly repudiates the jealous brother's calumny. It must have caused him a pang to think that such a thought could enter the mind of Jesus. The stained-glass windows of our churches are full of pictures of Jesus which dreadfully illustrate this anaemic idea of him.

Today, as both John Knox and J. A. T. Robinson have suggested in their works, contemporary ideas about sin demand a revision of our idea of the sinlessness of Jesus. It is clear from the Gospels when they are read without Mrs. Grundy's spectacles that Jesus was a rounded man of like passions with ourselves who knew the facts of life, and no pale young curate uninitiated into its unpleasant side. We should envisage his sinlessness (which itself is a deplorably negative word) in terms of his involvement in all the tensions and stresses of human life. He certainly felt temptation, lived a life of faith and of prayer, avoided no experience which would bring him alongside his fellow human beings, was little concerned with ritual purity and much with justice and compassion, exposed himself to accusations of immoderate eating and drinking and too close acquaintance with undesirable females, could become angry and despondent and indulge in sharp criticism of others, and yet preserved a fundamental integrity and quality of character which marked him out from others. He was not a bit like Tennyson's Sir Galahad, but perhaps Solzhenytsin may reflect for us dimly the courage, the wholeness and the attractiveness of Christ's character. A person concerned for his own moral purity in the nineteenth century meaning of that term is not the sinless Christ who can redeem the men and women of the twentieth century.

Paul, being a Jew and a former Pharisee, was deeply concerned about the relationship of Jesus to the Law. He had to face the fact that the expected Messiah of the Jews had come, and had been crucified by the Romans at the instigation of the Jewish authorities mainly responsible for maintaining the Torah. This indeed gave occasion to some of Paul's deepest insights. He presented Jesus as one who lived by faith in God and not by the Law, thereby attracting to himself its penalty and curse, and who thereby overcame the deadlock in which all men, Jew or Gentile, strove to please God by obeying a moral law and inevitably failed to do so. He said (as we have seen above, p. 110) that God 'made Jesus to be sin', that Jesus became a curse for us and that God 'condemned sin' in Christ's flesh.

These drastic words of Paul were scarcely appreciated by the Fathers (except perhaps by Augustine), and have not often been taken seriously since. We can however note two instances of their effect in the history of Christian doctrine. Luther took as literally as possible the words about Christ being made sin, and maintained that, though he was personally sinless, he became, in order to deliver us from the power of the Law, the greatest murderer, thief, adulterer, committer of sacrilege etc. there had ever been. Succeeding ages have, understandably, refused to follow this characteristically exaggerated idea of Luther. But Karl Barth taught, in his *Church Dogmatics*, that when the Word of God assumed human nature at the incarnation it was *fallen* human nature which he assumed, and not, as had usually been maintained hitherto, perfect human nature such as was Adam's before the Fall: 'He was not a sinful man. But inwardly and outwardly His situation was that of a sinful man. He did nothing that Adam did. But he lived life in the form it must take on the basis and assumption of Adam's act. He bore innocently what Adam and all of us have been guilty of. Freely he entered into solidarity and necessary association with our lost existence' (*Church Dogmatics* (English translation), 1.2.152).

Perhaps the best way to express the truth contained in these ideas of Paul, of Luther, and of Karl Barth is to say that the moral values expressed in Christ's self-offering and its vindication and acceptance by God render all human values precarious and ambiguous. So great is the sweep of this divine goodness that it leaves our ideas of goodness bankrupt, our respectability, our self-justifying, careful, calculating morality. We have no figures nor diagrams to plot the graph of God's self-giving. Dostoevsky here is a safer guide than Luther. He had a tendency in his novels to illustrate God's love and compassion by causing the most degraded, disreputable, and despised characters to perceive this love and compassion when the other more respectable and upright characters failed to do so. Similarly in his novel *Hard Times* Dickens caused the far from respectable circus-manager Sleary to utter his deepest insight into the nature of love. Novelists can sometimes teach theologians. The drunkards, the prostitutes, the rejects of society may be able to perceive the richness of God's undeserved love, his *agapē*, more clearly just because they have broken with conventional morality and have no hope of being justified or reinstated by it.

d. The Wrath of God

In the earliest parts of the Old Testament God's wrath can be dangerous and arbitrary: Uzzah was struck down by God's wrath because he tried (with the best intentions) to save the ark from falling off the cart. This does not mean of course that we are to accept the reason given for Uzzah's death in 2 Samuel. God is not unjust and arbitrary. Later in the time of the great prophets there is a certain noble anthropomorphism about the description of God's wrath. God is angry with his people because of their sin, but he is also grieved because he loves them. In Hosea 11 there is a moving description of how God cannot let his wrath have the last word; his love must conquer in the end. Such a description still tends too much to describe God in human terms to be thought of as a theology of God's wrath, but we can sympathize with Hosea's desire to do justice to God's attitude. After the exile, in the Books of Chronicles the wrath of God almost becomes an impersonal process, an automatic reaction to Israel's disobedience, manifesting itself in disaster.

The wrath of God is not a prominent feature in the New Testament, but it is there. It is expressed in two ways: there is wrath manifested at the last time. The wrath of God is to be manifested at the Second Coming against those who have disobeyed him; see Matthew 3:7; 1 Thessalonians 1:10; Romans 2:5,8. But there is also realized wrath; wrath seems to be a description of the present state of some people; this is to be found both in Paul and in John; see Romans 4:15; 12:19; 13:4. In these three passages the wrath of God is a process taking place now, not postponed till the *Parousia*, and it is spoken of in remarkably impersonal terms. It does not seem to mean God being personally angry with anyone. This is even clearer in John 3:36: 'he who does not believe in the Son shall not see life, but the wrath of God abides upon him'. Plainly here the wrath of God is not an event confined to the End, but a spiritual condition which unbelievers have brought upon themselves. In Revelation there are tremendous descriptions of the wrath of the Lamb and the wine-press of the wrath of God; but we must remember that this book conveys its message by means of symbols, and it is quite possible that both these figures refer primarily to the cross, and the author means to emphasize the appalling consequences of the rejection of God, and not to suggest that God or Christ is angry with anyone. There is a good parallel between the New Testament doctrine of the wrath of God and the Hindu doctrine of *karma*. Both doctrines mean that sin must bring its disastrous consequences.

In the history of the Church, ecclesiastics found threats about the wrath of God very effective in persuading unlettered laymen that what the Church required was also for their own health. At the Reformation however the concept of the wrath of God was brought into the doctrine of the atonement. Luther had the unusual idea of the wrath of God as the obverse, the other side, of his love: it was motivated by love but showed itself in punishment and terror and threat. God himself overcame his own wrath when Christ conquered it on the cross, along with the other 'tyrants' of oppressed man, sin, curse, law, and the devil. Calvin said that Christ died in order to propitiate the wrath of God. He just stopped short of the unique absurdity of saying that God loves and hates the same people at the same time by making the (to us quite unconvincing) suggestion that God hates the sin but loves the sinner. This is a wholly unbiblical doctrine: the New Testament never brings the wrath of God into connection with Christ's atoning work. We have already seen in II,6,(a) how disastrous such an approach to the doctrine of the atonement must be.

The liberal theologians of the nineteenth century tended to play down the idea of God's wrath. Albrecht Ritschl, for instance, dismissed it as an unfortunate carry-over from the Old Testament into the New. But the doctrine is not to be dismissed as easily as this. We must not indeed represent God as being personally angry with us. The New Testament never actually uses any verb, meaning 'to be angry' of God. Still less must we think of God as sending us special punishment in his anger. But we must retain the doctrine for two reasons. First we may retain it as a description of those who are not under grace but under law. We must not think of God as growing angry with such people and punishing them. It is rather that they punish themselves. They prefer to remain in the darkness. So 'the wrath of God' is rather a description of what they have done to themselves than a name for anything God does to them. The wrath of God is a condition of man not an affection of God. It is called 'the wrath of God' because this is God's universe and such people, whether they know it or not, are reacting against God.

Secondly, the doctrine of the wrath of God safeguards the fact that sin must have disastrous consequences, both for the sinner, and, because man is a social animal, for those connected with him. Sin cannot be shrugged off. God does not ignore sin. The fact that it has disastrous consequences is his arrangement, and this is God's universe. We can see the wrath of God working itself out both in the life of the individual and in society. To take a very simple example, the alcoholic is in fact experiencing the wrath of God, because he is experiencing the consequences of his own wrong-doing. It is not that God is punishing him; he is punishing himself. And of course his long process of deterioration has consequences not only for himself but for his family and friends. This does not mean that we should let him alone to bear the wrath unaided. On the contrary, we should do all we can to help him. But from the moral or religious point of view, in abandoning himself to alcohol he has abandoned himself to the wrath of God.

We can also trace the wrath of God working itself out in society; here the effects are much longer in manifesting themselves, and are often at their worst long after the people originally responsible for them have passed away. For example the centuries of African slavery in America are only now producing their long-term consequences in social unrest and violence. Those who suffer from this are not the people originally responsible for slavery, but it is nevertheless a clear example of what is meant by the wrath of God. The original wrong must have its consequences. To quote T. S. Eliot, who is thinking of exactly the same phenomenon in an individual life:

From wrong to wrong the exasperated spirit moves.

If we want another example we can find it in Northern Ireland. If the fathers of the present generation of Protestant Ulstermen had made a genuine attempt to integrate their Catholic fellow-citizens into Northern Ireland fifty years ago, that unhappy province would not now be plagued with its present disorders. The original wrong of bigotry and hatred is now working out its terrible consequences. If we want an example neither from the USA nor from Ireland, but from England, may we not perhaps find it in the industrial troubles which so dangerously hinder the economic recovery of Britain? The attitudes and restrictive practices of trade unionists today are the consequences of capitalist oppression and exploitation a hundred years ago, or less. This does not excuse, condone, or justify those who hinder economic progress, but it does give an intelligible account of them in the light of the New Testament doctrine of the wrath of God.

The wrath of God then is not a system of rewards and punishments, because, as we have seen, it is frequently the innocent who suffer as a result of sin as much as the guilty. This is the truth behind that dangerous assertion in Exodus 20:5 that God visits the sins of the fathers upon the children unto the third and fourth generation. God does not punish the innocent, but we do in fact inherit the consequences of our ancestors' wrong-doing, and this is God's ordinance.

The remedy for God's wrath is the cross of Christ. This was the supreme example of the innocent accepting the consequences of other men's sins, and it is also the supreme example of how the wrath of God can be transmuted into the victory of God's love. When we say that the wrath of God can be seen in the cross (cf. Romans 1:18), we do not of course mean that God was angry with Christ, but that the cross was the supreme example of the consequences of men's sins. Because Christ bore the cross and rose from the dead, it is possible for those who follow him in some sense to experience the same process. This is what Paul means when he speaks so mysteriously of rejoicing in his sufferings for Christ (see Phil. 1:29–30); and in Colossians 1:24 we even have the suggestion that one can 'make up that which is lacking in the sufferings of Christ'. The consequences of sin (whether one's own or other people's) borne in the spirit of Christ can be transformed so as to become eventually not a curse but a blessing. This is easy to write about but very difficult to experience. Only those who have conquered in this way have any right to speak about it, and they are not usually the sort of people who want to speak about themselves. This is perhaps the point where the Christian doctrine of the wrath of God differs most clearly from the Hindu doctrine of *karma* already referred to.

This leads on to one more related topic, the idea of reparation or making amends. Imagine any situation in which one person has seriously wronged another: we would most of us admit that, if the person who has done the wrong not only confesses his fault and expresses his contrition, but also makes some attempt at making amends, we admire him more than if he had made no such attempt. To take a simple example, immediately after the last war, when the full enormity of the Nazis' crimes against the Jews had been disclosed, a number of young Germans deliberately went to work at some socially beneficial project in the newly established state of Israel. They did it by way of reparation, not for what they had done (for they were too young at the time to be held responsible), but for what their elders had done. Of course any reparation that they could make could not possibly atone for the appalling wrongs inflicted on the Jews by the Nazis, but we must surely applaud their intention. In other words, where moral wrong has been done, reparation is morally admirable.

Now the idea of reparation is the truth that lies behind Anselm's famous book already referred to, *Cur Deus Homo*. Christ, says Anselm in effect, by his death made reparation for our sins. As a matter of fact the New Testament never applies this concept to Christ's death, but it does use it of Christians' labours and sufferings in the cause of Christ; see Colossians 1:24 quoted just now, and also such passages as 1 Corinthians 4:9–13; 2 Corinthians 4:7–12. The notion has been taken up in Catholic theology. The Blessed Virgin has been called 'Marie Reparatrice'; by her prayers she makes reparation for the sins of the world. And the devout have been encouraged to ask God to let his punitive wrath fall on them (who can presumably take it) instead of on the sinners who deserve it. Something like this is found in 4 Maccabees 17:21–2. This is a Jewish book written probably in the first century AD, in which the sufferings of the martyrs of the Antiochean persecution are described. In this passage they are represented as asking God to accept their innocent deaths as a reparation for the sins of Israel.

When it is expressed like this, reparation is being misused. It leads straight to self-righteousness and to a doctrine that one can earn merit with God by one's sufferings. But there may all the same be a place for the idea of reparation in Christian thought. The nun who took the place of the frightened teenager in the death-queue at the concentration camp was offering an act of reparation. Those who try to help drug addicts by accompanying them through their sufferings, and as far as possible bearing with them, are really making reparation. When Mother Teresa picks up and ministers to the foundlings and outcasts on the streets of Calcutta, she is bearing the consequences of other people's sins and turning them to blessing. To make reparation is Christ-like, God-like. It is to carry on Christ's ministry. It is to turn the wrath of God into praise.

e. Doctrine of Man
i. The Fall of Man
The doctrine of the fall has its origin in Jewish thought. The story in Genesis 3 as it stands does not necessarily imply that all Adam's posterity was permanently alienated from God, but this is the way in which it was understood in rabbinic exegesis by the first century AD. Rabbinic imagination had built up Adam and Eve before the fall as super-creatures, endowed with all sorts of magnificent qualities and features which they lost as a consequence of the fall. There is no sign of this in Paul, but he certainly says that because of Adam's fall, all his posterity are involved in actual sin (Romans 5:12–15). He does not say what Augustine, and after him Calvin, said, that because of

Adam's fall all men are born guilty sinners and subject to God's wrath. Indeed Paul seems to be more interested in the fact that Adam's fall involved death for all men than in the sinful condition which it produced. As we read Romans today we can very often substitute *homo sapiens* for 'Adam' without seriously altering the sense.

However Paul, and, we may be sure, all the other New Testament writers, regarded the events narrated in Genesis 3 as literal history. This conclusion was accepted by all the early Fathers with the exception of Origen, who boldly allegorized the fall story, denying that it was to be understood literally. This literal interpretation held valid for most Christians till well into the nineteenth century. It was assumed that man as a species had been created complete and that Adam and Eve were historical figures. This assumption was sharply challenged in the course of the last century by the findings of biologists, palaeontologists and geologists. These men of science began to suggest that the earth was far, far older than a literal reading of the chronology of Genesis implied, that man had not been created complete as a species, and that he had in fact developed over a period of hundreds of thousands of years from ape-like creatures. At first educated Christian leaders in this country indignantly denied these conclusions and accused their authors of denigrating man's glorious status and destiny. The controversy reached a dramatic climax at a meeting of the British Association in Oxford in 1860, when Samuel Wilberforce, Bishop of Oxford, confronted Thomas Huxley, the famous biologist. We know now that Huxley was right and the churchman was wrong on the actual matter of fact about which they were disputing. Adam and Eve are symbolic, not historical, characters, and man has evolved from the higher primates and was not created complete as a species.

It does not necessarily follow that the fall was not an historical event. We have, after all, a vast perspective of pre-history into which we can fit the event if we are determined to do so. History, recorded history, only begins about 3000–2000 BC, and *homo sapiens sapiens* (men with as much average brain power as we have) has been on the earth since 40,000 BC. You can even, given great ingenuity (not to say credulity), maintain that the fall originated with an historical couple somewhere in the depths of pre-history. Teilhard de Chardin, the famous Jesuit palaeontologist, does so in his major work *The Phenomenon of Man*. On page 206 of the English translation of his work he has a footnote part of which runs thus: 'At those depths of time when hominization took place, the presence and movements of a unique couple are positively ungraspable, unrealizable to our eyes at no matter what magnification. Accordingly one can say that there is room *in this interval* for anything that a trans-experimental source of knowledge might demand'. These words were written in the 1930's, though not published till after his death in 1955.

So one can still defend the theory of an historical fall if one is determined. But it is much better not to make the attempt. It is pretty obvious from the way Teilhard de Chardin writes that he does not himself believe in the historical existence of this couple, and one has every reason to suppose that he only wrote the footnote in a vain attempt to satisfy the ecclesiastical censors in the Vatican, who were at the time intent on maintaining the foolish pretence that responsible Roman Catholic scholars need not and must not accept a doctrine of evolution (they kept up this attempt for another ten years or so, but it has now been abandoned). In any case, since Teilhard de Chardin wrote those words further discoveries in palaeontology have revealed a long process of closer and closer approximation to *homo sapiens* which preceded his appearance about forty thousand years ago, and it is clear by now that these approximations ('hominids' is the technical term) must be regarded as moral creatures and not as mere animals. And these hominids were not in the slightest like Adam and Eve before the fall! There is no evidence for example for cannibalism in Genesis; there is in the caves where hominid remains have been found. It is therefore far more satisfactory from every point of view to admit that Genesis 3 is a parable, not history, that Adam and Eve are symbols for *homo sapiens*, and that God willed to create man by means of a long process of evolution. The story in Genesis 3 is a theological description, couched in symbolic terms, of man's relation to God.

Why must it be couched in symbolic terms? Why cannot it be expressed in scientific or philosophical language? Scientific language fails us here because man's relation to God is a moral question and science is not competent to tell us what we ought to do. Philosophical language fails because man's relation to God involves the concept of sin as the breaking of a relationship to God, and this is an area which philosophy will not treat – certainly not the philosophical tradition that prevails in this country today. We must therefore be content to say that the doctrine of the fall means this: man in his relation to God is always conscious of being a fallen creature. He is aware of guilt before God. He is not as God intends him to be. He has a divided self.

Here psychology (perhaps one should say psychiatry) unexpectedly comes to our aid. Freud could not be accused of a leaning towards the acceptance of Christian doctrine. But when he comes to try to explain the repressed and divided condition of man's psyche, he does in fact elaborate what looks surprisingly like a myth of a fall. Freud himself did not realize he was using mythological language; he thought he was being purely scientific. But his theory of the origin of the Oedipus complex is in effect a myth. Freud wants to explain why man has got a bad conscience, and the way he does it is this. At some point in pre-history, he claims, when primitive man was living in extended families presided over by a patriarch in each instance, the young men of the family wish to gain access to the females whom the patriarch-father had reserved for himself. They therefore kill their father (and subsequently eat him in order to gain his strength). But this gives them a bad conscience, so they compensate for the killing by deifying the dead patriarch and identifying him with the source of moral authority. This bad conscience, which we all inherit, he called an Oedipus complex after the character in ancient Greek legend who unwittingly killed his own father. Subsequent psychologists have laughed at the idea that Freud had in fact found out anything scientifically valuable about primitive man. But it is surely very interesting that Freud, faced with essentially the same phenomenon which the story in Genesis 3 tries to explain (man's divided psyche), should have had recourse to a myth, a symbolical explanation. As a matter of fact, if one is offered a choice of symbolical explanations for this phenomenon, that given in Genesis 3 is much preferable. It does not masquerade as a scientific account (however much Christians have mistakenly treated it as this), and it underlines the really significant elements in the relation between God and man: the fact that fallen man remains a responsible being answerable to God (Gen. 3:9–10); the fact that guilt involves a disordered sexuality (Gen. 3:7); the fact that guilty man always tries to shift the blame onto someone or something else (Gen. 3:12–13); the fact that there is no returning to a primitive state of innocence; we must go on through suffering to restoration (Gen. 3:24). Rightly understood, Genesis 3 is a magnificent parable expounding man's predicament before God.

There is one other sense in which the fall can be understood, not an alternative but a supplement to that which we have first outlined. Moreover it is also one which has a correlate in Freud. The fall could be understood in a social or anthropological sense as the impact on primitive man of civilization in the sense of more highly organized society. Imagine a primitive tribe hidden away in a mountain valley in Papua-New Guinea. Before they have been discovered by modern man, their social life has been very strictly ordered; everyone knows his or her role in society; everyone does what is expected of him at the time it is expected. Tribal laws, tabus, and ceremonies are carefully observed. There are very few rebels. Though this is not a paradisal society, it is a society in which social sin at any rate is almost unknown. Then comes the intrusion of modern man. New possibilities are opened up, new ways of living disclosed, it is realized that the tribal laws and customs are only relative, not absolute. At once the tribe begins to disintegrate, individuals to degenerate, and a general sense of meaninglessness to prevail, which can in certain circumstances lead to the actual death of the tribe. Is this not something like the account in Genesis 3 of man eating the fruit of the tree of the knowledge of good and evil? Freud's parallel is to be found in the rather pessimistic view which he took of the impact of organized society on primitive man. He imagined primitive man to have existed in a very free condition, so that he was able to obey his unconscious urges without hindrance (except for the actual consequences on other people; Freud admitted that primitive life was short as well as uninhibited). But with the coming of society or civilization man has to repress his urges, and is consequently unhappy and frustrated. Freud did not draw from this the conclusion that therefore we should try to return to the condition of the uninhibited savage; he was in favour of civilization, but he believed that it was to be had only at the price of psychic frustration. Thus when we rightly understood the doctrine of the fall, we find that it is a profound concept, capable of providing valuable insights about man's psyche and his existence in society.

Is the concept of 'original sin', then, to be explained away altogether? To do so would be to imitate the producer of the play in Sheridan's *The Critic* who in order to shorten the production of a play whose central character is Queen Elizabeth I cuts out every single appearance of the Queen on the stage. Man's consciousness of moral failure or paralysis is one of the central facts of his existence, witnessed to by authors who have no connection with Christianity as well as by Christians and Jews. *Video meliora proboque, deteriora sequor*, wrote the pagan Roman poet Ovid ('I see the better course and know that it is right; I follow the worse course'). The question is not, does this constant consciousness of sinfulness exist, but how are we to assess it, what are we to make of it?

It is certainly no use, as we have seen, trying to persuade twentieth-century man that this phenomenon represents our inheritance, physically imparted at each new conception by the act of procreation, of the sin and guilt of a single pair of human ancestors some thousands of years ago, mainly because they had eaten an apple which they were forbidden by God to eat. What has been said in this section already effectively precludes that. It was only because this ridiculous and dreadful theory was propounded by a man of gigantic intellectual power who lived at a period uniquely formative of the thought of the Middle Ages, Augustine of Hippo, that it gained such a hold upon the imagination of the theologians of the Church and became part of the mediaeval world-view. Augustine had much of great value to contribute in his insights about the working of the human personality and its relation to God, but when he propounded this disastrous doctrine he was attempting to give what he thought was a scientific basis to his own psychological observation. The sooner the Augustinian doctrine of original sin is buried in the sands of history the better. Thoughtful and responsible Christians should be ashamed to teach such a doctrine.

It is then simpler and more satisfactory to say that this sinfulness is just the survival in us of our animal past? Books such as *The Naked Ape* have recently suggested that much of our conduct can be accounted for by the operation in our subconscious selves of instincts, patterns of instinctive behaviour, which can be seen operating openly and unsuppressed in animals, instincts of aggressiveness, self-protection, herd-loyalty, and so on. Certainly nothing can be more completely self-centred than man in his least sophisticated state, a new-born baby. Yet this is too naïve an analysis of human sinfulness. Competent psychologists dissent strongly and justly from the kind of argument put forward in *The Naked Ape*. Of course our animal ancestry is part of our make-up. We have inherited a vast amount from the remote past of the race — our upright stance, our versatile thumbs, even our appendices. And we cannot confine this heredity to our physical frames; there must be a considerable heritage in our minds too. But man is in no aspect of his existence *simply* an animal, not even in his self-centredness. On the one hand the attribution of sin to the survival within us of the animal is not altogether fair to animals. The higher animals, even including birds and fish, follow some rules of what we might call instinctive or intuitive obedience worked out apparently in order to preserve themselves and their species. Among some animals (for instance elephants) these rules may be quite sophisticated. They are capable of self-sacrifice and of loyalty, and in some cases of friendship to man. On the other hand man's type of self-centredness is much more complex than that of the animals. In fact man's behaviour goes well beyond ordinary animal self-centredness. As a self-transcending, reflecting being, man's wickedness removes him from the wickedness of animals, as his goodness removes him from theirs. Predatory animals, whether they be lions, hawks or insects, may exemplify

'Nature, red in tooth and claw', but they do not add hypocrisy, deceit and self-righteousness to their ferocity. They do not burn other animals to death for the sake of their religious beliefs, nor condemn them to imprisonment on carefully contrived false evidence. Similarly man at his best, at his most self-giving, generous and holy, exhibits a different type of goodness from even the best of animal behaviour.

It is even less satisfactory to attribute this sense of sinfulness to the restraints of civilization and morality laid upon us by society. The Freudian explanation of the sense of guilt in effect sees it as the result of the repression of our natural impulses and the refusal of our conscious minds to acknowledge them in obedience to the rules of morality which our upbringing and education, themselves deeply embedded in the culture and society in which we live, impose on us. The logical conclusion of such an idea (though Freud did not draw this conclusion) might well be to throw off all moral restraints and glory in being superior to morality with the unscrupulousness of a Nietzsche or a Hitler. But the fact is that human beings are moral, whether they like it or not; it is part of being human to be aware of moral obligation, and those who are wholly unaware of it or whose awareness is deficient are rightly regarded as insane; that is to say that their humanity is in some way reduced.

Perhaps those theologians are nearest the mark who, ever since Kierkegaard, have fastened upon anxiety as the most important symptom of sinfulness in human beings. We here refrain from using the term 'original sin', for this is generally thought to imply the whole Augustinian doctrine. But it seems persuasive to suggest that anxiety is at the root of that proneness to sin which is a universal human phenomenon. It is our anxiety which drives us into the multitudinous forms of selfishness which we display. We are anxious about our survival, our success, our popularity, our sexual capacity, our status, our honour, our authority, our property, our future, and so on. And clearly this anxiety is involved with our consciousness of finitude; we know that our life is limited and precarious; we are conscious that we shall die, however we may attempt to conceal this unpleasant truth from ourselves. It is man's capacity to transcend himself, to, as it were, stand outside himself and view his life as a whole, which forces him to recognize his finitude, and this is close to the root of his proneness to sin. Animals do not display the same anxiety nor the same power of self-transcendence. And children, whose trusting, carefree, single-minded attitude to life adults often admire, display anxiety and self-transcendence in a much smaller degree.

It was not merely the writer of Genesis who observed and in his myth of Adam and Eve commented upon the proneness to sin of human beings. Many other writers in the Bible observed it, though we must not assume that they all attribute its origin to the story of Adam and Eve, which in fact receives little notice in the rest of the Old Testament: 'Behold I was brought forth in iniquity, and in sin did my mother conceive me', wrote the author of Psalm 51 (v. 5). The writers of the New Testament also take this sinfulness for granted as one of the permanent facts of the human condition, though once again we must be on our guard against reading the whole Augustinian theory into, for instance, the words of Paul. All the biblical authors, in accordance with the profoundest insights of the religious tradition of Judaism, interpret human sinfulness in the light of man's relation to God. For them sin is not just unethical or anti-social behaviour, it is disobedience to God. Man's anxiety drives him not only to self-assertiveness and pride, it impels him to defy God, to set himself up as God, to brush God aside and involve himself in something like a rebellion against the world as God has ordered it, the whole nexus of moral and spiritual order which God has designed for human society. Man therefore is in a constant condition of insurgence against his true advantage, against what he is meant to be in God's design. We need not believe in a pre-historic or pre-cosmic fall in order to accept this interpretation of human proneness to sin. We cannot believe in the myth of a fall as an explanation of how human sinfulness came about, but we can see that it contributes something towards analysing the phenomenon.

ii. The Image of God in Man

'Then God said, "Let us make man in our image, after our likeness". So God created man in his own image, in the image of God he created him: male and female he created them' (Genesis 1: 26,27). These are words which have been much pondered on through the ages. Philo, the Alexandrian Jew who was contemporary with St. Paul, and several others after him, decided that we were meant to distinguish between 'image' and 'likeness', but the text gives us no justification for making this distinction. Some monks at the beginning of the fifth century took this verse literally, supposing that the physical appearance of God is literally the physical appearance of man, and succeeded in making the pliant Theophilus, Bishop of Alexandria, at least say that he agreed with them; but ideas such as these must of course be dismissed as nonsense. Paul gave the idea of man's creation in God's image his particular Christological interpretation when he wrote that Christians were destined 'to be

135

conformed to the image of his Son, that he might be the first-born among many brethren' (Rom. 8:29); cf 1 Corinthians 15:49, where we are to bear the image of the Heavenly Man, and 2 Corinthians 3:18, where we are told that we 'are being changed into his likeness from one degree of glory to another'; so at Colossians 3:10, we are reminded that we 'have put on the new nature which is being renewed in knowledge after the image of its creator.' For Paul, Christ is the image of God; he may well have read into Genesis 1:26,27 the thought that man was created in Christ (the pre-existent Christ), and it is our calling to conform our lives and characters to his.

But if we ask ourselves whether, as well as this typically Pauline Christological interpretation of the passage, there is an interpretation which fits every man, the answer is not easy. What is there in every man, every human being, which mirrors God? The early Christian Fathers answered almost with one voice – 'Reason'. Man is distinguished from the animals by the fact that he can reason and they cannot. This reason (*logos*) in man is given him because he has been created by the Logos (Word/Reason) of God. This satisfied their minds, nurtured as they were on Greek philosophy, and in particular the philosophy of the Stoic school, which taught that everybody has a Logos in himself capable of responding to the universal logos which guided and ordered the world, interpenetrating it. Similarly, they saw reason as the inmost agent in the human personality, that which is characteristically human, and this exaltation of reason has had a long history in Christian and European thought.

But Augustine was a much more realistic interpreter of the human personality when he saw that which was characteristic of human kind, that which ultimately directs their actions and determines their characters, as desire rather than reason. Reason is in fact, immensely important though it is, no more than a tool of desire. And to make reason that which is God-like in us is to think of God in too intellectual, too abstract terms, as if he were the Great Mathematician rather than our loving and caring Father.

If we are to be true to the picture of God given us in the Bible, the wisest course is to envisage the image of God in us in terms of our moral freedom. When God made man, he made him, as far as we know, unique in the universe in that man alone is genuinely free to choose good or evil, to obey God and fulfil his own being freely and voluntarily, and if there are other morally free beings in the universe, this does not in the least infringe or affect our freedom. This means that God has given to man a reflection of God's own freedom. With this as an inescapable corollary follows the possibility of man making the wrong choice, abusing his freedom, introducing sin and moral evil into the world, and the atonement must in some sense be seen as God's strategy for meeting this situation, this inevitable result of his giving away to man something of his own freedom. But it also means that man enjoys a creative freedom, a capacity to create; it means that man has to a degree possessed by no animal an imaginative faculty which is the source of everything that is fine and good in human culture and civilization; art, poetry, drama, literature, architecture, technology, science, invention. Man's creativity is a reflection of God's, and God is a God who wants to see his creativity reproduced in his creatures, and wants not only creatures which are made to fulfil their ends biologically, as they are conditioned, as their elements or their instincts lead them, but also human creatures designed to respond to him voluntarily, spontaneously, gratefully. Man can also, of course, be creative in evil, can design ways of enslaving or torturing or exploiting nature and animals and his fellow-men with a diabolical ingenuity. But this is the price paid for freedom.

This freedom also means that man is – as far as we can make out – uniquely self-transcending. He can examine himself, to some degree objectify himself, place himself in his universe, his surroundings, his context both geographical and chronological. He can wonder, speculate, question, pursue almost indefinitely his insatiable curiosity. When he has secured for himself safety from his predators and enemies and ensured an adequate supply of food and clothing, he is *not* satisfied. At his worst he is bored and tries to banish his boredom with sexual activity (which ultimately leads to more boredom) or with bingo; at his best he turns to science or philosophy or art or literature or religion or exploration. But in one way or another his nature drives him beyond the satisfaction of his immediate needs. This self-transcending element or possibility in him is called 'spirit' by the theologians; it is a permanent part of man's personality, even when it is atrophied or stifled. In our contemporary Western society this self-transcending spirit-aspect of man is probably the best way of relating man to God. It offers the most hopeful avenue to God for man. We find it difficult or impossible in our urbanized civilization to approach God through nature, in spite of the often seductive arguments of D. H. Lawrence and people like him. For us this self-transcending freedom is the best pointer to God.

We must not of course forget that we are all also in a sense animal, that we have descended from animals and that we share a great deal in common with animals. We live by food much as they do; we need sleep and exercise as they do; we reproduce our kind as they do. We still preserve something of their instinctive life, perhaps of their herd-consciousness and self-protective impulses. But this dimension of spirit which we possess marks us off from animals. It is not even logical or satisfactory to say that man is animal +x, because it is the x which makes him man and which affects his whole nature, even his 'animal' element. To say that man is 'only an animal' is as reasonable as to say that *Hamlet* is only words. Man is not only greater than the animals but also more degraded than they. 'Be more than man, or thou art less than an ant', said Donne. Man is capable of heroism and self-sacrifice beyond that of animals (though animals are capable of self-sacrifice), and also capable of cruelty, sensuality and deceit which no animal could, or would, stoop to. Man's selfishness is therefore not simply the preservation in him of the animal instinct to survive, the enactment of the law of 'nature red in tooth and claw', but a deeper self-regard which represents a refusal of possibilities not open to animals, the 'heart bent in on itself' of Augustine. It is the price of his freedom.

But are we really free? A number of different theories have been produced and are still quite influential to prove that we are not free. It has been suggested that we are simply aggregations of reflex actions, i.e. that all our behaviour can be accounted for by regarding us as a vast complex of unconscious or automatic reactions, all of them in essence like the immediate, unthinking reaction which we make to the sound of a door banging behind us, or like the action of our mouths watering when we see food. It has been held that our behaviour is completely determined by subconscious pressures in our minds set up by our experiences in early childhood, or by the chemistry of our brains, or by social pressures and conditions. Now, it would be absurd to deny that we are to some extent conditioned by some or all of these factors, just as we are conditioned if somebody hits us on the head with a mallet. Our freedom, if we have freedom, is certainly a limited one. But if we are so determined by any or all of these forces that we have no freedom at all, then it must be clear to anyone who gives the matter the slightest thought that we cannot know this great truth, because our total conditioning prevents us from knowing any truth at all, including the truth that we are conditioned! Arguments for determination such as these usually collapse by cutting off the branch upon which they are sitting.

The fact is that we know in our inmost, unassailable selves that we are free moral agents, and that if we were not free moral agents we could not be human beings. When we speak of ourselves as 'persons' or 'personalities', we mean more than anything else that we are morally free beings. One could even say that being in the image of God implies being a person. Moral freedom, freedom to choose right and wrong, good and evil, is part of the essence of being human. There is nothing that we know with more unshakable certainty than that we can exercise free will. God has given us this dangerous and appalling gift and responsibility, and even though we may run away from it into totalitarian political systems and authoritarian religions, even though we may try to hand it over to Grand Inquisitors and Supreme Praesidiums and People's Chairmen, we cannot get rid of freedom. It is part of our birthright or curse as human beings, according to the way you look at it. We may think that God has made a dreadful mistake by admitting into the world so much evil and suffering as a result of our free will. Or you may admire God's generosity in taking the vast risk of sharing his freedom with us and in voluntarily choosing himself to endure the resultant suffering as he pursues his strategy of recovering us. But free we are and free we shall remain, even after 1984.

iii. Justification

Ever since the appearance of Article XI of the XXXIX Articles which said 'that we are justified by faith only is a most wholesome doctrine, and very full of comfort', the doctrine of justification by faith has been formally a part of Anglican doctrine, and it is usually treated of by modern Anglican writers upon doctrine (e.g. E. J. Bicknell, *A Theological Introduction to the Thirty-Nine Articles of the Church of England*, new impr. 1936, pp. 254–266; J. Macquarrie, *Principles of Christian Theology*, 2nd ed. 1966, pp. 304–305). But it is a long time since this doctrine figured at all prominently in Anglican thought, and a man could listen to sermons from Anglican pulpits for a very long time – indeed for a lifetime – without so much as hearing it mentioned.

But in fact the doctrine of justification by faith is a central ingredient in the thought of Paul, and unless we are prepared to abandon Paul as an interpreter of the significance of Christ we must attempt to understand it and to integrate it into our whole conception of the Christian faith.

The whole of Paul's thought is conditioned by his conviction that the Messiah long expected by God's chosen people, the Jews, had come, had been rejected by that people, had been put to death by crucifixion, and had been raised again by God. This realization created a revolution in Paul's thought; he had been convinced against the bent of all his previous training and ideas. If Paul had never referred to the drastic change in his own outlook (Gal.

1: 11–16), and if we did not have no less than three descriptions of
Paul's conversion in Acts (9: 1–19; 22: 6–16; 26: 12–18), we would
have had to postulate some such experience in order to account for
the character of his thought, his amazement at God's unexpected-
ness, his sense of experiencing total reorientation at God's hands.
That upon which all pious Jews had relied as their point of stability
in existence, that which expressed the very character of God himself
and set out for his people the way of righteousness and of salvation,
the Torah, had been pulled like a carpet from under his feet. The
Messiah had been executed according to the Law, and God had
vindicated the Messiah and not the Torah. This meant that for Paul
all familiar, reliable landmarks had been obliterated, all religious
security withdrawn. No wonder that he experienced a period of
blindness and later spent a long time in Arabia trying to sort out his
ideas.

The doctrine of justification by faith was the result of this
re-ordering of his ideas. And first it should be noted that this
doctrine is not simply a theological expression of Paul's internal
religious experience. This idea was for some time popular; it is one
of the ruling thoughts of the Moffatt Commentary Series (not least of
the Commentary in Galatians in that series), and is not absent from
Bicknell's jejune and timid treatment of the subject. But the doctrine
has foundations more solid than Paul's religious experience. It rests
upon the messianic claims made by Jesus and for Jesus and on the
death and resurrection of Jesus. Those passages in Galatians where
Paul is describing his relationship to Christ as a justified man, 'I have
been crucified with Christ; it is no longer I who live, but Christ who
lives in me, and the life I now live in the flesh I live by faith in the
Son of God, who loved me and gave himself for me' (Gal. 2: 20 etc.),
are not simply transcriptions of periods of exaltation and mystic
union in Paul's prayers, but something which applies, in Paul's
thought, to every baptized Christian. This is what happens when
men and women become Christians, are initiated into Christ,
undergo the revolution that comprises Christianity. These experiences are not confined to the saints and mystics; they are part of the
reality of God's handling of all men and women in Christ.

The result of the death and resurrection of Jesus Christ is that
both Jew and Gentile have been brought to a common condition of
bankruptcy before God. As Paul puts it, 'all men, both Jews and
Greeks, are under the power of sin. . . . The whole world' is 'held
accountable to God . . . there is no distinction; since all have sinned
and fall short of the glory of God' (Rom. 3: 9, 19, 22, 23). This
condition of bankruptcy, like the condition of the Unmerciful

Steward in the parable, is what Paul calls not being justified by works, i.e. not possessing any claim on God or favour with God based on sacred rites performed or holy law observed or upright conduct displayed or ethnic privilege pleaded. One could say that a great deal of all religion consists in attempts by man to exploit God in various ways. God is found to be useful as a final sanction for morality, or as lending a sacred dimension to the duty of upholding the *status quo*, or as providing supernatural fuel for stoking political or racial or even (finest use of all!) religious hatred. Or he simply is used to buttress man's endless self-esteem. Well, not being justified by the law or by works means the demolition of all possibilities of exploiting God. When the Unmerciful Steward is finally brought before his master, there is an end of all excuses and rationalization. The books are open; they have been examined. There is nothing the defaulting servant can do except to throw himself with desperate, imploring tears on the mercy of the man whom he has cheated.

But Paul knew much more about God than that he was the master of the delinquent steward. He knew that God was commending his love in Christ's death for sinners; he knew that the God who was to be found in the Hebrew Scriptures was a trustworthy God who was merciful and cared for his people, who had a good purpose which he was carrying out in history; he knew that Jesus himself had spoken of the undiscriminating, forgiving love of God, and had taught the need to approach God in faith. Indeed, to most of the writers of the New Testament Jesus was the great exemplar of faith. When therefore men were faced with this necessity to throw themselves on the mercy of God, Paul taught that they could do so confidently, relying on God's character and not on their own merits, for God was no capricious tyrant delighting in disappointing his creatures, but a God who was eminently faithful, worthy of faith, as he had proved even before the Law was instituted, in his dealings with Abraham.

But what did Paul mean by saying that God is righteous and justifies those who have faith (Rom. 3:26), or by the term 'the righteousness of God' which has been 'manifested' or revealed (Rom. 1:17; 3:21)? Careful study has been given to the Greek words that lie behind these expressions (*dikaio-ō* and *dikaiosunē*) by Sanday and Headlam, C. H. Dodd, Karl Barth and many other commentators on the greatest of all Paul's letters. Primarily, the resurrection was a vindication of Jesus Christ. In vindicating Christ God vindicated himself; he showed that he was, in spite of appearances, master of the situation, that (in Paul's words), 'the foolishness of God is wiser than men and the weakness of God is stronger than men' (1 Cor. 1:25). The resurrection was the great turning of the tables by

141

God on men, what the ancient Greeks called a *peripeteia*, an unexpected reversal of affairs at the end of a drama by some divine agency. In its fundamental sense God's righteousness was a demonstration that he was right, and that everybody else was wrong. But the motive of this reversal of expectation, this vindication of his rejected Messiah, was love, pure, undeserved, unexpected, unearned, gratuitous love. Henceforward God's relationship with men and women would be one of unalloyed graciousness, love, self-giving, even though God in this relationship continued to be master, as he must continue if he was to remain God. This relationship, this self-giving Paul calls 'grace' (*charis*). It means God's act of giving himself in undeserved love to those who will accept him. It governs and conditions all the Christian dispensation; it calls out in those who accept it (and they can only do so in the Holy Spirit) an answering love of the same unconditional, self-giving character which Paul calls *agapē* – 'charity', as the A.V. has it (the R.S.V.'s 'love' is inevitable but inadequate). It is obvious that all this new strategy of God in Christ demands an order and ethos of grace and love (*charis* and *agapē*), and that any idea of our earning God's favour or chalking up merit with God or putting God in any sense in our debt must be excluded.

When we accept God's offer of self-giving in Christ God is said by Paul to 'justify' us. The concept is certainly associated with the Last Time as the verb 'reveal' (*apokaluptō*) used by Paul shows. In Christ's death and resurrection and in the coming of the Holy Spirit God has brought about his Last Act, he has acted finally, distinguishing by this act between the ages. In Paul's account, the offer of justification reaches us with all the power and significance of the Last Age.

Subsequent thinkers debated anxiously about the true meaning of this word 'justify'. Did it mean that God *made* us righteous, as the mediaevals from Augustine onward tended to teach, that he infused goodness into us as we meet his grace? Or did it mean that God *accounted* us righteous, chose to regard us as righteous, without the question of whether we were righteous or not being raised? Or did it mean that God *imputed* a forensic or purely legal righteousness to us? This last way of thinking (which represents the thought of later Protestantism rather than of Luther himself) depicts God as indulging in a kindly legal fiction. If anyone, till very recently, travelled on British railways accompanied by a bicycle he was given for the bicycle a dog-ticket. One could say that caninity was imputed to the bicycle. But if anyone expected his bicycle at the end of the journey to come running up of its own accord to its owner and plant its front wheel on his chest, he would be very much mistaken. This was a matter of imputation, not impartation.

Manifestly it is wrong to imagine that when God justifies us he puts us in a position in which any of us can say, 'Now I am upright, virtuous, righteous; now I am 18½ per cent more virtuous than I was yesterday'. This would be to destroy the order of grace, as Paul plainly said (Gal. 2: 15–19). On the other hand, a justification which left us totally unaffected, merely the recipients of an empty title, would be worthless, as well as making God out to be ineffective. The best way to view justification is to see it as a dynamic calling from God. God gives us out of his generosity status as his sons, his beloved children, to live in his grace, in a new freedom, as brothers and sisters of Christ; and that gift calls us to respond to it, in a famous phrase to 'become what we are', to make real and effective in our lives what God has given and what we could not have unless he had given it to us, in our daily decisions and in the formation of our style of living. If we persevere in this response we may move on to what has traditionally been called 'sanctification', a state of holiness beyond that of simple justification. But whether we achieve this or not should be left to the judgment of others, not of ourselves. We are no judges of our own holiness. If at any point in the process of justification we attribute virtue or moral success to ourselves, we have misunderstood or denied our state of grace. This is the significance of Paul's remarkable doctrine that we have been crucified with Christ. It does not primarily refer to our religious experience nor to any ascetical practices. It means that what Paul calls our 'old man' – the kind of self which wishes to make claims for its holiness or goodness or popularity or wisdom or charm or ability or skill – has been, as far as God's act towards us is concerned, superseded, rendered obsolescent. We cannot compete in goodness, in self-abandoning resolute compassion, with God.

The Catholic way of refusing to accept the full force of justification by faith usually takes the form of imagining that we can put God in our debt, oblige him to reward our merits or achievements in some way. This is sheer illusion. God is not the sort of God who can be put in man's debt in any conceivable way or circumstances. The Protestant way sometimes takes the form of believing that God needs us, that he requires our hands and feet and minds to work for him, otherwise there will be no means at his disposal. This too is an illusion. God does not need us; it is an extraordinary miracle that he wants us. 'For if you keep silent at such a time as this,' said Mordecai to Esther, 'relief and deliverance will rise for the Jews from another quarter, but you and your father's house will perish' (Esther 4: 14). Sometimes however the Protestant form of denying justification by faith takes the subtler guise of justification by religious experience. 'I am not,' says the Protestant, 'justified by masses or pilgrimages or almsgiving. I leave such superstitious ideas to the besotted Catholic. But I am justified by my religious experience, by the wonderful and exalting sensations which I enjoy when I pray, by my profound faith, by my direct consciousness of salvation through Christ.' This is the last and most insidious form of justification by faith, and is quite widespread in some circles. It is as much an illusion as the others. My religious experience is *mine*, as much as my pilgrimages or my works of charity. This illusion Karl Barth in his *Commentary on the Epistle to the Romans* has justly stigmatized as 'the hideous and mistaken doctrine of modern Protestantism that we are justified by our secret knowledge of God'.

What does justification 'by faith only' mean? Clearly it means 'by faith and not by works'. But does it further mean, as Luther argued, 'by faith alone and not at first by love'? He was arguing against the scholastic theologians who had taught that we are justified by both faith and love, by faith working with love, and here they certainly had Paul on their side, for he had written 'For in Christ Jesus neither circumcision nor uncircumcision is of any avail, but faith working through love' (Gal. 5:6). Luther's contention that justification begins with sheer faith without love is quite unreal. We would not trust in God unless we loved him, nor love him unless we trusted him. But Luther had this excuse, that the scholastics argued from the fact that we love God when we believe in him that we thereby earn merit with him. Luther was right to reject this idea. The whole order of grace and faith and justification excludes the idea of merit. It is just as unreal to say that love earns merit as to say that faith can operate without love; we do not in our ordinary experience love people in order to earn merit with them; if we genuinely love them we do not ask or care whether we are earning merit with them or not.

Another important insight about justification by faith which theology owes to Luther, that great exponent of this doctrine, is that justification does not exempt us from sin. The battle against sin is not over when we are justified. Justification is not identical with redemption. We have the Holy Spirit as the first instalment of redemption, but the process is not complete. We must expect to find sin attacking us. We must wrestle with it, and must not be surprised if sometimes we fall. Luther coined the well-known phrase *simul iustus et peccator*. The Christian is at one and the same time a justified man and a sinner. This does not mean that he can sin with impunity, assured of salvation. But it means that he should not indulge in morbid scrupulousness about his own state of moral purity; in the words of that fine Anglican authority on the spiritual life, Evelyn Underhill, he should not always be taking out his soul and looking at it under a microscope. Self-regard, even regard concerning one's holiness, should not be part of a Christian's life. If one looks at oneself, Luther insisted, one finds nothing but evil and corruption and the old man; but if one looks at Christ, then there is liberty and joy and hope. This is why he could produce the apparently shocking maxim *Pecca fortiter*, 'Sin boldly' (but Luther never minded shocking people). If you do find yourself sinning, do not be cast down, but look to Christ.

Finally the relation between faith and works must be discussed. Luther was understandably sensitive on this point, because his whole original protest against the Mediaeval Church arose out of his conviction that it had turned Christianity into a vast machine for gaining salvation without troubling the Christian, without involving him in (to use the words of Kierkegaard) 'infinite personal concern', without necessitating his personal commitment to God. This machine for salvation was what he meant by the scriptural term 'works'. But Luther never denied that there was a connection between faith and works nor that works must flow from faith. In two separate places (Rom. 14:10 and 2 Cor. 5:10) Paul reminds his readers that they will stand before the judgment-seat of God or of Christ, and elsewhere (1 Cor. 3:10–14) he declares that everybody's work will be tried by fire, when its worth will be revealed, and even suggests that each will be rewarded or punished accordingly. We are justified by faith, but we are judged by love. Indeed, if our faith does not impel us to the right Christian conduct, there is something wrong with that faith. As Article XII of the XXXIX Articles (reproducing a well-used image) says; works 'are pleasing and acceptable to God in Christ and do spring necessarily out of a true and lively Faith; insomuch that by them a lively faith may be as evidently known as a tree discerned by its fruit'. There always have been, and presumably there always will be Christians who labour under a kind of neurosis which takes the form of believing that they are so securely saved that either they are incapable of sin or that what would be sin in others does not count as sin with them, or that the more they sin the more forgiveness and grace they will receive, and therefore they 'continue in sin that grace may abound'. Paul had to deal with people like this. The technical name for them is Antinomians. They have blinded themselves to the fact that however deeply we may rejoice in our salvation, we are not yet completely saved. In Keble's words, 'The grey-haired saint may fail at last'. We are judged by the effects in our lives of our faith, not by our feelings when we exercise faith. There is always a danger for Catholics so to objectivize the Christian faith that salvation becomes a matter of either manipulation or earning wages. There is always a danger for Protestants that their experience of salvation shall become bathed in a mist of subjective feeling which obscures from their consciences what might be justly called the stern realities of God's love and God's demand.

iv. Grace and Free Will

We have described grace as God's self-communication through Christ to those who are justified, his loving handling of them when they throw themselves in faith on his mercy. There is a constant temptation for those who think or write about grace – a temptation which we shall say more about when we reach the subject of sacraments – to speak of it as if it was either a very much refined liquid or a current of electricity. The poet Gerard Manley Hopkins in one of his less happy flights of fancy likened in a sermon the Church to a cow with seven udders, representing the seven sacraments. But we do not suck God in a liquid form. God does not flow in channels which men can control, even though he has appointed sacraments whereby we can approach him.

But how does God make contact with men and women? We continually ask God's help in our prayers, but we do not often pause to think how much help he gives us. The straightforward, common-sense solution of the problem is to use the old maxim, 'God helps those who help themselves'. If we wish to teach a child to walk, we do not spend all our time holding its hand. All our teaching must be directed towards making the child independent of our help. This seems to be the obvious way of envisaging God's help. He helps us to be independent of him, so that we are not always running back, to cling, so to speak, to his apron-strings.

Again, if we return to the subject of free will discussed above (p. 135–9), it would seem to be a matter of common sense to assume that our process of making choices starts, so to speak, from a neutral position in which we are choosing neither *a* nor *b* but debating about both, and we then decide freely for one or the other, and that our very freedom consists in standing, as it were, on an island between two rivers and being able to plunge into one or the other, starting off by being prejudiced in favour of neither. These apparently common sense ideas were very widespread in Christian antiquity; they were much influenced by Stoic thought, and in the fifth century particularly they were propagated by an earnest Christian monk and moralist called Pelagius who taught mainly in Rome and had been born in Britain (and in consequence British people have ever since been liable to be suspected, perhaps unjustly, of Pelagianism). The Pelagian version of 'God helps those who help themselves' was that God rewards merit by grace. When God sees that we are good, he gives us grace because he sees that we deserve it. Pelagius was by no means the first to teach that grace follows merit. The great third-century theologian Origen had taught something very like this (see Benjamin Drewery, *Origen's Doctrine of Grace*).

Augustine, that gigantic intellect and supreme former of Western Latin theology, taught a totally different doctrine. We have seen (above, p. 136) that he diagnosed the essential element in the human personality as desire, not reason. His analysis of the human soul, based partly on his by no means wholly respectable experience and partly on his study of Paul's thought, with a dash of Neo-Platonism, the latest form of ancient Greek philosophy, thrown in, led him to conclude that the idea of a neutral stance or an island between two streams for the will is an illusion. Our will lives by yielding to attraction. If a good purpose attracts it, then it becomes the servant of the good, if a bad then it is the slave of the bad. It does not have any room to stand untouched between the two, as far as a choice between moral objects is concerned. If it is choosing or has chosen the bad, then it is the slave of that bad choice which it makes and is in bondage. If it makes a morally good choice then it is the servant of that chosen end, and then, and then alone, is free. For Augustine God was the supreme good and a supreme good who drew people to himself by the attractive power of love. To opt for God therefore was to choose the highest good and to be most free. That phrase of the Book of Common Prayer 'whose service is perfect freedom' succinctly sums up Augustine's doctrine. When the will is obedient to, is the slave of, God, then it is free. This is what freedom means, and this is authentic freedom, compared with which the trivial capacity to choose x and not y, this book and not that book (which he admitted the will possessed), is unimportant. It can readily be seen that behind this account of grace and free will lies the conviction that the more we are dependent upon God the freer and stronger we are. This is the reverse of Pelagianism. It is, in spite of not being the common sense solution, the deeper, more penetrating analysis of the subject, corresponding more closely to what we know of the human will and personality, and supported by our own experience.

This solution raises inevitably the question, 'How much does God's grace contribute to our good actions and how much does our own will contribute?' Our first reaction is to try to answer this in mathematical terms. Perhaps we split the matter, God contributing 50 per cent and we 50 per cent; or, rather more reverently, we might suggest God 90 per cent and our will 10 per cent, or even, at the worst, God 99.99 per cent and ourselves 0.01 per cent! This kind of argument has agitated the theologians at intervals through the ages. We believe that the solution which was in effect reached by that great seventeenth-century theologian and scientist, Blaise Pascal, is the right one. We must throw mathematical logic to the winds and say that grace contributes 100 per cent and the human will 100 per cent. God's grace and man's will are not mutually exclusive. We are most ourselves when we are most under God's guidance.

We must not imagine that Augustine's agonizing about the slavery of the will was simply a quirk of the crabbed mind of the theologian. Very much the same problem is faced by psychologists and sociologists on a purely secular level. It is the problem of free will versus determinism. It is surely remarkable that the break-away from Christian assumptions which was consciously made by those who founded the modern sciences of psychology and sociology in the last century has not led, as was widely believed at the time, to an increased emphasis on man's freedom. The human sciences, freeing themselves from the shackles of Christian dogma, have not succeeded in doing very much to enhance the concept of human freedom. On the contrary, a hundred years after their emancipation, many of their students hold a doctrine of the slavery of the will far more absolute than anything that Augustine or Calvin ever envisaged.

The problem is, how can we explain man's behaviour without explaining it away? The perpetual temptation of the human sciences is to account for human behaviour entirely in terms of physiological, genetic, and environmental factors. What man thinks, says, and does, is wholly determined by his physical make-up, biological inheritance, and environment. This solution comes up against exactly the same objection as that which Pelagius used against Augustine: 'But we are free!' In fact we know that we are (within limits) free to do what we choose. If this sense of freedom is an illusion, then so is all our knowledge, including the knowledge that we are wholly determined. Somehow or other the human sciences have to find a way of explaining our freedom that does not explain it away, just as Augustine did hold that the will of fallen man was free, even though it was only free to make the wrong choice.

We can even find an analogy in the secular sphere to Augustine's solution to the slavery of the fallen will, obedience to God. God, Augustine held, was the true guide for man: 'Thou hast made us for thyself, and our souls are restless till they find their rest in thee'.

Similarly we are most free when we are obeying the true laws of our being. The athlete is free to do all sorts of things which the ordinary person cannot do because he or she has studied the laws of his physical being and has obeyed them. Their freedom comes not through arbitrary antinomianism, but through free obedience to the law of our being.

We can also find a sound analogy outside the sphere of theology for the sense of obligation to do God's will which the religious person experiences. If someone has genuinely attempted to obey God all his life, he will often express himself thus: 'I had to do this, I had no choice, I knew it was God's will'. And he will likewise not want to claim any credit for himself for anything he may have accomplished (compare Mark 10: 17–18; Jesus is not making a confession of sin but identifying God as the source of all goodness). 'It was not my doing, but God's', he will say. By such statements he does not mean that he was a mere puppet, moved by God without his own will. He is not making a plea of diminished responsibility. He is wholly responsible for his actions, but he is aware that God was working through him.

A good analogy is that of artistic creation: the true artist senses an obligation to express the conceptions and ideas which he has. Whether he is a writer, or a sculptor, or a painter, or a musician, he will often say about a work of his: 'I felt I had to do it'. This does not mean that he was under any external or physical compulsion such as the psychologist would identify. It means that if he had not executed this work he would have felt that he had betrayed himself. Indeed we sometimes find that some artists who in other aspects of life are very irresponsible and morally despicable nevertheless show remarkable responsibility and integrity about their artistic work. All this goes to show that man's subjective side is not a mere illusion or epiphenomenon or hang-over from childhood. Man is a creature of convictions, obligations, and vocations. It is in this sphere that his true freedom lies.

III · THE HOLY SPIRIT

7 The Nature and Function of the Spirit

a The Spirit as a phenomenon of the Last Time

It is usual to begin a treatise on the Holy Spirit with a section on 'The Holy Spirit in the Old Testament'. In fact, there is virtually no doctrine of the Holy Spirit in the Old Testament, and very little even in the first three Gospels. Throughout the greater part of the Old Testament 'Spirit' if linked with the activity of God is no more than a periphrasis for God himself, or an allusion to some peculiar access of strength or skill or wisdom given to some individual by God for a limited period, with almost no connection at all with the New Testament doctrine of the Spirit. There are a few eschatological passages suggesting an expectation of the Spirit being poured out in the Last Time (e.g. Isa. 44: 1–5; Ezek. 37: 1–14; Joel 2: 28–32), and it is stated once or twice that God is spirit, that is what he is composed of (e.g. Isa. 31: 1–3). But that is all.

In the Inter-Testamental period the idea grew up in Rabbinic circles that certain eminent men would receive the Holy Spirit when the Messianic Age dawned; meanwhile they could be described as 'worthy of the Holy Spirit'. But the conviction remained that the Spirit was a phenomenon associated with the Last Age, the Age to Come.

There is an extraordinary lack of mention of the Holy Spirit in the Synoptic Gospels. It is quite clear that even if the sayings of Jesus did contain a few scattered references to the Holy Spirit (e.g. Matt. 10:20, 12:31, 22:43; Luke 4:18, 11:13), the Holy Spirit did not figure prominently in his teaching. This has been explained variously by various scholars, but it must be recognized as a fact. It would not be true, either, to maintain that the importance of Jesus' utterances about the Spirit preserved in the Gospels compensate for their scarcity. They manifestly do not.

When, however, we turn to the Fourth Gospel, the Acts and the Epistles of the New Testament, the situation as regards the Holy Spirit changes abruptly. John's Gospel has its own careful and significant teaching about the Spirit, to which we shall turn presently, and the Acts and Epistles abound with mention of the Spirit. Acts has been called 'the Gospel of the Holy Spirit'. From the description of the descent of the Holy Spirit at Pentecost onwards, he is the main agent in the activity and growth of the Church. Christians pray in the Spirit, preach in the Spirit, are guided by the Spirit. The Spirit makes them bold, lends them eloquence, sends them visions. The famous saying 'it has seemed good to the Holy Spirit and to us' (Acts 15:28) provides the keynote for Acts. Indeed in the thought of the writer it is not the Bible nor the ministry which provides continuity and stability in the Church, but the Holy Spirit.

This impression is deepened when we reach the Epistles, most of which were written, it must be remembered, before any Gospels or Acts were written. Indeed the thought about the Holy Spirit in the Epistles largely explains the intense preoccupation of Acts with the Spirit. In the Letters of Paul, in Hebrews and in 1 Peter the Holy Spirit is the great eschatological event; he is God-at-the-end-of-the-world, the first instalment ('guarantee') of redemption (2 Cor. 1:22; 5:5; Eph. 1:14; 1 Peter 1:1–12); he is linked with the resurrection of the dead (Rom. 1:4; 8:9–11; 1 Cor. 15:42–46; 2 Cor. 3:17–18; 5:1–5; Heb. 6:1–5). The Spirit in the Church is the witness and pledge that full salvation is awaiting the whole creation (Rom. 8:18–25). The appearance, the crucifixion and the resurrection of the Messiah has, so to speak, precipitated the Spirit in advance into the world. The harbinger of the End is here now, offering salvation, renewing all things. His descent is intimately linked with the career of Christ. He gives to that career its validity and its ultimacy.

But the Spirit is also closely associated with the response of God's people to his mysterious and epoch-making Act in Christ. There is scarcely a reference to any form of religious activity or experience in the New Testament which is not associated with the Holy Spirit. It is because Christians are in the Spirit that they can recognize what God is doing in Christ (1 Cor. 2). It is because the Holy Spirit has been poured out in their hearts (*kardiais*, here = the intellects) that they recognize that Christ died for them and that God commends his love in Christ's death (Rom. 5:1–11). Christians pray in the Spirit; he prays in them and for them (Rom. 8:26–27). They live and make their decisions in the Spirit. Above all, in Paul's noble conception of the Church as the Body of Christ, Christians are bound together in the Body through the Spirit, because they have 'drunk' of the Spirit (Rom. 12; 1 Cor. 12; Eph. 4:1–7). It is the Spirit who distributes the gifts of ministry to individual Christians. In the Spirit they speak with tongues and discern truth and prophesy. He is the great Master, Lord and Dynamic of the Church. He opens the meaning of the Scriptures (1 Peter. 1:10–12) and gives freedom from the Law (2

Cor. 3). He is, in short, God in whom God's people return to God.

The doctrine of the Holy Spirit in the Fourth Gospel reads this concept of the Spirit into the earthly ministry of Christ, as it reads so much else, pressing, to use antique language, his heavenly work into his earthly. God is Spirit, so that his true worship should now be given neither in the Samaritan sanctuary on Mount Gerizim nor in Jerusalem, but in his Messiah, who has come (John 4: 19–26). The Spirit could not dawn, almost could not break, like Spring, till Christ was 'glorified' (7: 37–39). But now Christ has ascended and breathed his Spirit upon the Church (20: 19–23), so that people can now be born again by water and the Spirit (3: 1–9). And in his last discourse before his Passion the Johannine Christ tells his disciples of the coming of the Counsellor (the Paraclete or Comforter, 14: 16–18, 26; 15: 26–27; 16: 12–24) who will stay with them, support them and interpret to them his words and acts. Though John does not completely abandon eschatological language, he presents what C. H. Dodd aptly called a 'sublimated eschatology'. The Holy Spirit, the representative of Christ, is, for most intents and purposes, equivalent to the *Parousia*, the Second Coming. The fourth evangelist thus retains the eschatological character of the Holy Spirit, though in his own peculiar way.

The Holy Spirit in the New Testament, therefore, whatever other adjective may be applied to him, does not deserve the epithet 'spectral' which the repulsive English archaism 'Holy Ghost' suggests. He is not a pale understudy for Christ; he is not an Hebraic periphrasis for God; he is not a vague influence analogous to an electric current. He is a new dynamic, unpredictable (John 3:8) power and presence in the world. His arrival ushers in the New Age, makes all things new, gives his Church strength and vitality to resist the assaults of the world, the flesh and the devil. Because the Holy Spirit is here, things can never be quite the same again.

b. The Divinity of the Spirit

Worshippers in the early Church knew and appreciated the Spirit – but the theologians did not. Early Christians were deeply conscious of the Church as the living, healing, reconciling community where the risen Christ was to be found in his Holy Spirit. This is one reason why they did not attempt to prove the resurrection by appealing to historical evidence. The Church was the contemporary proof of the resurrection, as it was the proof of the presence of the Spirit. As soon as we begin to find traces of early Christian liturgical practice (as in Hippolytus' *Apostolic Tradition* which reflects the worship of the Church of Rome about AD 200), we find this consciousness constantly reflected. And in traditional formulae, the kind which preceded credal formulae, the Spirit is usually linked with the Father and the Son. As Matthew 28: 19 witnesses, from a very early period baptism was administered in the Triple Name. And when (with Cardinal Daniélou and Prof. G. Kretschmar, two experts in the early history of Trinitarian doctrine) we peer into that strange world of Judaeo-Christian imagery and thought, among the apocalypses and angels we usually see the Spirit ranked in one form or another with the Father and the Son.

But to the theologians the Spirit more often than not proved an embarrassment. In the first place, it was very difficult to see the Holy Spirit satisfactorily evidenced in the Old Testament. All the epiphanies of God – at the visit of the three mysterious men to Abraham, at the burning bush, at Jacob's wrestling, at Joshua's encounter with the commander of the hosts of God, at the visions of Isaiah and of Ezekiel, at Nebuchadnezzar's burning fiery furnace – were already bespoken for the Son/Logos. And the same applied to any available figures in the Wisdom Literature. A few faint-hearted attempts were made to distinguish the Logos from the Spirit in the Old Testament, but they amounted to very little. It taxed the ingenuity of ancient interpreters beyond even their powers to detect *two* separate distinct divine entities in the Old Testament.

In the second place, it was not even easy to make a case for the second divine *hypostasis* in the New Testament, that is to say, for the existence of the Holy Spirit as a divine 'person', even in the limited sense in which the ancients understood the concept of 'person', distinct from God the Father and from God the Son. There were passages where the Holy Spirit was treated like an impersonal influence, a wind or an invigorating liquid, and there were passages where he was treated like a person. But the doctrine was not clear and unambiguous. There were even passages (as we shall see below, p. 159) where the Spirit seemed to be confused with Christ.

Thirdly, at all times it is difficult for Christians to speak about the Holy Spirit, because he is God as we directly experience him. He is 'closer than breathing, nearer than hands and feet'. We respond with the inmost part of ourselves to God, not only with our intellects but with our wills and hearts. And of this nobody finds it easy to speak, or rather those who do find it easy to speak are more often than not those whom we think least worth listening to. When Pascal had his striking 'conversion', when he realized that God was 'the God of Abraham, Isaac and Jacob, not of the philosophers and scientists', he attempted to record in writing what he had experienced. His words are vivid and burning, but still how little do they convey of what he must have experienced! Shortly before his death the great mediaeval theologian and saint, Thomas Aquinas, is said to have declared that he would write no more, because he had in worship experienced God in some way that was beyond utterance. And can we then theologize about the Holy Spirit?

The consequence was that the theologians of the first three centuries of the Church's history, while they did not actually ignore the Spirit, found him difficult to fit in to their theology and tended to say little about him. They mostly recognize that he is the quickener and sanctifier of the Church, and that he gives illumination to Christians so that they recognize God in Christ, but he did not fit easily into the theological framework which (as we shall see below, pp. 173–8) was adopted almost everywhere during the first three centuries. The Apologists of the second century for the most part write as if they would have been happier with a Binitarian, Father-Son, distinction within the Godhead and not a Trinitarian one. Irenaeus (fl 170–200) gives a rather better balance, and Tertullian (fl 190–210), under the influence of Montanism, pays considerably more attention to the Spirit; but this interest displays itself rather in an increased ethical rigorism and concern for prophetesses who indulge in trances during the sermon in the eucharist than in anything more constructive. Origen in the third century dovetails the Holy Spirit into his sophisticated and ingenious presentation of an hierarchically graded Godhead. But the Spirit is not essential in his scheme. Eusebius of Caesarea, the most learned bishop of those who attended the Council of Nicaea in 325, the first church historian, who was universally regarded as a theological authority in his lifetime, has an utterly inadequate doctrine of the Spirit. For him the Spirit is a created power, subordinate to the Son/Logos. In all this doctrinal history, what is surprising is, not that the Spirit is neglected and subordinated, but that the theologians felt compelled to include him at all. Until the rise of Neo-Platonism to the powerful and central position which it occupied in the thought of most intellectuals from the middle of the fourth century onwards, contemporary Middle Platonist philosophy offered to Christian intellectuals a tempting scheme of two ultimate forms of reality, not three, the second derived from the first, which could be readily adapted to the Father and the Son. The remarkable thing is that they did not fall for this temptation and present the Church with a fully-fledged Binitarian theology. This suggests that they knew that the Spirit, no matter how upsetting to theological patterns, was of such great significance in the Christian scheme of things that he could not be omitted nor neglected altogether.

The course taken by the Arian controversy in the fourth century, however, entirely changed this state of affairs. This controversy resulted in the acceptance by the Church of the proposition that Jesus Christ was 'God of God, Light of Light, Very God of Very God, Begotten not Made, Being of One Substance with the Father', in other words it established what we today call the full divinity of Christ. We shall consider this development later (see below, pp. 171–8). But the Church's ablest theologians soon realized that the status of the Holy Spirit could not remain unaffected by this dogma. The Holy Spirit was so involved with the self-communication of God in Christ that if Christ was declared to be divine as unequivocally as this, the same divinity must be ascribed to the Holy Spirit. Athanasius himself in his *Letters to Serapion* attempted, not with entire success, to articulate a consistent theology of the Spirit's divinity. It was, however, largely the work of three men from the remote province of Cappadocia in Asia Minor that enabled the Church to attain the goal at which Athanasius was aiming, Basil of Caesarea, Gregory of Nazianzus and Gregory of Nyssa. They were assisted by the fact that by now Neo-Platonist philosophy, with its reduction of reality to three ultimate interrelated forms, had beome widely known and accepted. They used arguments drawn from Scripture, of course, but they were more conscious than their predecessors of the inadequacy of Scripture for their task. Basil tried to explain this by an unfortunate theory of unscriptural tradition handed on in the Church, a theory which has since been used more than once for purposes which Basil would never have countenanced. Gregory of Nazianzus was wiser in explaining that whereas the Father is seen fully in the Old Testament and the Son dimly, the Father and Son are seen fully in the New Testament and the Spirit dimly; the full knowledge of the Spirit must be sought, he implied, not only in Scripture but beyond Scripture. All three theologians appealed to the practice of baptism to support their doctrine of the divinity of the Holy Spirit. It was Eusebius of Caesarea who had first used this argument, against Marcellus of Ancyra in a Christological context. Athanasius had used it too, but the Cappadocians employed it with greater confidence and effect. They envisaged the function of the Spirit primarily as sanctifying and perfecting. They did not hesitate to present the Spirit as active in the whole world as well as in sanctifying the faithful, even though this function was already to some extent preoccupied in their system by the Son/Logos. The result of their activity was an addition to the Creed adopted in 381 dealing with the Spirit, in which he was not described as consubstantial or co-divine but as 'with the Father and the Son worshipped and glorified', a phrase intended and understood to state his full divinity.

We must agree that in two important respects at least the Fathers were right. First, once the step has been taken of recognizing that the doctrine of the self-communication of God in Christ demands a belief in the eternal distinction between Father and Son in the Godhead, a similar distinction applying to the Holy Spirit must follow. We shall consider later whether this recognition is necessary or not. But we must admit that the theologians of the fourth century were logical in developing the doctrine of the divinity of the Holy Spirit once the divinity of the Son had been established. The self-communication of God in Christ becomes an inexplicable moment of history frozen into an unattainable past unless we recognize also the self-communication of God in the Spirit. And secondly, they were wise in realizing (however dimly) that the status of the Spirit cannot be *sufficiently* witnessed to in the Scriptures, though of course he must and can be witnessed to there. The Holy Spirit is God active in history, God known in the life, worship and experience of the Church. It is therefore necessary to see him in history and in the life of the Church as well as in Scripture before we can see him properly. There is, as we shall see, a certain inevitable incompleteness about the doctrine of the Spirit because history has not yet finished, the redemption of the Church is not yet consummated, and God is future as well as contemporary.

In addition to these reasons which must have weighed with the early Christian theologians, however, there are a few other points concerned with the divinity of the Holy Spirit which we must consider. We can suggest four reasons, which vary in value and are drawn from various areas, for believing in the distinct divinity of the Spirit, but which together form an impressive argument. They are as follows:

i. *The Spirit is, and has been since the beginning of Christianity, a datum of experience.* We have already seen that since the resurrection of Jesus Christ the Spirit has been continuously available for those who approach God in faith. The post-resurrection era is the era of the Spirit. This is constantly witnessed to in the epistles of the New Testament and in the Book of Acts, and in this respect the witness of the early church is continuous. Christians encountered the Spirit in Christian worship, in the crisis of trial and martyrdom, in their daily experience. This is the significance of these 'triadic' formulae which we find so often in the New Testament (see 2 Cor. 13: 14; Matt. 28: 19; Eph. 4: 4–6). It is not that anyone in New Testament times had reached the conception of God as 'Three-in-One', but that when the fundamentals of Christianity were mentioned, the Spirit could not be left out.

ii. *We must have a third in the Godhead because the pattern of salvation is threefold.* We have seen that the primary attribute of God in the entire Bible is that he is a living God who acts for man's salvation. When we try to describe the salvation which he brought about supremely in Jesus Christ, we find that we cannot avoid a threefold pattern of action: we must speak of God acting for our salvation, acting for our salvation in Jesus Christ, acting for our salvation in Jesus Christ and thereby bringing men back to himself. If we analyse this we find we have God active, manifest, apprehended in three modes of being: sending, redeeming, bringing back; or God as original agent, God as redeemer, and God as sanctifier. If we believe that these three modes are authentic manifestations of God's being, and not mere accommodations to our ability to comprehend, then we must acknowledge him as existing as three-in-one.

iii. The last two reasons are drawn from philosophy, but are none the worse for that: *if we have two terms, we need a third to mediate between them.* Our reason does not seem to be able to rest with a Binity (two 'Persons' in one God); it must move on to a Trinity. Admittedly this is a Hegelian argument; Hegel maintained that our thought must move in this 'dialectic' fashion, from thesis to antithesis, and finally to synthesis. We need not accept this view, but in fact in the long history of Christian doctrine the dispute has been between Unitarians and Trinitarians. Almost no one has suggested stopping at Binitarianism. There must be some good reason for this.

iv. The last argument comes from G. L. Prestige, that distinguished patristic theologian of the last generation. *The three distinctions, he says, correspond to the three possible relations of God to the world.* He may be unrelated to the world, in the sense that he does not need the world, the world is not a necessity for his very existence. He could do without it, though in his love he wills to create it and care for it. This corresponds to the mode of being which we call God the Father. Secondly, he may be related to the world *ab extra*, from outside, as creator, as preserver, indeed as redeemer coming to save the world. This corresponds to God the Son. Thirdly he may be related to the world *ab intra*, from inside, as one acting within the world, most especially within men. This corresponds to God the Holy Spirit. Different people will value these arguments in different ways, but it is as well to know that the assertion of a third in the Godhead was no afterthought, but an integral part of Christian belief in the Godhead.

c. The Procession of the Spirit

We have already noticed that the doctrine of the Spirit is not so clearly set out in the New Testament that the Fathers were easily able to prove his divinity from Scripture. This is eminently true of the doctrine of the Spirit in Paul's writings. It is notorious that Paul does not always clearly distinguish between the person of the Spirit and the person of Christ.

This is due to the fact that for Paul the Spirit is not just God's holy spirit in the Old Testament now met with as the Holy Spirit in the new dispensation. On the contrary, for Paul the Spirit is intimately connected with Christ. The Spirit is only available to all Christians through Christ and in Christ. Essentially the same teaching is found in the Fourth Gospel; see John 7: 39, where a literal translation of the Greek is 'for it was not yet Spirit because Jesus had not yet been glorified'. Moreover in Paul's thought, as we have seen, the Spirit was the sphere or dimension into which the risen Christ rose, the means by which Christians everywhere have access to the risen and glorified Christ. Thus, if we wish to trace the line of the Spirit's activity from Old Testament times into New Testament times, that line must pass through Jesus Christ. The consequence of this is a confusion in Pauline thought about the relation of the Spirit to the risen Christ. It is not that for Paul the two are identical, but that in the activity and in the experience of Christians they tend to coincide. There is no harm in this, as long as we remember that this was the situation which the earliest Christian theologians after the New Testament period had to face. As far as the Spirit is concerned, we are dealing at one and the same time with a mode of God's being and a mode of his activity.

Even when it has been determined that the Spirit must be recognized as part of a Trinity, as a distinct mode of existence within the Godhead, in some sense parallel to the Son, it is by no means easy to determine satisfactorily his precise relationship to the other two 'Persons' in the Godhead. We must always remember that in speaking about what are called the 'immanent' distinctions within the Godhead (i.e. what God is eternally in himself apart from his relations with anything outside himself), in contrast to the 'economic' Trinity (i.e. God as we know him in his self-communication in Christ), we are treading on ground where we scarcely dare to enter. In such discourse we are in an area of speculation, justified, indeed, and more, necessitated by the data of Scripture and by the pronouncement of tradition and reason, but still delicate, obscure and in a large part beyond the capacity of human thought to compass and of human language to utter. We could be compared to scientists who are compelled to handle the subject of their work through complicated apparatus at several removes from their own hands. The men who actually brought the doctrine of the Spirit to its final form in the fourth century were well aware of these limitations, and frequently protested about the inadequacy of human thought and language to deal with the subject with which they felt bound to deal. Theologians in later ages have sometimes forgotten this wholesome intellectual modesty, and have written about these themes with a matter-of-fact dogmatic confidence as if they were dealing with the bills of lading for a ship instead of the deepest mysteries of the Christian faith.

One principle, however, we can with confidence propound as one which all writers in this difficult subject should observe, and that is that our knowledge of the 'economic' Trinity must be our guide as far as possible in drawing conclusions about the 'immanent' Trinity. Except for the aid of philosophy and common sense, we have no other source for drawing such conclusions. Whatever we finally decide about the intra-Trinitarian relations of the 'Persons', they must be in accordance with, and emphatically must not contradict what we know of the 'Persons' from Scripture.

It is particularly important to observe this principle when we consider the relation of the Holy Spirit to the Father and the Son in the Trinity. The data for determining this question provided by Scripture are scanty. Traditionally theologians have fastened on a few verses in the Gospel according to St. John to decide the matter. Here Jesus, in his last discourse to the disciples before his Passion, speaks of the Counsellor (or Paraclete or Comforter) whom the Father will send in his name (14:25,26), and says (15:26), 'But when the Counsellor comes, whom I shall send to you from the Father, even the Spirit of truth, who proceeds from the Father, he will bear witness to me', and later (16:13,14) 'When the Spirit of truth comes, he will guide you into all truth: for he will not speak on his own authority, but whatever he hears he will speak. . . . He will glorify me, for he will take what is mine and declare it to you'. On the strength of these words, traditional theology has always affirmed that the correct way to describe the relation of the Spirit to the Father is 'proceeding' or 'procession', corresponding to what is called in the Son 'generation' or 'filiation'. This is indeed impeccable reasoning as far as it goes, but it does not go far. The word 'proceeding' is about as neutral as it could be; when the fourth century Fathers were asked to say how the Holy Spirit existed distinctly in a way differing from the way in which the other two 'Persons' existed distinctly (as the Father existed as the unoriginate source of Godhead and the Son as begotten), they could only give some such answer as 'processionwise', and when further pressed to explain what this meant, they very honestly replied that they did not know. In another part of the Fourth Gospel, Jesus is described (20:22) as breathing on the disciples and saying 'Receive the Holy Spirit'. It has accordingly sometimes been the custom to speak of the relation of the Spirit to Father and Son as 'spiration'. But of course this scarcely advances our knowledge further either.

Over these matters there has arisen through the centuries an acute controversy between the Eastern and the Western Church. Does the Spirit 'proceed' from the Father only or from the Father and the Son? One point at least can be made absolutely clear here. The Creed of Constantinople of 381 which was the formula generally reckoned as settling the Arian controversy simply said of the Holy Spirit 'who proceeds from the Father'. It did not add 'and from the Son', the Latin for which phrase is *Filioque*. This was a creed unambiguously accepted by the whole Church, East and West. It is indeed still the central formula of the Christian faith, which must be the formula destined to unite the divided Church, if that Church is ever to be united. During the early Middle Ages the custom grew up, starting in Spain, of adding the words *Filioque* at that point in the creed, which was of course said or sung in Latin. The first Holy Roman Emperor, Charlemagne, at the end of the eighth and beginning of the ninth centuries made two separate attempts to persuade two different Popes to make this addition to the creed of the Church in Rome, because he had found it in the creed of his own church at Aachen and was anxious to impose liturgical uniformity throughout his dominions. They both refused, alleging quite correctly that though they believed and accepted the *doctrine* embodied in the *Filioque* clause, they had no right nor authority of themselves to add to the creed of the whole Church without the consent of a General Council. Two hundred years later, in 1012, in an evil hour a German Emperor persuaded a German-born Pope, his own creation, to add this clause to the creed of the Roman Church. The *Filioque* clause has consequently ever since been a bone of contention between East and West, with the further complication that there now seems to be involved in the argument the right of a Pope to alter the creed without calling or consulting a General Council. Christians who do not belong to the Roman obedience must unequivocally recognize that the Eastern Orthodox Church – indeed all churches of Eastern origin – have the right clearly on their side. The right of the Pope to alter the creed without calling a council of the whole Church is precisely one of those papal claims to authority which should be most strenuously resisted, all the more because earlier Popes guided by better principles refused to recognize that they had such a right. Christians who use the Nicene Creed in their liturgy should as soon as possible delete this clause from their creed.

But the question still remains, should we *believe* that the Holy Spirit proceeds from the Father and the Son or that he proceeds from the Father only? The contention about this point has waxed so violent that we must here remind ourselves how slender are the premises from which it is possible to argue in either direction. The words of Jesus as given to us in the last discourse in John's Gospel are most unlikely to represent the *ipsissima verba*, the actual words, of Jesus himself, but are rather an interpretation of his significance by the evangelist. Anyway Jesus never did at any point directly lay down Trinitarian theology, as it were over the heads of his disciples, for the ultimate benefit of later ages. We must not attempt to transcribe the words of Jesus, nor of any other figure in the New Testament, directly into the more speculative realms of theology. The history of the interpretation of the much better attested words 'This is my body' ought to warn us of that fallacy. What we have to ask ourselves is, taking the picture of the relation of the Holy Spirit to the Father and to Christ given us by the whole New Testament, not merely by six verses in the Fourth Gospel, are we to say that the Spirit comes from the Father only or from the Father and the Son? We can answer with some confidence that the words 'from the Father through the Son' characterize the thought about God's activity which prevails through the whole New Testament. It would therefore be wrong to suggest that in the immanent relations of the 'Persons' of the Trinity the procession of the Spirit is wholly independent of and unaffected by the Son; it would be equally wrong to suggest that the Spirit *originates* from the Son. We can therefore accept the *Filioque* clause as good doctrine if we interpret it as meaning that the Spirit proceeds from the Father through the Son, but not otherwise.

What we cannot say is that the procession of the Spirit within the Holy Trinity is in some way different from the mission of the Spirit towards the world. The Episcopalian communion in the USA has recently refused to delete the *Filioque* clause from its creed when its General Convention was drawing up a new Prayer Book and had an opportunity to do so. This was unfortunate. The attempt by some of the American bishops to ameliorate this bad situation by declaring that while the Spirit proceeds from the Father and the Son in his mission to the world, he proceeds from the Father only in his relations in the immanent Trinity, was positively disastrous. Karl Barth always insisted with all the force of his powerful mind that what we know of the economic Trinity we must believe of the immanent Trinity. God's being is identical with his act. We have no access to occult or mystical or philosophical information which could justify us in abandoning this principle. What we know about the self-communication of God through Scripture and our own experience must be the rule for what we infer about his inner Trinitarian life.

8 Our Experience of the Holy Spirit

a. How do we know that we have the Spirit?

When we turn from these high realms of theology to consider the apparently simple question, 'How do we know that we have the Spirit?', we find that this question is not as simple as it appears. Some schools of thought are ready to answer this question at once with a short formula, 'I feel the Spirit in my life' or 'I received the Spirit in baptism', or 'I have received the baptism of the Spirit'. But there are difficulties about all these cut-and-dried answers. Baptism is indeed not only a means of God's activity towards us but also a pledge; that is to say it is a sign or seal, outward, independent of our fancying, imagining, or experiencing of God's presence. Baptism prevents us being at the mercy of our own subjective experience; we do not invent it; we do not administer it to ourselves. It comes to us, as it were, from outside. And if baptism confers the Spirit, then it is a guarantee that we have the Spirit. But does baptism operate quite as mechanically, as objectively, as that? When we baptize infants are we, so to speak, inoculating them with the Holy Spirit? This is a repulsive idea. We must allow faith a place in Christian initiation; Christianity is both a communal and an individual religion. The individual must make his own response to and in baptism; that response can only take the form of faith. Here we are again thrown back upon our own subjective selves. If baptism were an automatic conferring of the Holy Spirit, we would do well to hire a fleet of helicopters and by means of mass sprinkling from the air to distribute the Spirit wholesale among the unchristianized populations of India and Africa and the Far East.

On the other hand, to determine that we have the Holy Spirit because we feel his operation in our lives, and for no other reason, is equally unsatisfactory. This is in fact to subordinate the activity of God to our own experience of him. This is the peculiar temptation of Protestantism once it has lost the austere discipline imposed upon it by its mighty originators, Luther and Calvin. The joy and triumph of the believer in God's unmerited dealing with him gradually changes into the pride and self-righteousness of the believer in his experience of God's gracious dealing with him. Feelings, emotions alone, are very dangerous guides to our spiritual state. The Christian who judges whether he is justified and whether he has the Spirit by whether he feels justified and Spirit-filled will soon reach a position in which he judges every feature of the Christian faith – theology, ministry, sacraments, prayer – by the extent it rouses in him what he considers the right religious emotions. 'The heart' said the prophet Jeremiah, 'is deceitful above all things'. We all have an endless capacity to deceive ourselves not least concerning our spiritual state.

Least satisfactory of all is the claim to possess the Spirit grounded on the conviction that the believer has undergone a 'baptism of the Spirit'. This 'baptism of the Spirit' is a profound spiritual and emotional experience in which the Christian feels himself exalted closer to God than ever before, and experiences new and powerful conviction of God's presence and power in his life, and it is often accompanied by such phenomena as prophesying or speaking with tongues (*glossolalia*). Now we do not wish to disparage or set aside such experiences as these. Christians should respect the spiritual integrity of those who describe themselves as having undergone such experiences. Indeed we should by no means ignore the so-called 'Charismatic Movement' which has made such an impact on the Church of our day in all its various forms, but rather be thankful for it and welcome it. But to speak of a 'baptism of the Spirit' as contrasted with water-baptism is altogether mistaken. The witness of the New Testament, as we shall see, is not altogether consistent on the relation of the Holy Spirit to baptism. But it never suggests that there awaits believers beyond baptism in water a further baptism in the Spirit (who was presumably absent from water baptism). The only meaning to give to this alleged 'baptism in the Spirit' is that it represents a deeper and richer experience of the Holy Spirit than is normal or usual. It should be remembered that the vast majority of Christians through the ages (including the authors of this book) have never received 'baptism in the Spirit'. The use of this term is altogether too like a repetition of baptism. And to repeat baptism, unless in the most unusual circumstances, is to insult Christ.

To the question, 'How do I know that I have the Spirit?' we must give much the same answer as Luther gave to the question 'How do I know that I am justified?' He answered in effect: you are baptized; you believe in Christ and preach or teach his gospel; you see the fruit of the Spirit in your life. None of these three ingredients of the answer should be isolated and made to bear the whole weight of the argument. Baptism is indeed a salutary guarantee that we do not save ourselves, we do not manufacture our own initiation into Christ in the depths of our own consciousnesses. Christ comes to us in and through the Church. But we also believe; we respond to God's advance towards us, and respond as responsible persons, committing ourselves to him in faith, and experiencing the forgiveness, the reconciliation, the joy and peace which this encounter with God affords us; we enjoy the privilege of prayer and of worship. And we see in one way or another, without self-righteously claiming credit for them, some of the fruits of the Holy Spirit in our lives. All these represent assurance that we have received the Holy Spirit. The assurance is not infallible and does not amount to scientific demonstration. God is personal, and personal relationships are not to be conceived of in these terms. But in the three points just stated we have quite sufficient assurance that God has in Christ graciously given us his Holy Spirit, or, to put the matter in another way, that we experience God the Holy Spirit.

b. Christ and the Spirit

Analysis of religious experience is a delicate matter. But we suggest that Christians today might profitably ask themselves some questions about what they think to be happening in their religious experience, at least as far as their experience of Jesus Christ is concerned. We may start this discussion from a very simple and well-known hymn:

> Jesus loves me, this I know
> For the Bible tells me so.

We must not, of course, demand a nicety of theological expression from popular hymns, especially from popular hymns for children. But we believe that this hymn lends itself to a contemporary tendency towards what one can only call 'Jesuolatry', or what the eminent Orthodox theologian Professor Nissiotis called 'Christomonism'. This is a concentration upon the person of Jesus, either confining itself to his earthly ministry, and regarding him as a kind of 'conversion of the godhead into flesh', so that it can be flatly said 'Jesus is God', or else accepting that he is the mediator of the Word of God and Second Person of the Trinity, but ignoring altogether the activity of the Holy Spirit. It is possible to concentrate so intently upon Jesus that God the Father and God the Holy Spirit are forgotten. The impression created, for instance by J.A.T. Robinson's book, *The Human Face of God*, (which nevertheless has many good points in it and is by no means to be despised) is that Jesus is the representative of God the Father, and that, in our present state of culture, God the Father must be regarded as absent. The Bible does not tell us that Jesus loves us, but that God in Christ loves us, and if God does not love us in Christ then the fact that Jesus loves us (whatever that may mean) brings very little comfort. It is not true to say that the human being Jesus is God without qualification. We are not intended to take every incident of his life, his spitting on the eyes of the blind man, his grasping the hand of Jairus' daughter, his eating a meal in the house of Simon the Pharisee, as actions directly done by God. Jesus Christ is the image of the invisible Father, but not a physical image. God does not speak in Aramaic.

The same reasoning applies to the relation of Jesus of Nazareth to the Holy Spirit. Jesus has through the resurrection been brought into the sphere, the world, or Spirit. God communicates himself to us in the form and character of Jesus Christ. But the way in which he reaches us, the way in which we experience him, is as God the Holy Spirit. The Holy Spirit is God communicating himself to us here and now in the form and character, in the Spirit, of Jesus Christ. He overcomes the limitations of time and place. He has inaugurated the new order, what Paul called the new creation, in which his people can anticipate their final redemption, when, time-bound though they still are, they have been enlightened (baptism) and have tasted the heavenly gift (eucharist) and have become partakers of the Holy Spirit, and have tasted the goodness of the Word of God and the powers of the age to come (Heb. 6:4,5). They have a foretaste of eternity because they are in God the Holy Spirit. The Holy Spirit is God our contemporary who looks forward quite as much as backwards. He is not a transparent understudy for a man Jesus who has somehow taken on the lineaments of God. He is indeed the God of Jesus Christ, but this does not mean that he binds us to adopt the sort of Christology implicit in Holman Hunt's *Light of the World*. It means that we can enjoy the freedom which Jesus Christ has won for us, freedom in God who is quintessentially free. It is one of the operations of the Holy Spirit at regular intervals to explode the images of Christ dear to conventional religion. This is part of his work as Giver of Life.

c. Is the Holy Spirit confined to the Church?

In the Catechism in the Church of England's Book of Common Prayer, the Apostles' Creed is thus effectively and succinctly summed up:

> First, I learn to believe in God the Father who
> hath made me, and all the world;
> Secondly, in God the Son, who hath redeemed me,
> and all mankind;
> Thirdly, in God the Holy Ghost, who sanctifieth
> me, and all the elect people of God.

In fact this statement sums up much more than that rather random selection of articles, the Apostles' Creed; it sums up the whole Christian faith. It draws, as it were, three concentric circles, the second inside the first and the third inside the second. But the point to be noted here is that it links the Holy Spirit firmly with the Church. This is a right and proper thing to do, but we must for a moment consider how he is linked with the Church. The traditional Roman Catholic idea that the Holy Spirit is the soul of the Church which is the Body of Christ is quite unsatisfactory. The picture of Christ with the Church as his body and the Spirit as his soul borders on the ridiculous, and gives the dreadful impression that the Spirit is imprisoned within or restricted by the Church. Any idea that the Church gives access to the Spirit as a container gives access to a liquid must be rejected at once. On the other hand the idea which it is not unjust to attribute to Karl Barth that the Church appears and reappears sporadically in history as the Spirit fills it or not, much as the Cheshire Cat in *Alice in Wonderland* assembles itself for a time and then gradually vanishes, is equally unsatisfactory. The Church may be more or less faithful to its Lord at different times and in different circumstances, but to say that at any time the Holy Spirit deserts the Church would be positively impious. God is faithful, even though man may break faith. The important point to realize is that the Holy Spirit is Lord and Master of the Church. The Church does not decide its own history and destiny, nor does it control the Spirit. The Spirit controls it. Can we say that the Holy Spirit is the Vicar of Christ? It depends what is meant by Vicar. If it means a representative of an absent Christ, certainly not. But if it means that the Holy Spirit brings the presence of God in Christ to us here and now, the term is unexceptionable. Best of all is the insight peculiarly characteristic of the Eastern Orthodox Church that the Holy Spirit is the Life of the Church. It is only by his indwelling vitality that the Church exists, continues, survives, and functions. He gives meaning to its message, authority to its ministers, effectiveness to its sacraments, reality to its whole tradition. The continuity of the Church ultimately rests upon the continuity of the Holy Spirit – a continuity which may be consistent with his causing or tolerating a number of discontinuities in ecclesiastical history.

In the Old Testament tradition the spirit of God and the wisdom of God are not always clearly distinguished. For example in Ecclesiasticus 24:3 the wisdom of God is identified with the spirit of God that brooded over the waters of creation in Genesis 1:2; and in Wisdom 7:25 wisdom is called 'a breath of the power of God'. So these two terms, 'wisdom' (with which 'word' was often associated) and 'spirit' lay ready for Christian thinkers to use when they came to work out a doctrine of God which required that distinctions in the Godhead should be recognized. In effect the two words most generally used by Christians in this context were 'word' and 'spirit'.

The New Testament offers very little speculation about God's activity outside the Church; on the whole one gains the impression that New Testament writers would be likely to speak in terms of the Word (Logos) active at large in the universe, and of the Spirit when they consider God's activity within the Church. Indeed in one New Testament document, the Book of Revelation, there is a certain tendency for the Church almost to usurp the function of the Spirit. There is some uncertainty in the Fathers as to whether the divine wisdom in the Old Testament corresponds to the Son or the Spirit. The fact that in both Hebrew and Greek the word for 'wisdom' was a feminine noun inclined the balance rather towards the identification of wisdom with the Spirit. One important tradition in Patristic theology (the Alexandrian) was very ready to see God's activity in the writings of some of the ancient philosophers, most notably Plato. When this claim was made they always held that it was the divine Logos who had been active among the Greeks, not the Holy Spirit.

It is also true to say that the Spirit always has been closely associated with the Church in Christian tradition: we worship God through Christ in the Spirit. When we speak about some occasion when we have been particularly conscious of God's presence, we most naturally say: 'I was aware of the Spirit'. We talk about a revival of the Spirit in the Church rather than of a revival of the Word. We associate the Spirit with the sacraments; indeed the Eastern Orthodox Church has a special doctrine about the eucharist which teaches that at a certain point in the service, the *epiclēsis* or invocation of the Holy Spirit, it is the Spirit who descends and effects the change in the bread and wine. Thus the Western Church generally entered the twentieth century with the conviction that the activity of the Spirit was confined to the Church, and that if we are to speak of any saving activity of God outside the Church (which was by no means widely admitted), we must speak of the Logos.

This distinction has been challenged in modern times. Tillich for example has deliberately used the term 'Spirit' for God's activity outside the Church as well as inside it, because he regards 'Logos' as too intellectualist a word. God's activity is not confined to the intellect. At the same time there is a much greater readiness among theologians today to admit the activity of God in other religions. The question faces us therefore, should we say that the activity of the

169

Spirit is confined to the Church? Or are we ready to recognize the Spirit's activity outside the Church?

This is not just a question of words: we have already claimed that, according to the New Testament, the coming of Jesus Christ inaugurated the dispensation of the Spirit, so that he was henceforth constantly available to all who approach God in faith. But can this be said at all about non-Christian religions? On the other hand, in I,4,(a) we professed ourselves ready to encounter God in other religions, and we insisted that we must not deny out of hand anybody's religious experience.

Perhaps the best solution to the problem may be this: where it is a question of religious experience shared with devotees of other religions, we may well say that we are in the presence of the Spirit; for example when Christians share in worship, or prayer, or meditation, with devotees of other religions, and when they thereby experience the presence of God, we must not be afraid of confessing that it is the Spirit whom we encounter. After all, God, if he is known at all by non-Christians, must still be the God whom we know in Christ encountered in the Spirit. However much he may seem to us to be veiled, met with in however strange a context, that is the God whom we experience. Hence we must use the language of the Spirit. But when it is a question of the concepts, or images, or myths, in other religions where we claim we can in some sense recognize God in Christ, then we may more appropriately use the language of the Word or Logos, because here it is revelation that is in question. For example, it is the Logos who is found in the *bhakti* cult in Hinduism, or in the idea of *boddhisatvas* in Buddhism. In neither context is the term 'Son' appropriate: that surely must be reserved for domestic use within the Church.

To put it briefly, we must avoid two extremes: on the one hand we must not attempt narrowly to confine the activity of God's Spirit within the Church: see John 3:8. On the other, we must not so adulterate and emasculate the idea of the Spirit that he becomes merely equated with the influence of Christianity. To quote the great nineteenth-century poet Gerard Manley Hopkins, whom no one could accuse of wishy-washy Liberalism,

> Because the Holy Ghost over the bent
> World broods with warm breast and with – ah! – bright wings.

IV · THE HOLY TRINITY

9 The Doctrine of the Trinity

a. The Development of the Doctrine of the Trinity

In order to understand the doctrine of the Trinity it is necessary to understand that the doctrine is a development, and why it developed. At 1 John 5:7 in the Book of Common Prayer and in the Authorised Version there are printed the following words, 'For there are three that bear record in heaven, the Father, the Word, and the Holy Ghost; and these three are one'. This is a late interpolation quite certainly absent from the original text. It was added by some enterprising person or persons in the ancient Church who felt that the New Testament was sadly deficient in direct witness to the kind of doctrine of the Trinity which he favoured and who determined to remedy that defect. It is, however, significant that the interpolator perceived that the New Testament gives no direct witness to this doctrine. It is a waste of time to attempt to read Trinitarian doctrine directly off the pages of the New Testament. The doctrine is an interpretation and development of the witness of the New Testament, not a direct transcription of its words.

The reason why the doctrine of God as Holy Trinity developed was the indispensable need of producing a specifically Christian doctrine of God. As long as the Church existed in a mainly Jewish milieu, the eschatological doctrine of primitive Christianity presenting a Messiah who had come, had been rejected and crucified, had risen from the dead, and would shortly come again, could commend itself to believers. But once Christianity had emerged into a Gentile environment Christian thinkers were compelled to face the question, 'What is your Christian doctrine of God?' It was all very well to speak about messiahs who come and depart and return, and to retail Jewish history, but what difference did Jesus Christ make to their account of God? There were several different accounts of God already current, the Platonist, the Aristotelian, the Stoic, and mixtures of these. It was obviously inadequate for Christians to reply that they accepted Jewish monotheism and they also thought that Jesus Christ was a very important person. What the intellectuals of the Graeco-Roman culture into which Christianity was spreading expected of this new faith before they could consider it seriously was some account of how the being of Jesus Christ was related to the being of God. They wanted to know whether Christians intended to integrate what they believed about Jesus Christ into what they believed about God. Granted that the world was not going to end very soon with stars falling, and the sun extinguished, and the moon turned to blood and angels sounding trumpets, this was an entirely just and reasonable demand to make on Christianity. Sooner or later Christianity would have to answer this question if it was to remain credible as a missionary religion claiming universal authority. There are even some attempts (but not many, and those not much developed) to answer this question in the New Testament, in Colossians 1, for instance, and Hebrews 1 and above all in John 1:1–14.

The answer to this inevitable pressure towards a coherent Christian theology was given by the Church through a process of theological exploration which lasted at least three hundred years. This process has often been represented by theologians in grandiloquent terms as a majestic pondering or an unerring homing towards the truth or an heroic preservation of the faith against the malignant attacks of heresy. In fact it was a process of trial and error (almost of hit and miss), in which the error was by no means all confined to the unorthodox. In the process of discovering the best way of stating the Christian doctrine of God, theologians like Justin Martyr, Irenaeus and Tertullian, who were in their day regarded as pillars of orthodoxy, held some doctrines which would have been regarded as rankly heretical two centuries later. The process did not give the impression of developing in a straight line of clear and consistent orthodoxy, infallibly guided by some precious instinct for the truth, but rather of a history of search in different directions to solve immediate problems, of a pendulum swinging from one extreme to another, of vicissitude and uncertainty and disagreement and revision and reassessment, of new fashions clashing with old loyalties, resulting in a gradual general advance, like the history of any other humane discipline. Science, literary and artistic criticism, and historical research advance by a process of trial and error. So does theological development. It would be foolish to represent the doctrine of the Holy Trinity as having been achieved by any other way.

Two points must, however, be borne in mind when we come to consider the development of this, the most important dogma of the Christian faith. First, the process of development was carried out not only in biblical terms, biblical words and thought-forms, but also in the terms and thought-forms of contemporary Greek philosophy.

Here the Church had no alternative. It was impossible (and still is impossible) to develop the interpretation of the Bible in purely biblical language, for the obvious reason that in this process it is precisely the meaning of the words of the Bible that is under question. The only tools available to the intellectuals of the Church were those of Greek philosophy. Roman philosophy did not exist save as a pale imitation of Greek philosophy, and Greek philosophy formed the main pabulum for higher education throughout the whole Roman Empire. It would have been absurd to expect the Church to develop its thought in terms of Indian religion or Buddhist philosophy, which were very little known in the late Roman Empire and only professed by distant peoples. The Bible itself provided no consistent philosophy at all. The Greek philosophy which was available to the Church in the second, third and fourth centuries was not the Platonism of the *Phaedo* or the *Republic* or the *Parmenides*, nor the Aristotelianism of Aristotle himself. Many centuries had passed since these great masters had taught, and philosophical thought had changed. The philosophy available to the Church was an eclectic mixture of Platonism, Stoicism and Aristotelianism, with parts of the first two predominating, and Aristotle supplying not much more than his picture of the three-storey universe and his logic. Starting on a biblical basis (and it *was* a biblical basis) the Fathers of the Church proceeded to make with these materials a superstructure of dogma, yielding to the inevitable pressure of history.

The other point to remember is that the theologian of the early Church was by no means Hilaire Belloc's 'remote and ineffectual don'. He was a pastor, writing for people who were all worshipping Christians, not university professors. Among the pressures playing upon early Christian thought as it developed was the piety of multitudes of Christians. The main factor, for instance, in developing the doctrine of the full divinity of Christ was the practice of worshipping and praying to Christ in the contemporary Church. The main reason why theologians (perhaps a little against the grain) had to take account of the Holy Spirit was because contemporary Christians experienced him.

The development of the doctrine of the Trinity followed a line dictated in its first stage largely by the needs of contemporary philosophy. Jesus Christ was identified with the *Logos*, a term which could apply equally to the Old Testament image of the Word of God and the concept known both to Middle Platonism and to Stoicism as the universally active and illuminating principle of rationality in the universe. The beginnings of this tradition of doctrine, as adopted by Christian theologians, visible in the writings of Ignatius (early second century) and of Justin (mid-second century), seem, curiously, to have been largely or wholly independent of the Fourth Gospel. But undoubtedly the espousal of that gospel by Irenaeus (fl c. 170–200), which brought Johannine teaching into the mainstream of Christian thought, contributed greatly to fixing the Logos doctrine as the traditional, orthodox, Christian scheme for achieving a doctrine of God. The Logos was described as a power or faculty within the Godhead which was put forth, made distinct but not separate from God the Father by his will and providence at a certain point in order to create the world, reveal himself in it and accomplish man's redemption. The relation of this Logos to the Father was differently described by different writers. In Justin the Logos came near to being the authorized messenger of an unknowable High God. In Irenaeus and Tertullian he was represented as the mind and plenipotentiary of the Father, representing fully and faithfully the will and act of the Father, his Son and image and 'hand'. In Origen (186–255) he appeared as the second stage in a graded Trinitarian godhead, resembling the second of the two forms of ultimate reality into which Middle Platonist philosophy had resolved all phenomena; he was undoubtedly divine, but no less certainly a mediator in his own nature between ultimate divinity and transitory, created things. In all versions of this Logos scheme, the Logos is directly identified with Jesus Christ, who is thought of as a continuation in incarnate form of the being of the Logos. In all (with the possible exception of Irenaeus) the Logos scheme is regarded as a useful way of solving the main problem of contemporary philosophy, viz. how the supreme God, or ultimate reality, can come in contact with the world of change and decay at all. And in all without exception the Son/Logos is regarded as in a greater or lesser degree subordinate to, less than, the Father. Only in Origen's system is the Son thought of as having existed eternally as a separate entity within the Godhead. Most theologians before the Council of Nicaea in 325 assumed without arguing that God must have become a Trinity for purposes of creation, revelation and redemption. The Holy Spirit was (as has already been intimated, see above pp. 153–7) included in this Trinitarian account more as a concession to tradition and experience than because his presence was demanded by the philosophical structure which usually lay behind the doctrine. But included he was; the pre-Nicene doctrine of God was decisively, though perhaps weakly and in some cases confusedly, Trinitarian.

The Arian controversy in the fourth century tested, shook and altered this doctrinal tradition of the Son/Logos. This was a long, confused, process whereby different schools of thought in the Church worked out for themselves, and then tried to impose on others, their answers to the question, 'How divine is Jesus Christ?'. It is quite misleading to represent this controversy as a contest between self-confident, well-defined orthodoxy on the one hand and blind, perverse heresy on the other. At the beginning of the controversy nobody knew the right, most satisfactory answer. This is one reason why the controversy lasted more than sixty years and gradually involved every conceivable authority; general councils, Popes, Emperors, bishops alone or in parties, and the faithful at large (who tended to make their contribution in the form of riots). If ever there was a controversy decided by the method of trial and error, it was this one. But gradually a consensus emerged. It was indeed a consensus assisted by the support of the Eastern Roman Emperor, Theodosius (379–395), but it is unlikely that Theodosius could have succeeded in imposing the revised Nicene Creed of 381 as orthodoxy had it not been supported by a consensus of opinion. Previous Emperors had tried imposing ecclesiastical order by decree without consensus and had failed. This consensus was in effect the full doctrine of the Trinity, that God existed as three Persons but one Godhead, having eternal distinctions within his being corresponding to what were known in revelation, in the history of salvation, in the witness of Scripture, as Father, Son, and Holy Spirit. The main contributor to this doctrine in the earlier period of the controversy was Athanasius, Bishop of Alexandria from 328 to 373, who was a passionate defender of the full divinity of the Son, and in the later period the three great Cappadocian theologians, Basil of Caesarea, Gregory of Nazianzus and Gregory of Nyssa, who developed a more deliberately Trinitarian doctrine.

One point concerning this doctrine must be made clear immediately. The English word 'person' is a most misleading term; it should, in our opinion, be discarded as far as possible and is only used here because it is a traditional term and cannot thus far be omitted. Used in a Trinitarian context 'person' does not mean, and its equivalents in the languages of the ancient Church, *hypostasis*, *prosopon* and *persona*, did not mean what 'person' means to us today, i.e. centre of consciousness, personality, with all the psychological depth and complexity which attach to those terms in modern thought. To the ancients 'person' (*hypostasis*) had no particular psychological attachments; it meant, approximately, recognizable, separately existing entity; its associations were ontological, not psychological, that is, it signified that the *hypostasis* really and distinctly existed; it told nothing about the mind or consciousness or feelings of the *hypostasis*. The theory that the ancients believed, in declaring God to be three 'persons', that God had three centres of consciousness or comprised three personalities is a quite mistaken one. And the idea that we today are justified in adopting such a belief, because the advent of idealist philosophy or modern psychology has enabled us to do this, is altogether astray and likely to lead to a thinly disguised form of tritheism, even though this idea has been adopted by some eminent names (such as those of William Temple, of Leonard Hodgson and of Wolfhart Pannenberg). Clumsy though the expressions are, the terms 'mode of being' (Barth) and 'way of existing' (Rahner) are preferable to the word 'person' in Trinitarian contexts. God has three modes of being God, or three ways of existing as God. This is what the Fathers meant by saying that God was three persons but one God. God is only one personality and has only one centre of consciousness (to use words which rely heavily on using the analogy of human experience to apply to God), though he expresses his personality and his consciousness in three different modes of being what he is.

The theologians who developed this doctrine of the Trinity used, as we have seen, the Greek word *hypostasis* to describe the three ways of existence in the Godhead, and the word *ousia* (essence, substance, Latin *substantia*) to describe the united Godhead, what the three 'Persons' (ways of existing), not so much had in common, but were in common. These terms of Greek philosophy inevitably influenced the way in which the Fathers thought about the doctrine of the Trinity. They saw to it, for instance, that the doctrine was expressed in static terms concerned with substance and ontology rather than in dynamic terms suggesting movement and process. They stamped upon the Christian doctrine of God an idea of God's immutability (changelessness) and impassibility (incapacity to undergo human experiences) which was entirely Greek and not native to Judaeo-Christian thought. The Cappadocians at least, if not Athanasius, had in the back of their minds the basic structure of Neo-Platonism, the last great flowering of ancient Greek philosophy, which reduced all reality to three (the Middle Platonists had identified two) forms of reality which could be represented as like (but were by no means identical with) the Christian Three. But we must not run away with the idea that the doctrine of the Trinity as it emerged at the end of the fourth century was simply a surrender by Christian theologians to Greek thought. It put an end to the traditional (one might almost say 'orthodox') doctrine of the Son/Logos. Never again would the doctrine of the Son be used as a convenient philosophical device, for now the subordination of the Son to the Father was decisively rejected. The Son would never again mean some indefinitely divine super-angelic or infra-theistic being mediating between God and the world, but that Self which God gives when he communicates himself. This represented the firm termination of a line of doctrine in the field of what Harnack called 'the acute Hellenization' of Christianity.

The great theologians mainly responsible for forming the doctrine of the Trinity in both East and West were all well aware of the difficulty and delicacy of their task. Athanasius and the Cappadocians spoke more than once of the inadequacy of words to convey their thought, and the insufficiency of their thought to grasp the nature of God. And it was on the subject of the meaning of 'Person' in a Trinitarian context that Augustine uttered his famous remark that he only wrote in order not to say nothing. Some later documents were not as nice nor as perceptive, as the deadly confidence which pervades the Athanasian Creed demonstrates. We must, however, observe an important difference between the manner of approaching the doctrine of the Trinity of the Cappadocians, who set the custom for Eastern theology thereafter, and of Augustine, whose huge intellectual power continued to dominate Western theology for a thousand years and more after his day. The Eastern writers started their understanding of God as Holy Trinity from the Father. The other two modes of being ('Persons') derived from him, the Son by generation, the Holy Spirit by procession. But they thought that each mode, Son and Spirit, was God in his own right, not simply by reason of his relation to the Father or to the other. This was because ultimately the doctrine of these theologians had been worked out from the acceptance of the history of salvation or the data of revelation. God had revealed himself as God through the career of Jesus Christ and also through the presence and activity of the Holy Spirit. But Augustine had encountered the doctrine of the Trinity when it was already formed, as an inherited dogma. His thinking on the Trinity therefore started from the *ousia*, the substance, that which the three ways of existing had (or were) in common. Consequently he regarded the ways of existing as constituted by their relation to each other, not as existing as God in their own right. The Father existed as unoriginate, unbegotten, the generator of the Son and sender of the Holy Spirit, the Son as begotten by the Father and (as we have seen) co-sender of the Spirit, the Spirit as proceeding from the Father and the Son. To put the matter succinctly, for Augustine the 'Persons' *are* the relations. He found great difficulty in determining what relation more than a passive one the Spirit should be thought to have to the other two. He suggested that the Spirit is the bond of love (*nexus amoris*) whereby they are united. This conclusion has consequently entered traditional Western thinking on the subject of the Trinity. It is however, an unsatisfactory one, and has not commended itself to Eastern theology. A bond of love suggests a less than personal entity, but God in his mode of being as a Spirit must be personal, as he must be in his other modes of being. Further, it is not clear how the Father must be conceived as loving the Son and the Son the Father if each represents the same God existing in a different way as God. Love is, of course, the motive of God's action and characterizes his very nature, but if we begin to think of God loving himself in his different modes of being God, we shall find ourselves in strange waters. We can indeed conceive of God the Holy Trinity as representing a kind of outgoing and return of love, if we transpose the relation of the Father to the Son and Spirit and theirs to him into dynamic rather than static terms. This is perhaps the nearest we can come to doing justice to Augustine's doctrine of the *nexus amoris*. Another unfortunate consequence of Augustine's way of approach to the doctrine of the Holy Trinity was that it probably encouraged the later idea to be found in Western theology that any of the 'Persons' of the Trinity could have become incarnate or been sent as Spirit irrespective of their distinctive characters and their roles within the inner life of God.

Such is, in very brief compass, the developed doctrine of God as Holy Trinity. There can be no doubts now, after the work (done in very different ways) of such scholars as Newman and Harnack, that this doctrine represents a development. It is a far cry from the Gospel of Mark to the Athanasian Creed. The question to be decided is not, is this doctrine a development, but is it a right, proper and necessary development? The doctrine has been attacked often and on many grounds. It has been thought to be an unnecessary intrusion of philosophy into Christianity, an expensive space flight of metaphysical speculation; so thought Schleiermacher, the great German originator of modern Protestant theology who lived from 1768 to 1834. It has been regarded as an undesirable appendix of complex and unwarranted theology attached to the person and career of Jesus which merely complicates Christianity without enriching it (Wiles and Lampe). It has been stigmatized as a turning of the Christian gospel into a piece of Greek philosophy. We have to ask ourselves how far we can assent to what the Fathers made of the Christian faith as they inherited it, and how far we must conclude that they betrayed Christianity by burying it under a heap of doctrines which were really alien to it.

It has already been suggested (see above pp. 171–3) that the doctrine of the Trinity was formed in response to pressures which were unavoidable and which could not have been ignored without gravely injuring Christianity. It has also been argued that if the theologians of the Church were to attempt to construct a Christian doctrine of God, the only materials available to them, apart from those to be found in the Bible, were those supplied by Greek philosophy, and that it was impossible to achieve this task using the words of Scripture alone. But in the course of completing this exacting and necessary task – and the fact that theologians took three hundred years at least to complete the task suggests at least that they took it seriously – the Fathers did not import philosophical ideas wholesale into the doctrinal tradition which they inherited. In the first place, the Platonism which they used was not pure Platonism, even by the standards of the fourth and fifth centuries. Recent studies (not least those of Professor C. Stead in his book *Divine Substance* (Oxford 1977)) have shown that the word *ousia* which figured so largely, whether simply or in compounds, in the theological vocabulary of the fourth century was used in ways so diverse and so loose as considerably to weaken its original or primary meaning of 'substance'. The world-soul of Greek philosophy with which more than once the Christian philosophers identified the Son/Logos was in fact a noticeably different concept in the hands of (for instance) the Neo-Platonists, for Plotinus' world-soul was transcendent to and not immanent in the world. In short, as E. P. Meijering observes in his *God Being History*, the Fathers used Plato indeed, but it was *their* Plato, Platonism adapted for Christian uses and changed in the adaptation. Gregory of Nyssa, in his long controversy with the extreme Arian Eunomius, is well aware of the danger of turning biblical doctrine into complex Greek metaphysics, and more than once accuses Eunomius of doing so, not without humour. We have seen, in the ending of the old Logos doctrine, one striking example of the rejection of Greek thought. Secondly the Fathers managed to preserve in their development of Christian doctrine a number of Christian ideas which are apparently incompatible with Greek philosophy. The creation of the world by God out of nothing had been part of Christian orthodoxy since the end of the second century, and this was a concept which Greek philosophers, with few exceptions, would have repudiated. The incarnation is another doctrine repugnant to Greek thought; yet it is the very centre of the theology taught by the Cappadocians. Another is the view of history as a significant unilinear process controlled, or even interrupted, by God. There were indeed many areas, such as psychology and anthropology, where most of the Fathers unreflectingly adopted Greek categories of thought, because the Bible did not very obviously throw light on them, though even in these areas there are some striking exceptions. But it is unfair to accuse the theologians of the fourth and fifth centuries of compromising or abandoning the fundamental doctrine of the Christian faith. 'Dogma', said Harnack, 'was in its conception and development a production of the Greek spirit on the ground of the Gospel'. Meijering agrees, but maintains that in this enterprise the Fathers did not desert that ground. Perhaps the greatest contrast in this area is between the Hebraic conviction that God is completely independent of the world and only acts on it and through it because he chooses to do so on the one hand, and on the other the Greek conception that God was the highest manifestation of reality, the highest conceivable form of what was there already, sometimes so metaphysically remote and abstract as to be beyond speech and knowledge, but still conceivable, so to speak, in a series and in that sense bound to existence. The Fathers never overcame this tension, but they did not compromise nor betray it.

The most common recent accusation against the doctrine of the Trinity achieved in the fourth century (at least as far as theologians in this country have criticized it) is that, having laboured with great effort to establish the existence of the Son and the Spirit as distinct entities within the Holy Trinity, the ancient theologians then declared that these distinct 'Persons' could not be distinctly experienced. It was, they maintained, impossible for men to experience the Father and/or the Son separately from the Holy Spirit. All our experience of God is experience of God the Holy Spirit. It would be just as effective, say Wiles and Lampe, to teach that we always in all circumstances experience first God, God the Father or God as Spirit, and thereby save ourselves a great deal of trouble and of unnecessary and doubtful theological speculation. Trinitarian theology appears to amount to much the same result as Unitarian.

The first answer to make to this criticism is to observe that to assume that we cannot know the existence of Son and Spirit as distinct from the Father unless we experience them distinctly is to subject theological truth to the criterion of religious experience, a proceeding which we have already found unsatisfactory (see above, pp. 144, 164–5) and one which is likely to have an impoverishing effect upon theology. Next, we must repeat the argument already traced when we were treating of the Spirit. The Holy Spirit in the New Testament is not just a periphrasis for God as he is known in the Old. He is the eschatological event, the anticipation of the End, the harbinger of resurrection, the pledge that God has in Christ decisively intervened in human affairs. The Fathers did indeed in their treatment of the Holy Spirit flatten and dim this eschatology, but they did not jettison it. For them the advent of Christianity meant discontinuity, an inrush from heaven into human affairs, the presence here and now of God who stands at the end of history, the Alpha and the Omega, indeed the actual giving of himself by God to men: the eschatological note of primitive Christianity was re-expressed by patristic doctrine in the sense of ultimacy which they attached to Jesus Christ. The doctrine of the Trinity is their attempt to guarantee, establish and safeguard this ultimacy, to ensure that in Christ God was moving, acting, offering and judging, decisively committing himself. They saw this doctrine as the inescapable logical consequence of regarding Jesus Christ in this way. They envisaged and expressed it in terms drawn from the only source available to them, Greek philosophy, but they did not embrace the ideas of Greek philosophy so slavishly as to lose the significance of the original Christian truth.

As our last point, we must turn from the Fathers and ask whether, even if we decide that they in their day and circumstances were justified in forming this doctrine, we, many centuries later, need endorse or indeed take any notice of it at all. The answer must be that if the career of Jesus Christ represents God authentically communicating himself, then in God there must be a Self who communicates and a Self who is communicated. And if we are wise we shall follow Karl Rahner in deciding that only the Son could become incarnate, just as only the Spirit could descend to gather a people to respond to the Son. Only a Trinitarian shape of doctrine can safeguard the authenticity of God's self-revelation and self-communication. We deliberately use the word 'shape' because we do not believe that any formula for Trinitarian doctrine can be thought of as eternal or demanded by dogma. We have had occasion to criticize and in large part discard one important term which is traditional to this doctrine, that of 'person'. But that a Trinitarian account of God must be regarded as an essential part of Christian faith we do assert.

One final point should be mentioned, though in the present theological climate one might well hesitate to bring it up. The doctrine of the Trinity was the choice of the Church; it represents the consensus of the undivided Church. It has been ratified by the faith and worship of the vast majority of Christians for well over a thousand years. It cannot be said that recent discoveries in history or science have seriously threatened it. There is no reason for regarding it as superstitious or antiquated or frivolous. The God of Christian faith and experience is a triune God. If the verdict of the Church has any authority at all, it must be accepted when it commends to us the doctrine of God as Holy Trinity, Father, Son and Holy Spirit.

b. The Holy Trinity as a Mystery

Curiously enough, the Church as a whole has never committed itself to any one formula to describe or define the doctrine of the Trinity, as it has to some extent in the case of the doctrine of the incarnation. The word 'Trinity' does not occur in either the Apostles' or the Nicene Creed. The nearest thing to an official formula is the so-called 'Athanasian Creed'. This is a very misleading name for it, since it was probably composed (in Latin not Greek) long after Athanasius' death, at the end of the fifth century. A more accurate name for it is the *Quicunque Vult* (the opening words in Latin, meaning 'Whoever wishes (to be saved etc.)'). This is a full statement of the doctrine of the Trinity, but it was never accepted by the Eastern Orthodox Church and has no claim to be called a catholic creed.

We speak therefore about 'the doctrine of the Trinity' not 'the formula of the Trinity'. As a doctrine it is of course a construction of men, not a divine revelation; but it is a construction based on the Christian experience of God in Christ, just as is the doctrine of the incarnation. It may at first seem strange that a doctrine which is not at all clearly stated in the Bible, and did not begin to be formulated until the third century AD, should be regarded as an integral part of the Christian faith; but a moment's consideration will show that there is nothing surprising in this. God does not develop and grow, but man's understanding of God does. It took Israel of old centuries to learn the fact so obvious to us, that there was only one God. It was not until the sixth century BC that this great truth was set down with absolute clarity by the great prophet of the Exile. Even later came the understanding (if it came at all before Christ) that God was interested in Gentiles as well as Jews. The great new development represented by Jesus Christ took an equivalent time to be understood and absorbed in its full implications. Just as Israel had to come to the realization that there really was only one God and that this had always been the case, so Christians had to come to the realization that there are distinctions within the Godhead and that this has always been so.

A parallel from physics may help. For centuries intelligent Western man has talked about physical matter: philosophers made theories about it: theologians have contrasted it with mind or with spirit, and so on. Only in the last two or three hundred years have scientists produced an account of what the ultimate unit of matter must be like. They contended, especially in the nineteenth century, that the ultimate unit of matter must be a hard particle, an unbreakable atom like a minute billiard ball: but in the twentieth century even this supposedly scientific account of matter has had to be modified, and today scientists prefer to use two alternative models in order to imagine the ultimate unit of matter: sometimes it is useful to picture it as a particle and sometimes as a wave, and it is impossible to commit ourselves permanently to one model to the exclusion of the other. If our understanding of physical matter, with which we think we are so familiar, can alter so much in the course of a few centuries, it is not surprising that our understanding of God, who by definition must transcend our intellectual capacity, should have to undergo development. Of course the parallel of the electron, like all parallels, breaks down ultimately. We cannot be sure that our conception of the electron may not have to change some time in the future, whereas Christians may be confident that in saying God is three-in-one they are not making just a provisional estimate.

If God is three-in-one, Holy Trinity, can we experience him as such? When we meet him in prayer, in meditation in the eucharist, do we know him as three-in-one? Some Christians have claimed they do, for example some of the mystics, and even some modern Indian Christians who have been influenced by Indian ways of thinking about God: but on the whole it seems to us a strange claim. God is known as personal; he encounters us as personal moral demand, as love in a personal form, as the infinitely desirable, infinitely other, infinitely intimate, but always as the personal. It is not easy to see how this can be reconciled with the claim that we can experience God as Trinity. Perhaps what is meant by those who make this claim is that, through their communion with God they can understand how, or why, he must be three-in-one. Compare Dante's vision at the end of the *Paradiso* of God the Holy Trinity as three concentric circles with a man's face in the centre: but this was a vision, not direct experience.

Many Christians unfortunately regard the doctrine of the Trinity as a total puzzle or an intellectual burden. We remember Dorothy Sayers' amusing portrayal of the predicament of the average Christian (which she herself certainly did not share): 'The Father incomprehensible, the Son incomprehensible, the whole thing incomprehensible'. To approach the doctrine this way is to misunderstand it. Rightly understood, the doctrine of the Trinity should have a liberating effect on our apprehension of God. If there are distinctions in the Godhead, this, so to speak, should give God more scope for our understanding him, more for us to hang on to. A very eminent Sikh, speaking about Hinduism and Christianity as contrasted with Judaism and Islam, once said that religions which recognized distinctions within the Godhead seemed to be able to get closer to God. Far from regarding the doctrine of the Trinity as an intellectual burden, we should look on it as a step forward in our knowledge of God. Helen Oppenheimer, that distinguished modern Christian philosopher, has remarked in a recent book that the Christian understanding of God as three-in-one, compared with the Purist Monotheism out of which it sprang, is like Einstein's theory of relativity compared with the old Newtonian physics.

The Holy Trinity is not only to be acknowledged and (partially at most) understood. He is also to be worshipped. Indeed it is perhaps in worship that we come closest to understanding the doctrine of the Holy Trinity. The Collect for Trinity Sunday in the Book of Common Prayer begins with these words: 'Almighty and everlasting God, who hast given unto us thy servants grace, by the confession of a true faith, to acknowledge the glory of the eternal Trinity, and in the power of the Divine Majesty to worship the Unity. . . .' This is the right relationship. We acknowledge the Trinity and are thereby enabled to worship the unity. What we worship must always be a mystery or he would not be worthy of our worship: but the mystery of the Holy Trinity is not a dark mystery or an enigmatic mystery, it is a bright and dazzling mystery, one which attracts us by its very splendour, and sets us wondering what it will be like to explore that mystery in eternity.

c. Analogies to the Trinity

We must be able to use some analogies to enable us to think about the Trinity, otherwise the doctrine becomes not a mystery but a puzzle. We must not expect too much of these analogies: no analogy is perfect. They all break down at some point: but we must use them and refine them as far as we can so as to try to find as close an analogy as possible.

Ever since the time of Tertullian at least (early third century), Christian theologians have been using analogies to illustrate the doctrine of the Trinity. Tertullian uses two: the sun, the ray proceeding from the sun, and the sunbeam as it is reflected by some object on earth. This might claim some sort of scriptural backing since in Hebrews 1:3 Christ is described as the *apaugasma* of God, which in that context probably means 'reflection'. Tertullian's second analogy is the spring, the river, and the lake. Either of these could be useful. Both suffer from one grave defect: they are spatial analogies; but the Trinity is spirit. We need an analogy drawn from the realm of spirit.

The Cappadocian Fathers did not venture often to suggest analogies in our experience to the Holy Trinity. They sometimes tentatively advanced the analogy of three men belonging to the same human race. This is at once recognizable as a very bad analogy, and when Gregory of Nyssa at least used it he did so only with considerable qualification and with awareness of its inadequacy: but Gregory of Nyssa produced another and better analogy, that of three different disciplines, like theology, medicine and law, coexisting in the same mind, as well as one or two less sophisticated suggestions.

Augustine in his masterly work *De Trinitate*, written very early in the fifth century, has a thorough discussion of what are the best analogies for the Trinity. He is convinced that such analogies are best found in man, because man is made in the image of God, and therefore one should expect to see in man some reflection or vestige of the triune God who made him. He first proposes as an analogy the act of seeing. In every act of seeing three things are involved: the object which we see, our vision, and our awareness or consciousness. These would correspond to Father, Son and Spirit: but this is unsatisfactory, says Augustine, because we are still in the dimension of space. God is spirit, so we need a more spiritual analogy. The one which he finally judges to be the best is simply this: the mind knowing itself. In the act of self-knowledge we can distinguish what Augustine calls *memoria*, *intelligentia*, and *voluntas*. By these he means 'the contents of the mind', 'the act of thinking' and 'the will' respectively. All these three are involved in the act of self-reflection. What is excellent about this analogy is that it is entirely unmaterial, and that we have three real distinctions within one undoubted unity, the self. It is therefore undoubtedly a very valuable analogy for the Trinity. Augustine himself points out where it breaks down. We would naturally say that memory, intelligence, and will 'belong to' or 'are part of' the self, as if the self was a whole within which they are to be contained, or to which they belong. We must not speak of the Trinity in these terms, since that would give us Father, Son, Spirit, and a fourth, the Godhead: but in the Trinity the Godhead *is* Father, Son and Spirit. The 'Persons' are not three examples of one species or three species of one genus.

In the early part of the eleventh century Peter Abailard, one of the most acute minds of that, or any other, century proposed a new analogy for the Trinity, one drawn from the realm of logic: think of the subject as agent (in the nominative), the subject as addressed by another (in the vocative) and the subject as spoken about by someone else (perhaps in the accusative). It is the same person but in three different roles, all of which may exist at the same time. It may seem a little confusing, but it reminds us of Karl Barth's profound statement that the Trinity is not three 'I's' but 'I' three times over.

Modern theologians have not really improved very much on the efforts of their predecessors as far as finding illuminating analogies is concerned. A school of Anglican theologians, notably C.C.J. Webb, Leonard Hodgson, and Helen Oppenheimer, has emphasized very much the social aspect of the Trinity. They favour the family as an analogy for the Trinity, because this gives a model in which there is movement and reciprocal relationships. We have discussed this approach above and would certainly consider that the family is not a satisfactory analogy, since it seems to lead straight to Tritheism, and to ignore the fact that the word 'person' when used in Trinitarian theology does not have the full meaning which it has in ordinary English usage. Our judgment is that on the whole the best we can do by way of analogy is to offer a modified version of Augustine's model. In our conscious life we can distinguish three elements, thinking, feeling, and willing. No conscious act can take place without these three elements being present; we cannot separate them, but we can distinguish them. Here is a very nearly completely spiritual analogy for the relation of the 'Persons' in the Trinity to each other, drawn from our daily experience, but yet implying an element of mystery (nobody knows how these elements operate) which admirably reflects the mystery of the triune Godhead. It suffers, of course, from the same defect as Augustine's, but that is inevitable.

Hinduism provides some interesting parallels to the doctrine of the Trinity. Some years ago, if you had received a letter from India, the stamp might have had a picture of a famous statue with three faces. This was a statue of the *trimurti*. The *trimurti* is the concept of God as manifested in three aspects, Brahma as creator, Vishnu as preserver, and Siva as destroyer. It presents a remote parallel to the Christian concept of the Trinity. We must bear in mind, however, that this *trimurti* is not regarded by Hindus as the ultimate truth about God; it is more in the nature of an accommodation to our finite minds. This is certainly not what Christians believe about the Trinity.

A very able Indian theologian, who died early in the nineteenth century, Brahmabandav Upādhyāya, made an interesting suggestion. about how the doctrine of the Trinity could be expressed using the terms not of Western, but of Indian, thought. He pointed out that Hindu theologians were accustomed to speak of God as *sācchidān-*

anda. This is a compound word made of three elements: *Sat,* which means reality or being, *Chit,* which means mind, and *ānanda,* which means bliss or experience of God. These three correspond very accurately to Father, Logos or Word, and Spirit, or man's experience of God. In fact there is no reason why Indian theologians should not use this term for the Holy Trinity. The fact that a completely different culture could come to so very similar a concept of God must surely suggest that the doctrine of the Trinity is not some sort of a quirk of Western minds, but a profound and valuable way of thinking about God. The differences between the Hindu and the Christian way of understanding God remain despite this similarity, not the least of which is the Christian insistence that he must always be thought of in personal terms, and the Christian claim that he is supremely revealed in Christ: but the resemblance is interesting and encouraging. In declaring that God is three-in-one we Christians are not merely indulging in logical paradoxes; we are moving into a deeper understanding of the mystery of God's being.

V · CHRISTIANITY AND HISTORY

10 Development and Orthodoxy

Our consideration of the doctrine of the Trinity will have left the reader sufficiently aware that there is such a thing as development in doctrine. But the subject of development cannot be left there. It is indeed one of the foremost theological subjects under debate and discussion today. The difficulty which the theologian has to face here is that of deciding, granted that the doctrine of the Trinity is a legitimate development, whether any or every further development of doctrine is legitimate. The doctrine of the Trinity was certainly not the last claimant for the title of true development. We have already (see above, pp. 86–88) surveyed briefly the developments represented by the findings of the Councils of Ephesus (431) and of Chalcedon (451), without being able to regard them with entire satisfaction. The next few centuries saw several more developments of doctrine proclaimed by general councils, a modification of Chalcedon in 553, a condemnation of Monothelitism (the doctrine that Christ has only one will) in 680 and the declaration of the propriety of giving veneration to icons in 787. All these developments have been approved and regarded as legitimate dogma by the Eastern Church and also, though with rather less enthusiasm, by the Roman Catholic Church. The Roman Catholic Church, indeed, has since the Middle Ages been adding developments in doctrine at a greater rate than any other Christian body. The Orthodox reckon that the last authentic general council took place in 787, but the Roman Church has added in its reckoning another fourteen to these, the latest of which is the Second Vatican Council which took place in our own lifetime. Not all these fourteen councils produced developments in doctrine, but many of them did, and in addition Popes have sometimes on their own initiative promulgated dogmas which are in effect developments without summoning a general council. The most striking of these Roman developments are the dogma of Transubstantiation declared in 1215, the dogma of the Immaculate Conception of the Blessed Virgin Mary (1854), the dogma of the Infallibility of the Pope (1870), and the dogma of the Corporeal Assumption into Heaven of the Blessed Virgin Mary (1950).

The first theologian to call attention effectively to the fact that doctrine has developed and that serious theologians must determine their attitude to this phenomenon was John Henry Newman in his book *The Development of Christian Doctrine* (1845). He asked pertinently of the Church of England, which he had just left for the Roman Catholic Church, whether, if the Holy Spirit guides the Church into all truth, it was to be understood that the Spirit had ceased to guide the Church since the fifth century, which was the last point at which the Church of England formally admitted that a general council had rightly defined doctrine. He might have added that the same question could be addressed to the Orthodox Church, substituting the eighth century for the fifth. Newman's own attempt to answer the questions raised by development in doctrine in his famous book can hardly be said to have succeeded. It is a classic work, but its best friends must admit that it is not so much confused as involved and indecisive. Newman's mind was a subtle, almost devious one; his methods of argument often seem to escape the net of logic. But he had the great credit of having perceived the problem and raised the question.

It is impossible to deny that development has taken place, even in those early dogmas which are accepted by the vast majority of Christians, though many of Newman's opponents in the nineteenth century, such as Mozley and Salmon, were surprisingly obtuse about recognizing the truth. Some Roman Catholic theologians between Newman's day and the Second Vatican Council were inclined to accept the full force of what was implicit (though never quite explicit) in Newman's argument, and to declare boldly that development has taken place, is taking place, and should not be restricted or discouraged, as long as it is understood that the Catholic Church has the right to develop doctrine in whatever direction it liked. This total rejection of the norms of Scripture and tradition has however never been the official doctrine of the Roman Catholic Church, and today would find very few supporters. An exactly opposite argument which paradoxically produces pretty well the same result has recently been advanced by some scholars, all of them Protestants and some of them Anglicans. They state boldly that there are no workable criteria of doctrine, neither Scripture which is too restricted, too obsolete and too ambiguous to be of any use; nor tradition, which is self-contradictory and full of ideas alien to Christianity; nor reason, which cannot operate where it has such intractable material to work on; not even religious experience can guide us here because it is too subjective a norm to stand alone. On this view therefore there is neither orthodoxy nor heresy. Christianity is whatever happens when Christians interpret the Bible and worship, and it is Christianity because it happens. This is an argument of despair and of nihilism. Even though it may appeal to a number of theologians at the present time it is inconceivable that such a recipe as this for the swift disappearance of Christianity in a host of contemporary cultures could endure. It is curious that its end result is in fact the state of total independence from Scripture and tradition occasionally advocated by Catholic theologians. Extremes indeed meet.

It must be realized in connection with this subject that development of doctrine has never been plain sailing. Development has usually been called forth by some controversy, and controversies do not make for a calm and steady appreciation of truth. Again, doctrinal development has very often been involved with the interpretation of Scripture; and it has perhaps been made plain enough in the earlier pages of this book that interpreting Scripture is a difficult and complex process demanding sensitivity and flexibility, qualities not to be found among all theologians in all ages. Two observations may however safely be made here. The first is that the assumption that the only way to bring about doctrinal development rightly is by means of a general council should be challenged. It is a a *priori* ridiculous to imagine that because the Anglican and Orthodox Churches have not formally agreed to any dogma for hundreds of years therefore they assume that no doctrinal development has taken place. The formal registration of dogmas by general councils is not necessarily the best way of dealing with development. Anyone who has gone in any detail into the workings and proceedings of, say the Council of Chalcedon or the First Vatican Council will not easily come away filled with admiration for this particular means of managing the Church's doctrine.

The question may also legitimately be raised whether some of the doctrines advanced by general councils are sufficiently universal and central to deserve the name of development if not of dogma. It is doubtful if the findings of the Second Council of Constantinople in 553 condemning certain passages in some writers of the past were of more than local or ephemeral interest; and it is hard to justify the view that the question of giving reverence to icons, which formed the subject of the Council of 787, was something that seriously affected the vital interest of Christian faith, however dear it may have been to the Eastern Church. Both Orthodox and Anglicans, in different ways, tend to express new understanding of doctrine in the form of liturgy, of worship, rather than in the registration of a new insight by the hierarchy in the form of a dogma imposed as *de fide* on all the faithful. Reformed traditions have in the past tended to express new movements, or critical declarations of doctrine, in the form of a confession, like those of Augsburg, of Westminster and of Barmen. Again, doctrinal development can take the form of a general response in the thinking of the Church to a new phenomenon in contemporary society, such as the reappearance of Aristotelianism in the twelfth and thirteenth centuries which resulted in the rise of scholasticism, or the emergence of historical criticism which has increasingly during the nineteenth and twentieth centuries demanded from the Church a reassessment of its faith.

Newman never gave a satisfactory reason for concluding that Reformations, deliberate attempts to return to earlier doctrine on the grounds that it was purer and truer, should not form legitimate phases of development. After all, the same phenomenon has been observed in other religions, such as Judaism and Islam. This was partly because the 'models' for development which he chose were almost all taken from the world of organic growth, the emergence of the oak from the acorn or of the man from the boy. Here certainly a pruning or cutting back of development is out of place. But there is no reason to assume that the right 'model' for the development of doctrine should be taken from the realm of nature, rather the contrary. In fact any concept of the development of doctrine which is so to speak rectilinear or one purely of growth in bulk is *eo ipso* not likely to be helpful, because generally speaking human thought does not develop as simply as that and is more subject to vicissitude and chance and the pressure of contingent circumstances than any such similes suggest. To think of the development of doctrine as the growth of an empire ('wider yet and wider shall thy bounds be set'), or of a coral reef enlarged age after age by the toil of millions of insects, is quite unrealistic, unhistorical, schematic. The fact alone that contemporary Catholic theologians admit that much of the theological protest of the Reformers was justified, and that Orthodox theologians today deplore the Romanising tendencies which were visible in many parts of their Church during the eighteenth century, should establish this point.

If we are to place the phenomenon of development in Christian doctrine in a proper theological perspective we must search further for an analogy or 'model' for it in human experience. We believe that such an analogy is available. It was once fleetingly suggested by Newman and has since been considered by Maurice Wiles in his *The Re-Making of Christian Doctrine*, but has hardly been given sufficient attention. It is an analogy of literary criticism. If we consider for instance the course of Shakespearean criticism since its origin in the seventeenth century we shall find that it has pursued a varied and by no means direct or straightforward course. Different ages have estimated Shakespeare differently. We can cite the young Milton's rather patronizing lines:

> And sweetest Shakespeare, fancy's child
> Warbling his native wood-notes wild.

We can observe Colley Cibber in the eighteenth century altering *King Lear* to give it a happy ending, read Macaulay's opinion of Shakespeare, which seems to have been mainly a literary and not a dramatic one, sympathize perhaps with Matthew Arnold's 'Others abide the question; thou art free', witness the multitudinous ways of presenting Shakespeare on the stage today, culminating in the unspeakable folly of giving a tragic – or at least a squalid – ending to *Measure for Measure*. Yet all this continuous assessment of Shakespeare, in spite of some folly and some perversity, has certainly added to our understanding of him. Further, Shakespeare's plays are not merely literary productions. They can be acted and were intended to be acted, just as Christianity is not merely a set of doctrines but a living religion which can inspire behaviour, prayer and worship. And yet for all this ongoing tradition of exploring Shakespeare, we cannot actually consult the man himself, know his work as he knew it, any more than we can consult or speak with Jesus or the apostles. The analogy is not complete; if it were it would be an allegory and not an analogy. But it is sufficient to show that we can reasonably understand that there has been a development in Christian doctrine representing a deeper understanding of the original self-communication of God in Christ without any actual addition to the original communication, and that we need not abandon in despair the search for norms of doctrine.

It is easy to suggest the general principles which should lead us in seeking norms of doctrine – Scripture, tradition and reason. Creeds and confessions of the past are obviously useful but should only be used after it has been thoroughly understood that they, like all documents, like the Bible itself, are conditioned by the age in which they were produced and cannot represent absolute immutable truth. We have already seen good cause in this book to be critical about some aspects of some of them, e.g. the Chalcedonian Formula and the Athanasian Creed. The Apostles' Creed is of very little use except as a museum piece because it is simply a bare summary of a few doctrines and not all of these the most important. It does not, for instance, mention the doctrine of the Trinity, nor of the incarnation, nor of the atonement. Creeds may roughly be regarded as landmarks in the history of Christianity useful in their own measure and within their limited scope. Similarly piety, the test of religious experience, is not to be disregarded or underestimated; we have seen several examples of its effect on Christian doctrine, perhaps the most striking of which is the condemnation of iconoclasm. But it is equally true that piety alone cannot stand as the supreme norm of doctrine, and doctrines which appear to appeal to piety or Christian devotion alone, unsupported by Scripture or tradition, such as that of the Corporeal Assumption into heaven of the Blessed Virgin Mary, must be regarded as suspicious and inauthentic.

One principle in estimating norms for doctrine which should command acceptance is that which is called the 'hierarchy of truth'; it was mentioned in the Second Vatican Council and is widely entertained among both Catholic and Protestant theologians today. This means the recognition that within Christian belief there are central truths and less central or secondary or peripheral truths. This certainly was a principle accepted by those theologians who in the second and third centuries wrote of 'the rule of faith', and it is an obvious conclusion of common sense. The idea which has usually been popular at periods and among churches where 'triumphalism' and ecclesiastical imperialism were in the ascendant, that the whole of Christian belief is a seamless garment, a vast interconnected tapestry of doctrine, so that if even the smallest part is attacked the whole becomes unravelled and collapses, is a piece of nervous propaganda rather than a serious argument. We can tolerate neither the contention of the Orthodox that the rejection of the *Filioque* clause is *articulum stantis aut cadentis ecclesiae* (a doctrine by which the Church stands or falls), nor of the stricter Baptists that the practice of infant baptism (vulnerable though it certainly is to criticism) renders suspect the orthodoxy and purity of doctrine of the churches which use it. Orthodoxy must apply to the central doctrines of the Christian faith. It must leave the others undecided; it must tolerate a great deal of diversity; it must be enormously flexible, continually self-critical, full of understanding and readiness to adapt itself to new ideas, new situations, and endlessly tolerant of the limitations and vagaries of the human mind.

But that there is such a thing as orthodoxy and that it must not be lost, and that in the last resort the Church has the right to determine it can hardly be doubted if we look not merely at the long vista of past history but attempt to imagine what the future has in store for Christianity. Such orthodoxy will no doubt bear the shape of the three basic doctrines of Christianity, its doctrine of God, its doctrine of God's relation to history and its doctrine of God's relation to man;

in other words, of the Trinity, of the incarnation, and of the atonement. It is true that today it is peculiarly difficult to determine the limits of the Church, and even more difficult for the Church to express its mind. It is true that we live in an age of rapid change, intellectual as well as social, and that scholarship, which is today more than ever indispensable for determining doctrine, can never give more than a relative approximation to truth. But the movement towards the unity of divided Christian bodies and an impulse towards the common exploration of Christian truth by Christians and scholars of all traditions are well under way and can hardly now be stopped. Christians have, by and large, ceased to fight each other and are beginning to join hands. We need not despair either of the Church or of the Church's gospel.

11 The Last Things

a. Eschatology

The New Testament is full of the expectation of the imminent return of Jesus Christ. They called it the *Parousia*, a word used in secular Greek for the personal visit of a supreme ruler. Only in the Fourth Gospel are there signs that the *Parousia*, though not denied, was beginning to be replaced by the belief that what really mattered was Jesus' presence with his disciples in the Spirit. One of the latest books of the New Testament witnesses to the fact that some Christians were beginning to ask why the imminent *Parousia* had not arrived (2 Pet. 3:4f).

Today this belief in an imminent *Parousia* is an embarrassment to intelligent Christians. It is true that every Advent many clergymen remind their flocks that, though the Lord has not returned yet, he may return at any moment, and we should be ready for his return: but these words ring hollow. If the clergy really believed this, they would not make long term plans which everyone else makes, like life insurance, pension schemes, and mortgages on houses. An event that has been just round the corner for a thousand years is a non-event. Thinking Christians should not behave as if the *Parousia* was a genuine possibility.

Is the language in the New Testament about the end, then, simply to be ignored as a primitive Christian misunderstanding? We hope to show that this is not the case, but that the eschatological nature of Christianity is still meaningful today.

In the first place, God is still in control of history. History is not a meaningless succession of events, but has point and purpose and is proceeding towards a goal appointed by God. Here if we will we can read Teilhard de Chardin with his concept of Christ as the goal not just of history but of evolution. This is no naïve illusion of a society that will grow steadily better and better until the millenium arrives. On the contrary, it is during the deadliest and most desperate times that Christians are most convinced that God is in control and that human history has a purpose. We may be sure that one of the books which Christians in Russia and parts of Eastern Europe value most today is the Book of Revelation.

Secondly, though we can no longer believe in an imminent return of Jesus, we must retain the sense of *ultimacy* which that belief originally expressed. The New Testament represents Jesus as the last Act of God; he is so important that the only significant thing that can happen after his appearance is the end of the world. This Jewish way of expressing the ultimacy of Jesus Christ was still retained in the transposition of doctrine more clearly visible in the Fourth Gospel than in any other document. C. H. Dodd brilliantly described it as 'sublimated eschatology'. The Church discovered during the period when that transposition was being made that the significance of Christ was such that it must survive even the abandonment of the expectation of an early visible return. It discovered, in short, that he represented the ultimate offer and demand of God. This ultimacy Christian eschatology preserves, and eschatology therefore remains an essential ingredient of Christianity.

Thirdly, ever since it dawned upon the world, authentic Christianity has had an eschatological flavour about it. From the first Christians claimed that in Jesus Christ God had accomplished something new, in some sense the last important event had happened. Hence Christianity at its best has always had a demanding, a forward-looking, an expectant quality. It does not allow its devotees to sit still; it makes constant demands on them, it expects them to show their faith by their actions. In this respect Christianity contrasts with the great religious tradition of India which on the whole has been world-denying and quietist as far as history is concerned. This expectant, eschatological quality of Christianity can be corrupted: it shows itself not only in missionary activity and social reform, but also in crusades and persecutions: but it is there, part of the very genius of Christianity, the eschatological enzyme. We Christians claim that in Jesus Christ God newly and decisively communicated himself to men and that this decisive newness is to be met with in the Church. We in the West find this hard to believe because in many parts of the West the Church appears conservative and backward looking, more concerned with the past than with the future. We ought to be able to point to some indications of this newness and expectancy in the contemporary Church. What are the eschatological signs in the Church of today?

There is the world-wide extension of the Church, a comparatively recent phenomenon. Christianity is the most universal religion in the sense that it has established itself in more parts of the world than any other great world religion. In some areas of the world it is growing fast, e.g. East Africa, South America, South India. Even in a situation such as that in the United Kingdom, where the Church is in decline, some of the liveliest and most intelligent Christians are most concerned with the Mission of the Church. The public image of the missionary today is absurdly out of date. Most modern missionaries are well educated, intelligent, and broadminded Christians. Here is a constantly recreated source of new life in the Church.

Next, why is it that the Christian Church is usually the first victim of the modern totalitarian state, and that very often the strongest defenders of human liberty in conditions of oppression are Christians? If one looks at the historical record of the Church, one would expect exactly the opposite. In the history of Europe and America the Church has often been the great enemy of individual liberty, the suppressor of free thought and in some places, such as South Africa, some professing Christians are the allies and apologists of oppressive regimes. Nevertheless it is the Christians who resist totalitarianism; it is the Christian Church that has survived in Russia after sixty years of unprecedented persecution. It is the Christians who have provided more martyrs in this century than in the whole of previous Christian history. The Church's ability to survive discrimination and persecution is an eschatological sign. The new life of God in Christ is there. Here is something transcending history. The testimony of Jesus is the spirit of prophecy (Rev. 19: 10).

Again, in many parts of the third world Christianity appears as the forward-looking, active, renovating, force. It is Christianity that has brought education, modern medicine, modern agricultural technology. Christianity has pioneered woman's liberation, democratic government, mass literacy; Christianity in these places contrasts with long-established or ethnic religions as the religion of the future, the new vital force. It is indeed true that there are historical reasons for this: the missionary movement of the last century went hand in hand with the imperialist expansion of the Western countries into the third world, an expansion made possible by superior Western technology: but this provokes deeper reflection: was it just a coincidence that modern science and technology grew up in a Christian culture? Was there not something about Christianity, an acceptance of the world as God's gift, a forward-looking attitude towards human history, that made the beginnings of the scientific attitude possible? In any case Christianity is the first world religion that has had to face the onset of modern science. Our experience (often bitter experience) of how science alters our world-view should be made available to the adherents of all religions. We have coped; we are coping; we will not renounce science, nor yield our place to science when scientists make unjustified claims about either God or man. We are still the religion that looks forward and is inextricably concerned with history.

b. Christianity and Marxism

It is this concern with history that has provided in our days the talking point between Christianity and its most immediate ideological rival, Marxism. At first sight there would seem to be nothing in common between Christianity and the ideology of Communism. Marx was a convinced atheist and regarded religion as a sort of drug. Soviet Communism assumes that religion is a diseased state of mind and it actively harasses and supresses organized religion of any kind; but in the last fifteen years there has developed a form of neo-Marxism or liberal Marxism which has reacted against the rigid determinism of Stalinist Marxism, and has returned to the earlier philosophical writings of Karl Marx, in which he shows himself more interested in a doctrine of man. It has repudiated the 'orthodox' interpretation of Marx, which represents him as teaching that man is a part of nature and that man's role in history is completely determined by social and economic forces. This liberal Marxism concedes that man can stand over against nature, that he can transcend himself, and that he experiences a dimension of transcendence. From this it follows that man's history is not determined; he can fashion his own history. History is open; he can be master of his own destiny.

One of the most distinguished of these neo-Marxists is Roger Garaudy, a professor of philosophy in France, who, in three successive books written between 1965 and 1977, has described his gradual approximation towards Christianity. In the last of these books he declares himself to be a Christian: he believes in God in Christ, though he remains a convinced Marxist anxious to bring about the revolution. What has attracted him about Christianity, he says, is that it has an open attitude towards history and therefore towards the future. Because Christians believe in a living God, they are free to try to fashion history according to God's will. The death and resurrection of Jesus Christ have shown both what sort of a God God is, and how he can change tragedy into triumph. God is therefore seen as the God of the future, who invites men to fashion history along the path which he wills for their good.

This does not mean that there are no fundamental differences between Christianity and Marxism. Professor Garaudy's interpretation of Marxism has not yet been subjected to the final test, being entrusted with political power. It cannot be said that either Christianity or Marxism has been very successful in resisting the corrupting influence of power: but it is immensely significant that it is on the topic of one's attitude towards history that Christians and Marxists find their best ground for dialogue, and it is one of the clearest indications that the dropping of the belief in a literal *Parousia* does not mean that Christianity ceases to be an eschatological faith.

But not only is Christianity influencing some forms of Marxism: Marxism is also influencing Christianity. A number of modern Christian theologians, who might be said to be disciples of the theology of liberation, have borrowed some very important elements in their theology from Marxism. The most distinguished of these theologians is J. Moltmann, particularly in his book *The Crucified God*; and he has now been followed by J. Sobrino, who, in his book *Christology at the Crossroads*, has attempted to work out a Christology on these lines. Such theologians view Jesus Christ primarily as liberator, describe him as having made a supreme protest against unjust social conditions, and maintain that God is primarily to be found in the poor and oppressed. They tend to repudiate metaphysics; both Moltmann and Sobrino maintain that God can *only* be known in Christ, a position remarkably reminiscent of Karl Barth's: and both put great emphasis on *praxis*, i.e. the practical living out of Christianity. Sobrino at least claims that we can only know God by following Christ, and that *praxis* is the means of knowing Christian doctrine. We may well agree that Christians must not shrink from the challenge to exhibit their belief in life, and Marxism may well be justified in claiming that a Christianity which does not manifest in practice the redemption which it preaches is meaningless. But the claim that the truth of Christian doctrine can only be known by means of *praxis*, which is certainly taken from Marxism, is itself in danger of lapsing into nonsense. The Marxist is bound to the dogma that meaning is the result of production, itself a throw-back to a very much outdated notion that science itself is a union of theory and practice. The Christian form of this dogma is to say that doctrine cannot be formulated in conceptual terms, but must be experienced in life. Such thinking could degenerate into a sort of anti-intellectual mysticism.

c. Resurrection, Heaven, and Hell

Even though we cannot take the *Parousia* in a literal sense, for every Christian there are still certain last things. There is death and what comes after death. In the Creeds we say we believe in 'the resurrection of the body' (Apostles' Creed) or 'the resurrection of the dead' (Nicene Creed). For many centuries Christians tended to understand this in a literal sense, and theologians argued that God could, and would, restore the physical units of our bodies at the resurrection. In fact it is not by any means certain that this is what Paul meant when he wrote about the resurrection of the bodies of Christians. He writes in 1 Corinthians 15: 50 'Flesh and blood cannot inherit the Kingdom of God, nor does the perishable inherit the imperishable'. Today at any rate we do not need to understand the phrase 'resurrection of the body' in the literal sense of the resurrection of the physical particles of our bodies.

Most thoughtful Christians in the West, if challenged to say what they *do* mean by 'the resurrection of the body' would probably reply by saying 'the preservation of the personality'. This is not a mere evasion, for the personality is something more than just the mind or 'the soul'. It means that which makes me precisely the person I am with all its implications. My personality is that deepest part in me which can respond to the personal God. We use the term 'resurrection' because the survival of the personality is not something that happens automatically like the immortality of the soul in Platonic philosophy. Plato held that the soul was naturally immortal and could not perish. There is no support for this view in the New Testament. All the writers of the New Testament hold that resurrection is the gift and act of God, as Christ's resurrection was. The traditional view following Paul's schema (see 1 Thessalonians 4: 15–18) was that the resurrection of Christians will only take place at the *Parousia*. In the meantime those who die in faith will somehow be preserved by God without bodies: but if we do not accept a literal *Parousia*, we are free to think of the individual's resurrection taking place at death. Speculation about the nature of our environment after death is quite fruitless. We must be content to know that we will be in God's hands.

There is much in the New Testament about heaven and hell, almost all of it expressed (as it must be) in highly symbolical language. A great deal of damage has been done through the ages by Christians understanding this language in a literal sense, so that we either have a vision of an eternity of sitting on a damp cloud harping, or we have the daunting prospect of burning in literal, physical fire for ever. All this symbolic language is intended to convey just one thing: heaven is being in the presence of God; hell is being cut off from God. We must add one qualifier: either of these conditions depends in the last resort on our choice; neither of them is something which God does to us against our will.

Let us take hell first. Hell means being cut off from God, or to be more accurate, cutting ourselves off from God. Hell can therefore begin in this life. In extreme instances (alcoholism, drug addiction, for example) we can see some unfortunates already entering hell.

Not, of course, that anyone is predestined to hell; there is always time to repent. So God does not send anyone to hell: but he will not compel them to turn to him. Indeed he cannot compel anyone to turn to him voluntarily: that is a contradiction in terms. The most commonly used term for hell in the New Testament is *apōleia*, which means 'destruction'. This suggests that, if there are people who go on resisting God's love to the very end, their fate will be annihilation. Eternal punishment is totally incompatible with all we know about God as revealed in Christ. Whether there are, or will be, any who will go on resisting to the point of annihilation, we do not know. The New Testament does not provide light here, and speculation seems profitless. This doctrine of hell abates nothing of its terrible quality. Hell is terrible and should be feared: but we should not fear God in that sense, and few people nowadays can be frightened into the Kingdom.

From all this it follows that we are very far indeed from dispensing with a doctrine of judgment. The judgment of God is a real, historical process that is taking place every day. We are judging ourselves all the time, destining ourselves either for a closer life with God or for the outer darkness. Death itself will no doubt bring a crisis of judgment, a moment of truth, but it will not be a new judgment, rather one that sums up and focusses all that has gone before. It will not be an arbitrary decision of God, but a revelation of what we really are, i.e. what we are in God's eyes.

The survival of the human personality after death is, of course, an assumption that must not be made lightly. The intimate involvement of the human personality with the physical organism in which it functions has been demonstrated even more clearly by recent discoveries in the field of neurology and cybernetics. On the other hand, no philosopher nor scientist has yet been able to convince the majority of his colleagues that the human mind is exactly and precisely identical with the human brain. Immaterialist accounts of the mind are still possible, as Bertrand Russell once very honestly admitted. Further, in the last twenty years or so respectable philosophical and scientific opinion has begun taking much more notice of evidence which suggests that the human personality survives death, even though the whole subject is still shrouded in darkness and to a regrettable extent the chosen field of the fraud and the crank. Christians have assurance of life after death from their religion, but they cannot afford arrogantly to ignore the fact that this is a field where science and philosophy and even the witness of other religions have a right to be heard also.

There has been a traditional disagreement between Catholics and

Protestants about the nature of the life after death. Catholics have claimed that most people will have to enter purgatory, an intermediate state in which the soul purges itself of all the sinful stains it has acquired in this life, before being ready to enter heaven, the nearer presence of God. At the Reformation Protestants rejected this doctrine because it had been abused. The Pope was in effect claiming on his own authority to shorten the time spent in purgatory by the issue of indulgences etc. (a practice which has not, unfortunately, been wholly abandoned yet). Protestants therefore held that the soul on death goes straight to heaven or hell, there to await the general resurrection at the *Parousia*. Anglicans are not committed as Anglicans to either view, but it would seem very reasonable, and more appropriate to our experience of God in this life, to believe that there is an intermediate state. Most of us are simply not ready for heaven, if by heaven we mean the immediate presence of God. We need a period (we cannot help using temporal words, unsuitable though they are) during which we can undergo that thorough repentance, turning around, rejection of selfishness that most of us have aimed at but not by any means fully attained in this life. Of course the suggestion that any ecclesiastical authority is competent to calculate how much of purgatory can be remitted by applying the merits of the saints, still more the practice whereby the authority makes financial profit by means of this process, is to be completely rejected as a piece of gross arrogance.

This does not mean that in purgatory we are cut off either from earth or heaven. Our friends on earth can pray for us, especially at the eucharist, where we join the whole company of heaven in worshipping God. It is a mere Protestant prejudice to hold that a Christian should not pray for the dead. If someone you love has died, what more and what better can you do for him or her than to pray for them? If we really believe in life with God after death, we will want to pray for the departed. Nor are we cut off either in this life or the next from the prayers of those who have gone before us out of this life. What is dangerous is to be too literal or too well informed about the prayers of the saints. We have absolutely no information on this matter from the New Testament. All we know is that the faithful departed do pray. This is a topic surely on which Christians must not be dogmatic and must tolerate divergent opinion. The Catholic Church of the future will have room for those who ask for the prayers of the saints and for those who do not. Perhaps it would be true to say that those who have had most experience of death and suffering are often most conscious of the reality of the Communion of Saints.

d. Providence and Predestination

Paul wrote to the Romans (8:28) that 'in everything God works for good with those who love him', but he ended this part of his letter by applying to Christians a quotation from Psalm 44:22, 'For thy sake we are being killed all day long; we are regarded as sheep to be slaughtered', and he expects his converts to endure 'tribulation, distress, persecution, famine, nakedness, peril and sword' (Rom. 8:35,36,37). He himself, as he tells us, had endured every sort of calamity caused by accident and by human malice. It is evident that for Paul God's providential care for his people is entirely compatible with their having to encounter worldly disaster and ill success. The idea that God is likely to emancipate his chosen ones from the slings and arrows of outrageous fortune is confined to the Old Testament. The New Testament is marked with the sign of the cross.

Christians throughout history, and not least Protestants in the heyday of Calvinism, have at times tended to forget this and to apply to the Church, or to themselves as the élite of the Church, the promises of worldly prosperity given to individuals or to Israel as a whole under the Old Testament, and – worse – to follow certain trains of thought in the Old Testament which directly identified worldly success with God's favour and worldly failure with God's displeasure. There is no justification at all for Christians to make these assumptions, tempting though they may be. From a purely worldly point of view, Jesus was a complete failure, Pontius Pilate a distinguished and successful official, and Barabbas a very lucky man. However we conceive of God's providence operating, we can be sure that it does not operate upon those lines. We can of course easily perceive that integrity, honesty and self-control are more likely to bring a man worldly success, and dishonesty, self-indulgence and improvidence likely to ruin a man. But it is also true that calculating ruthless selfishness will often bring success in this life and unselfish generosity and humanity will bring obscurity and even misfortune. We cannot judge God's activity by calculations such as these.

We believe in God's providence by faith, not because we can see it writ large in the careers of our more virtuous and successful friends and acquaintances. We believe that God controls history and that he is good and wise, and our belief in his providence is part of our trust in him. This does not rule out the possibility of our seeing events which happen in our lives and in particular circumstances applying to us as providential, even though we do so only in faith. It is open to us to believe that God sometimes lifts for a moment the curtain of mist which envelopes our life here and permits us occasionally to see his providence clearly working. But we cannot and must not pretend to see the whole strategy, and we must be honest enough to admit that sometimes things happen which appear to us to be most unprovidential, for instance when young people die suddenly or when some frightful example of cruelty or selfishness on a large scale occurs. On such occasions we are not called upon, in the words of the Irish poet, A. E. Russell, to 'crucify the mystery with words of good cheer'. It is better to be silent, and to recall that God chose to redeem the world by means of a man tortured to death, and that in the words of the great philosopher George Berkeley, 'rational happiness is not to be had in this life', and even then the mystery of pain and evil confronts us inexplicably. We should not try to explain it. Natural disasters, such as volcanoes, floods and earthquakes, frightful and destructive though they are, must be regarded as part of the condition the human race accepts for living on this planet. To say that God might have designed a better planet is cheap but unconstructive. As Bishop Butler constantly reminded the readers of his *Analogy of Religion*, we do not know the principles upon which God made and upon which he governs this world. We can only believe in him and trust him as a loving and good God. Perhaps against the instances of inexplicable evil we can weigh the equally inexplicable instances of good, the examples of those who run leper colonies, sacrifice their lives for others and voluntarily live alongside people in poor and wretched conditions in order to serve them and ameliorate their lot.

Some people find it difficult to reconcile prayer with God's providence. If God really loves us he will care for us. What difference can prayer make? But prayer is not primarily a pulling of strings with God; it is a speaking to and an act of faith in our heavenly Father. Jesus spoke eloquently of God's providence which extends even to sparrows, but he prayed long and often and taught his disciples to pray. Prayer is also a declaration of freedom, a sign that we do not believe that we live in a closed universe, that God is free and capable of ordering events according to his will. It is a sin to imagine that the effects of our prayer are calculable or automatic; this is indeed to treat God as a machine. But we have no right to assume that our prayer is ineffective and that the answering of our prayer in some way is beyond the scope of God's providence. Part of God's sovereignty is his resourcefulness.

Some theologians have recently been prepared to speak of God taking a risk in his policy towards mankind. It is not difficult to see how they can arrive at this conclusion. If we believe that God made the human race and that he not only permitted men and women to have free will but positively wished them to have it, that the creation of freely obedient and responsive beings was, so to speak, the whole point of the exercise, then it is hard to avoid the conclusion that God has communicated to man a share of his own freedom and creativity and has in so doing permitted something to enter the universe which he does not control, something quite new, genuinely unpredictable. Indeed the incarnation could be regarded as God's strategy to achieve control of this new thing. The poet Edwin Muir pictures Christ on the cross as 'riding against the Fall'. This is God, as it were, wagering himself against man's disobedience, making a throw to recapture man's allegiance by himself experiencing man's lot and making himself vulnerable to man's malice. But if we allow this way of looking at God's providence, we must be sure of two points. First, God is planning to recapture the lost position, so to speak, by persuasion and not by coercion. The pressure which God puts on man is moral only. He is not a Zeus punishing Prometheus. Secondly, we must believe that God will win in the end, just because he is God. Theories of a God who is only partially in control of the universe, of a constitutional monarch of the cosmos gravely hampered by strikes, will not do. God must and will bring about what he wants, if only (as Origen perceived) because he is eternal and man is not. But he has chosen to implement his strategy by the pattern of crucifixion – resurrection, weakness – strength, death – life, in that order. Nothing will alter his decision to win by suffering and love.

Language about God's decision should prepare the reader for a brief consideration of the thorny subject of predestination. The Bible, both in Old and New Testaments, in several places speaks of God as exercising predestination, i.e. as determining events beforehand and not least as determining the moral decisions of individuals (e.g. in hardening Pharoah's heart at the time of the Exodus). Paul could write in Romans 'for those whom he foreknew he also predestined to be conformed to the image of his son, in order that he might be the first-born among many brethren' (8:29), and he proceeds in the ninth and tenth chapters of the same letter to give what looks like an account of God both as predestinating some to salvation and also as condemning some to damnation long before they were born. The state of mind of Christians in the primitive Church, who expected an early end to the world, found these views congenial, but later Christian theologians did not. Origen, for instance, (and not Origen only) was willing to allow that God foreknows all that will happen, but not that he preordains it. For Origen, too, the idea that God condemns anyone to hell eternally was abhorrent; to add that he predestined them to this fate long before they were born is only to add a further degree of inadmissibility to the doctrine. Augustine, on the other hand, embraced what is called 'the double decree' enthusiastically, insisting that God both pre-destines a fixed number of people to salvation and reprobates the rest to eternal punishment in hell. The Middle Ages on the whole were cool towards a wholehearted acceptance of the 'double decree', but as Augustinianism returned with great power during the Reformation (which might be described as a quarrel between two sides of Augustine's mind), so did his doctrine of double predestination. Though Luther accepted the doctrine of predestination, Calvin adopted it much more fully and effectively, making the 'double decree' one of the central doctrines of his system.

The doctrine of predestination cannot be washed out of the New, Testament. But it can be pointed out that both Old and New Testaments witness quite as fully (indeed more fully) to man's moral freedom. There is in the Bible no whisper at all to suggest that man is a puppet or a machine operated by God. Here, as in other instances which we have seen, we face what appears to be an inconsistency in the biblical evidence. One cause of a doctrine of predestination is the conviction (which runs all through the Bible) of the sovereignty of God. 'Does evil befall a city unless the Lord has done it?', says Amos (3:6). 'I form light and create darkness, I make weal and create woe', says the Second Isaiah (45:7), speaking for God. The ancient Jew was so deeply convinced of God's mastery of events that he found it difficult to imagine that anything happened without God's direct agency in causing it, and he extended this even as far as the motives in men's hearts and their decisions and behaviour. A deep conviction of God's guidance in an individual's life will also often convince him that God has chosen him before he had any power of choice himself, as we see to be the case with Jeremiah (Jer. 1:4-10), and Paul (Gal. 1:15,16). But when all is said and done a doctrine of predestination must in the twentieth century remain an erratic boulder among doctrines. It is clearly impossible to retain it in its traditional form (even in the milder mediaeval version of it) if we are to adopt the views on man's freedom which have been advanced in this book. And if we favour universalism in any form (the theory that all men will in the end be saved), the traditional doctrine of predestination becomes quite unacceptable. Liberal theology, of which Clement of Alexandria and Origen in the third century were the first great representatives, has always inclined towards universalism. Some have even found universalist tendencies in Paul, relying on the eighth chapter of Romans, however ill this view may sort with his other views.

Recently Karl Barth has produced a new and attractive doctrine both of predestination and of reprobation. He rejects decisively Calvin's 'double decree' and throughout his great *Church Dogmatics* he flirts with, but never decisively adopts, universalism. He deals with predestination by a doctrine which is even more centred on Christ than that of Augustine or of Calvin; he accuses the traditional doctrine of predestination of having made no serious attempt to integrate Christ's work into its scheme. God has indeed predestined to salvation, he says, in that he predestined and determined from eternity the incarnation of his Son; all predestination must be concentrated and focussed on Christ. Similarly God has reprobated also, in that he decreed that his Son when incarnate should become a curse and be made sin for us. Consequently Christ has absorbed and removed reprobation, which is now no longer operative. And those who wish to be saved can, so to speak, inherit a predestined salvation by accepting God's offer in Christ. This is certainly not the traditional doctrine of predestination which envisages God working with a remorseless and mathematical determination, and which threatens all the rest of Christian doctrine with reduction to meaninglessness. But it is a delightful and stimulating adaptation of it, inspired by a deeply Christ-centred theology, and cannot be accused of liberalism.

Finally this section must deal with the subject of man's destiny. What has God in store for man when he reaches his fullest consummation, that credible but wellnigh inconceivable goal which Paul summed up in the pregnant word 'glory'? Whether this is to take place in each individual's personal experience beyond this life or in some winding-up of history at the end of the world is strictly irrelevant. The Greek tradition, from Athanasius onward, speaks of man as destined to become God. Indeed, more than a century before Athanasius Irenaeus had said that the Son of God became what we are that he might make us what he is, which apparently comes to the same thing. The Greek theologians speak openly of man as ultimately destined for divinization, *apotheosis*. Orthodox theologians, and others who sympathize with them, stoutly defend this language, though they are careful to explain that this does not mean that man becomes equal with God or absorbed into God. The only biblical text that they can cite to support this view is 2 Peter 1:4, 'that you may . . . become partakers of the divine nature'. Elsewhere the New Testament suggests that we may become partakers of God's life, but not of his nature.

We do not like this kind of language however carefully it may be guarded from misunderstanding. Until the Nicene Creed became absorbed into European culture the word 'god' (*theos*, *deus*) had a wide variety of meanings, ranging from a remarkable human being such as a philosopher or an emperor, through a large range of demigods or indefinitely divine beings, to God Almighty, the exclusive sole God of the Jews. But once the Nicene Creed had become thoroughly assimilated, there was no room left for ambiguity about God. There was only one, and twentieth-century man, no matter how godless he may be, knows only one meaning for the word 'God'. Even when the atheist denies God, he denies one God, not many; when people swear by God profanely it is by the single almighty God by whom they swear. It is therefore most undesirable to reintroduce into contemporary discourse another, long abandoned, use for the word 'god', one which has no meaning at all, and should have no meaning at all, for modern man. Here the Greek tradition ought to be prepared to abandon its entrenched conservatism for the sake of avoiding serious misunderstanding. If there is any meaning in describing man in his glorified state as god or as a god, then the meaning is a bad one which threatens to blur the boundary between man and God, between the Creator and the created. On this subject there can be no compromise. Man is not God, and never can be. The doctrine of the incarnation is neither that of God turning into man nor of man being deified.

The Western, Latin, theological tradition has consistently tended to speak of man's destiny in other and better terms. Taking its cue from Augustine, it has spoken of man as destined for 'blessedness' and for the vision of God, of man enjoying eternally the sight and the presence of God in tranquility and joy. All these words are of course inadequate to describe what they are trying to convey, but there is here a choice of inadequacies and we should opt decisively for this one. It was Lucifer who wanted to become God and who tempted Adam and Eve with the prospect of becoming 'like God' (Gen. 3:4). In place of this serpentine prospect we should substitute the beautiful and mysterious vision at the end of Dante's *Paradiso*. What matters for us in the end is not what we become, but what we contemplate.

VI · CHURCH, SACRAMENTS, AND MINISTRY

12 The Divided Church

a. The Church and Ecclesiasticism

Imagine a great section of rock which breaks away from a cliff and falls down onto the beach below. At first it will remain in the shape it bore when it broke away; but gradually by the action of the waves it will be broken up into smaller fragments, and finally, if long enough time is allowed, those smaller fragments will be ground down into rounded pebbles. By this time there will be no possibility of piecing the pebbles together so as to reconstruct the section of rock that originally fell. The rounded pebbles simply will not fit into each other.

This is an allegory for what has happened to the Western Church since the Reformation: the section of rock that fell from the cliff is the mediaeval Church. The pebbles represent what the various denominations into which that Church split have now become. It is not a question of fitting the divided parts of the Church together again: four hundred years of denominational rivalry and existence as independent churches have now so altered the 'denominations' that they cannot simply fit together again. Each denomination is structured so as to be independent of all the others. The consequence is that working for the unity of the Church, a common aspiration nowadays for some Christians, is inevitably regarded as a spare-time occupation. The average clergyman or minister is first of all bound to look to the needs of his own denomination (after all that is what he is paid to do). He cannot be expected to give more than occasional attention to the needs of Christians in other denominations. We thus have a situation today in which, though almost everyone admits that closer co-operation between the denominations is to be desired, in fact the denominations go on along their own paths. They do not pay any attention to the other 'churches' in the things that really matter most to them; worship, pastoral care, appointment of clergy.

The next few pages, to the end of section VI,12,(a), apply particularly to the Church of England and to one or two of the major denominations in Europe; they are not directly applicable to the churches of the USA, though American readers may find them sufficiently relevant to be of interest. Attempts at corporate reunion have been made, and have gained some limited success, notably the setting up of the United Reformed Church in England, a union between Congregationalists and Presbyterians: but a much bigger projected union, that between the Church of England and the Methodist Church in England, has failed, primarily because the Church of England could not face the dislocation which the union would have caused to its structure. The Church in the West, it seems, is permanently frozen into mutually exclusive denominational structures.

In the meantime however denominational structures are being eroded by lay action at the grass roots. Compared with the situation in England thirty years ago, there is today in practice in England a very wide measure of intercommunion. Christians take communion at the eucharists of other denominations and are not excluded. This is even true to a limited degree of the Roman Catholic Church. Also Christians in effect accept the clergy and ministers of other denominations as if their orders were valid, whatever be the official view of the denomination to which they belong. It seems therefore as if there will be a slow but steady approximation towards a state of general intercommunion and mutual acceptance of clergy, quite apart from any formal theological agreement or acts of union. This is unsatisfactory, because a rightly planned union could ensure that all the uniting churches were afforded the opportunity of sharing in all that is good in the traditions with which they unite, and the pragmatic, recognition-all-round method does not by any means ensure this: but even pragmatic union is better than no union at all.

b. The Mediaeval Hangover in the Church of England

The Church of England and the Roman Catholic Church in particular, and the Free Churches to a lesser degree, find themselves caught in the last quarter of the twentieth century in a mediaeval hang-over. That is to say, the whole structure and ethos is based on the assumption that there are two classes in the Church, male clergy who have all the power and know-how, and the laity (of both sexes) whose primary functions are to obey and to pray. This is a very sweeping generalization, because this mediaeval division between clergy and laity has been greatly modified of late in the Church of England (though not very much in the Roman Catholic Church). The Church of England now has a democratic constitution: laity serve on the General Synod, which has the final authority in the Church. The office of reader is now widely used and is open to women as well as men: but in two very important areas the mediaeval hangover still persists.

First, in the area of pastoral care: it is still assumed that the clergy are the shepherds and the laity are the sheep. Thus the image of pastoral activity is one in which the clergyman plans, gives advice, rebukes, and teaches: but in fact outside the official organization of the Church, this is not how pastoral care is carried out most effectively. There has grown up a widespread activity known as 'counselling' which proceeds on quite different lines. The relation of counsellor to counselled is not that of one who gives advice, rebukes, or teaches. It is more an enabling relationship, whose aim is to help the client to face his own problem, to come to his own decision. Consequently the clergyman, with his image of one who gives authoritative advice, often finds himself bypassed. This does not mean that the world runs its pastoral activity better than the Church, because the Church (thank God) is not co-terminous with any denomination or with all the denominations put together. Also the counsellors outside the Church structure are often themselves committed Christians: but it does mean that the priest-laity relationship in churches in an advanced industrial society is in urgent need of overhauling. What goes on inside the official Church is often less effective pastorally than what goes on outside it.

The second area in which we suffer from a mediaeval hang-over is our treatment of women inside the official structure of the Church. In almost all other organizations and walks of life; education, medicine, law, politics, diplomacy, business, women can rise to any position and are treated as colleagues and equals. Men are expected to be willing to serve under women, to treat them as absolute equals, to give them equal opportunities of advancement. Nobody could claim that this is true of the Church of England or the Roman Catholic Church. On the contrary, full-time work in the ministry of the Church of England offers only the most miserable prospect even for the most highly qualified woman: she cannot be ordained, and therefore cannot gain any of the influential positions in the Church. Her pay is miserably low, even compared with the by no means princely salaries of the clergy: when there is a question of redundancy, it is the woman worker who is the first to be axed. Quite apart from any theological question about the ordination of women, it is extremely dangerous for the future of the Church when the moral standards of the world outside are higher than those within the official structure of the Church: but undoubtedly this is the case as far as concerns the Church's employment of women. Most clergy simply do not know what it is like to work in genuine partnership with women, and too many clergy view the prospect of the ordination of women with suspicion because they are afraid of encountering more talented rivals.

This is not to suggest that there is no teaching ministry in the Church. There certainly is, but it is no longer confined to the clergy. Theology is now being studied in this country by more men and women than ever before in the history of Britain. Most of them are laity and intend to remain so. This means that the clergy are no longer the only experts in doctrine and tradition, and among the best qualified in theology today are many women. This is only just beginning to affect the life of the Church, but it is bound to do so widely in the end. This too will modify the relation between clergy and laity and will move us further away from the traditional 'Catholic' conception of how the priesthood should function.

We have prefaced our account of the Church with these two sections, because we believe that the divided nature of the Church, and its inability completely to adjust itself to functioning adequately in the last period of the twentieth century, in themselves constitute a sort of crisis for the Church. Unless it can improve its achievement in these two areas, it will not matter very much how we define the nature of the Church, for there will be very little Church left to define.

13 The Nature of the Church

There are two ways of regarding the origin of the Christian Church, both of them having some support in Scripture, and neither incompatible with the other. The first is to see the Church as a human institution founded by Jesus either when he praised Peter at Caesarea Philippi for acknowledging him as Christ (Matt. 16: 13–20) or when he breathed on the apostles after the resurrection (John 20: 19–23) or (as neither of these utterances is well authenticated historically) simply when he called his twelve apostles and gathered round him a band of disciples. There can be no doubt that this band of apostles and disciples constituted the continuing link between the days of the Lord's ministry in the flesh and the earliest days of the primitive Christian community after the resurrection. Here is one account of the origin or foundation of the Church, and one about whose historical reliability there can be no doubt. It should be noted that this is not to be confused with an account of the origins or foundations of the *ministry*. In the beginning the earliest apostles and disciples *are* the Church, not what we today would call the ministry (see below pp. 249–63), and if privileges are given or promises made to them these apply to the Church as a whole.

The other way of regarding the foundation or origin of the Church is that to be found in the letters written by Paul or attributed to him. Here no reference at all is made to Christ's foundation of the Church in the days of his flesh, but the Church springs out of the resurrection and the descent of the Spirit. The Church here is that community of people who are members of Christ's Body and who live in the Spirit. It is a charismatic, eschatological community consisting of those who have died with Christ and hope to rise with him; it is in fact quite simply those who are in Christ. Its members share Christ's sufferings, his riches, his poverty, his tribulation and his victory. They are intimately related to the risen Christ and also closely bound to each other. They have an extraordinary sense of liberty and of joy. This is the Church of Romans 12 and 1 Cor. 12 and 2 Cor. 8 and Ephesians 4.

It is clear from all the documents of the New Testament that the primitive Church united both aspects, even though different Christian groups and traditions have since then attempted to separate them or to express one and suppress the other. The early Church certainly exercised authority and was surprisingly conscious of possessing

Christ's authority. It forgave or retained sins, admitted to communion or excommunicated, sent missions, decided policy, such as the admission of Gentiles emancipated from the necessity of circumcision, faced and overcame crises both internal and external, and at the same time its constitution was, by the standards of the Church today, anarchic. It had no fixed creed, no liturgy of its own, no permanent ministers, no New Testament. Its early eucharist, if we are to judge by 1 Corinthians 10 and 11, must have presented a picture of sanctified chaos. At its meetings for worship people freely spoke with tongues and interpreted (both men and women) and prophesied, and uttered slogans like 'Come, Lord Jesus!' We cannot determine from Acts whether reception of the Spirit preceded baptism or baptism reception of the Spirit and what part (if any) the laying-on of hands took in Christian initiation, quite possibly because the early Christian community itself had not decided these matters. This primitive Church managed to combine unity and diversity, authority and freedom, spontaneity and discipline, in a manner which has hardly ever been reproduced since and which we can only envy. Above all, the primitive Church seemed to have a capacity for unanimity, for acting as a whole and taking decisions not by head-counting nor by leaving the decision to an authoritative leader but by reaching an unanalysed agreement of all. Whatever developments therefore later occurred in the structure of the Church and its institutions must be reckoned as occurring within the Church as expressions of its life and its capacity to adjust to changing circumstances. There is no group set over the Church nor established as independent of the Church as a whole. No authoritative individual derives his authority from Christ by a line of command separate from the rest of the Church. No specially commissioned élite within the Church was marked out from the beginning as bearing authority distinct from the authority of the rest. Christ's authority comes to the individuals or groups from the Church and in the Church. Christ is present in his Spirit giving authority, and the whole Church bears and expresses that authority. It may of course delegate or entrust that authority to individuals, but it is from Christ in the Church that all authority is derived.

It is a far cry from the primitive Church to the heavily clericalized, institution-ridden, deeply divided Church of today, laden with nineteen centuries of ecclesiastical history. But when we say 'the Church of today', we beg the question. Which and what is the Church of today? We could answer that question in a number of ways. We could attempt to identify the true Church among the hundreds of Christian bodies laying claim to the name of Church, and stigmatize all who belong to the others as outside the Church. Or we could confine the brand of authenticity to a few major bodies characterized either by having what we consider the correct form of ministry or what we estimate to be geniune catholic doctrine (recognizing three 'branches' of the Church, Catholic, Orthodox and Anglican, and no others), and unchurch all the rest. Or swinging to the other extreme, we could declare that God alone knows who are his own, and that it is impossible or undesirable to determine any limits for the Church at all, or we could confine the Church to those who have had what seems to us the authentic experience of Christ.

The attempt to determine the true Church in a hard and fast way by its ministry has a number of drawbacks. It is liable to die the death of a thousand qualifications, as more and more exceptions or partial exceptions to the original hard-and-fast rule have to be made. This is the case with the theologians of the Roman Catholic Church today. Again, the claim of exclusive authenticity is usually based on dubious and uncertain historical grounds, such as the assumption that Jesus himself directly founded an episcopal ministry. This applies to Catholics, Orthodox and Anglicans. Finally we cannot help thinking that there is something profoundly alien to the mind of Christ in denominating one's own community the true Church and then looking out over the bulwarks of this safe citadel in order to determine the status of other Christians. The Good Shepherd did not stay in his fold secure in the conviction that his was the authentic, genuine, Catholic fold. The proper attitude towards lost sheep is to get alongside them. Anxiety as to whether we belong to the true Church or not is dangerously near being sub-Christian:

> Is the window bar made fast, is the door under lock and bolt? . . .
> Does the watchman walk by the wall?
> Does the mastiff prowl at the gate?

This is not the proper state of mind of those who have been called to the glorious liberty of the sons of God.

To attempt to determine the true Church by calculating which denomination preaches and teaches Catholic doctrines is a task of great complexity and uncertainty, as perhaps the preceding chapters in this book have shown. To subordinate the Church to the test of religious experience is to launch out onto a chartless sea of subjectivity. Only those whose knowledge of religious experience is narrow and restricted would be foolhardy enough to undertake such an enterprise.

All the approaches to the subject hitherto have implicitly assumed that we can define Christ by the Church. Where the Church (defined by one criterion or another) is, there is Christ. Might it not be better to reverse the process and to define the Church by Christ? Where Christ is, there somehow in some form the Church must be. If we recognize anybody as knowing Christ, believing in him and belonging to him, that person must belong to the Church, because the Church is inseparable from Christ. We have not perhaps solved the problem, but at least we may have approached it in the right order. We still have to determine how one belongs to Christ. We might answer, 'By baptism', if that answer had not been seriously prejudiced by the widespread practice of infant baptism, which divorces faith from baptism. We might answer, 'By faith', but here once again we launch ourselves onto a sea of uncertainty. How much faith? What sort of faith? How do I test whether my faith has decisively united me to Christ and kept me in him continuously? This answer comes perilously near to saying that we will ourselves into Christ, and this conclusion is emphatically contradicted by all Christian tradition. Again, the Church is a community and indeed there is nothing whatever in the New Testament to suggest that it is not a visible community. A visible community cannot be recognized by an invisible sign – faith. Certainly all through the ages baptism has been recognized by the great majority of denominations as the sign and means of entry to the Church, and baptism has always been (though too often clumsily and inefficiently) associated with faith. We must conclude that the normal way to describe members of the Church is to say that they are those who have been baptized and who have faith in Christ. We must recognize that there appear to be exceptions at both ends, to to speak; there are those who have been baptized but who have never shown any faith at all; their membership of the Church must be purely nominal, if it can be said to exist at all. And there are those who obviously have faith but have not been baptized. We must not restrict the Holy Spirit by unbreakable rules. These people must be thought to belong to the Church. But normally we can define the Church by both faith and baptism; nobody having both these signs should be regarded as outside the Church. It is, of course, possible to try to refine further here and to begin the process of detecting an inner Church or a more Catholic Church or a truer Church within the Church. But this is in effect to say that some people are more in Christ than others, even that some people have more Christ than others, that Christ is more available to some people than others. This restricting of Christ must be distasteful and wrong. This whole question must be distinguished from the question about the best form of ministry or the best form of organization for the Church. These are unaffected by any decision which we may make about the definition of the Church, which must depend upon our view of faith and of baptism.

Another point which must be considered is the relation of the Church in God's design to the empirical Church, the Church as we encounter it in ordinary life. The Church is not simply just another human organization like the United Nations or the Red Cross. It is divine as well as human, indwelt by the Spirit as well as subject to the assaults of the world, the flesh and the devil. The Church is given, not made by human hands, as the sacraments of eucharist and baptism are given and the Gospel is given. What is the relation of this given Church to the Church as we know it, shabby, unsuccessful, groping, frightened?

Several answers could be given to that question. It is possible to see an almost exact identity between the given Church and the empirical Church; at times during the Middle Ages this disastrous theory was, if not entertained, at least apparently put into practice. It is a disastrous theory because the obvious failings and sins of the Church, laity and clergy, institutions and pretensions, give the lie to the idea directly and only compromise the holiness of the Church. Another solution is to say that though individuals in the Church are sinful the Church as a whole cannot sin and cannot be misled. This is the answer both of Orthodoxy and of Rome. But if all the Church's members are to a greater or lesser degree sinful, how can the whole be sinless? Christ is sinless but if the theory means no more than that it ends in a truism. The picture of sinful people composing a sinless Church and fallible people producing an infallible Church is a strange one. Where precisely is the Church sinless? Where precisely is the Church infallible? The Orthodox and the Roman Catholics have concrete answers to this last question. The former say that the utterances of general councils are infallible, the latter that the utterances of the Pope in certainly narrowly defined circumstances are infallible. But the Orthodox allow that there has been no general council for 1192 years and the Catholics that it is very difficult to be sure when precisely the Pope is fulfilling the conditions laid down for infallibility. These theories seem more academic than practical.

Perhaps the best way of looking at this difficult question is to recall once more the Christians' conviction that they are living in the Last Age. Christians are people *in via*, still on pilgrimage, people who stand between the Cross and the End, living in an age which has yet to be consummated. Grandiose claims for the empirical Church should be submitted to the 'not yet' of the New Testament. God has created and gathered his Church in his Spirit and given it a dynamic calling, as he has given each individual Christian a dynamic calling in justifying him in Christ. It is the Church's task continually through history to become what it is, to answer its calling to reach in truth and integrity and in its own obedience and faithfulness that status which God has for his own part originally given it in Christ. This is why it is right and proper to be concerned about unity, about ecumenical rapprochement, about orders and ministry and the continuity and the structures of the Church, even though these questions today may seem *vieux jeu* and not as exciting nor as essential as others. The relation of the empirical Church to the Church in God's design is the relation of the Church *in via* to the Church consummated and perfected. But because the Church is the Body of Christ, because it is indwelt by the Holy Spirit, it still must strive to respond, to approximate, to fulfil its calling, to achieve greater unity, greater honesty, greater charity.

The New Testament offers us many different images of the Church. The Church is described as a flock of sheep: (e.g. Luke 12:32; John 10:7–21; 21:15–17; Acts 20:28,29; 1 Peter 5:2,3); as a temple (e.g. 1 Cor. 3:16, 17; 2 Cor. 6:16; Eph. 2:21; 1 Peter 2:4, 5), as an ark (1 Peter 3:18–21), as an olive tree (Rom. 11:19–24), and as a family (e.g. Gal. 6:10 and Eph. 2:19). Surprisingly, in view of the development of the Church in the Middle Ages, it is never described as an army. We shall here confine ourselves to two of the most important and widely-used images, that of a people on the march and that of the Body of Christ.

That the Church should be thought of as a people is not surprising, because at an early point Christians began to regard themselves as a new people of Israel, superseding the old. It was an easy step to think of the Church in a hostile and potentially dangerous world as travelling through the wilderness, subject to the same discipline and open to the same temptations as Israel in the wilderness of old. This is one of the dominant images of the Church. It occurs again and again in the Letters in the New Testament (e.g. Rom. 9:25, 26; 10:21; 11:1; 15:10; 1 Cor. 10:7; Heb. 4:9; 8:8–13; 10:30; 13:12ff; Titus 2:14; Rev. 18:4); perhaps most obviously in the eleventh and twelfth chapters of Hebrews and 1 Peter 2:1–9. It is significant that it should have been taken up as one of the main images of the Church used in the Constitution on the Church of the Second Vatican Council. This particular image brings into prominence the provisional nature of the Church's existence. The Church is a people on a pilgrimage, moving towards a future whose outlines it cannot wholly foresee, living in an in-between age, waiting for a goal, an objective, a consummation. It plays down the idea that the Church is a body where everything is decided, taped, formally defined, magisterially fixed. It points to the eschatological dimension of the Church. It emphasizes that the Church lives by faith. It suggests a Church whose limits are not precisely fixed. It prepares the Church for encounter with vicissitude and adventure and opposition. It suggests a Church which has found it necessary to dispense with unnecessary baggage, to submit to the process of what Pope John XXIII called *aggiornamento* (bringing up to date), a Church whose face is turned to the future. It is altogether admirable as an image of the Church in the twentieth century.

The image of the Church as the Body of Christ is confined to the Pauline writings in the New Testament. As a matter of fact we must make a distinction here: in 1 Corinthians and Romans the Church is referred to as the Body of Christ (1 Cor. 10: 16–17; 12: 12f, 20, 27): but in Colossians and Ephesians, which many scholars believe to have been written by a disciple of Paul after his death (Col. 1: 18; 2: 19; 3: 15; Eph. 1: 23; 2: 16; 4: 4; 5: 30), a different figure is used; Christ is the Head, the Church is the Body. This latter figure presents no real difficulties; it is simply a striking way of presenting the close link between the risen Christ and believers, like the 'vine and branches' figure found in the Fourth Gospel: but the figure actually used by Paul, wherein the Church is equated with the Body of Christ, presents difficulties. Partly these are caused by the various senses in which Paul uses the word *sōma*, usually translated 'body'. It is used for Christ's risen body, for the Church as the Body of Christ, for the risen bodies which Christians will receive at the *Parousia*, for the actual physical body in this life, and for the body of Christ to be discerned at the eucharist. We can perhaps best approach the problem by asking: why did Paul work out this doctrine of the Church as the Body of Christ? The answer seems to be that he wanted to explain how Christians, who have not yet experienced the resurrection of the body, are related to Christ, who has. His solution was to say that they are related to Christ by becoming members of his Body. By this he seems to mean the area or dimension in which those who are 'in Christ' (i.e. Christian believers) live: but Christians are living in the period between the coming of Christ and the *Parousia*, hence they are part of his body rather by anticipation. In this respect the Spirit is a pledge of the full state which is to come; so that, though they are members of Christ's body in one sense now, they are moving towards the full inheritance, i.e. the time when, at the *Parousia*, they will have the same sort of environment (which Paul calls a 'spiritual body') as Christ has now (see 1 Cor. 15: 42–44; Phil. 3: 20–21).

The doctrine of the Church as the Body of Christ is therefore a thoroughly eschatological one. It only makes sense in a context of keen expectation of the future. This is quite consistent with Paul's use of 'body' in an eucharistic context also: the eucharist is the rite in which we encounter the Lord in the Spirit and look forward to his coming. The early Christians behaved at the eucharist as if they were already in heaven. Charles Wesley, with his fine sacramental theology, hit it off very well when he called the eucharist the 'antepast of heaven'. The body of Christ broken for us at the eucharist cannot be dissociated from the community of the faithful as the Body of Christ. When Paul speaks of some Christians at the eucharist 'not discerning the body' in I Corinthians 11:29, he means not recognizing the community of the faithful as the Body of Christ.

But we do not believe in a literal *Parousia*. What relevance then has this doctrine of the Church as the Body of Christ to us? It can have a double significance for us: it can serve to remind us that God in Christ really has established a new relationship with man. This perplexing figure of 'the body' ought to help us to appreciate the radical and intimate nature of that relationship: and secondly, the forward-looking quality of the figure need not be lost on us. As long as we think of the Church as the Body of Christ, we can hardly forget the eternal dimension, the far greater majority of Christians who have died, but who share membership of the Body with us. In a way which the figure of the pilgrim people of God cannot do, it serves to remind us of the Communion of Saints.

But there are dangers in this figure of the Church as the Body of Christ: we must not presume upon it so as to endow the Church with the qualities of Christ. This is a temptation to which the Catholic wing of the whole Church is prone. On the strength of this figure the Church has been described as 'an extension of the incarnation'. It has at various times been termed infallible, impeccable, divine. There is no trace of this in Paul's thought and this sort of language too often leads to arrogant and triumphalist claims being made on behalf of the Church, or (worse still) on behalf of Church leaders. The Church is the Body of Christ, but she is also an assembly of sinners. Let us remember Blaise Pascal's dictum: 'Mankind is made up of two groups of people: sinners who think that they are righteous, and saints who know that they are sinners.'

For all this, the Church does collectively learn some wisdom as it moves through history. It does not lose awareness of its own history, or if it does it suffers damage to the fullness of its life. This awareness of history is what we call the element of catholicity. Too often catholicity has been presented as a sort of qualifying test: Christian bodies which did not measure up to a required standard of catholicity were disqualified from full church status. A more satisfactory way of regarding catholicity is to look on it as an element that is present in the life of every body of Christians in a greater or lesser degree. It is the awareness of history, the readiness to consult tradition, the sense of continuity with the past. It should not be allowed to harden into an inflexible rule that makes the past into the Church's tyrant, but the attempt to repudiate catholicity altogether always ends in failure. The Church cannot ignore its past. The usual marks of catholicity are a careful preservation of ministerial succession, emphasis on the authority of the ministry, possession of a fixed liturgy, encouragement of monastic orders for men and women, the use of icons or statues in churches, greater emphasis on the visual element in worship. Today, with the growth of the ecumenical movement, catholicity is not confined to those parts of the Church which are traditionally regarded as 'catholic', i.e. the Roman Catholic Church, the Orthodox Church, and to some extent the Anglican Communion. Nearly all denominations are now open to the influence of a more catholic conception of how the Church's life should be ordered, just as large sections of the Roman Catholic Church have woken up to the need for constant reformation in the life of the Church.

14 Sacraments

a. Baptism and Confirmation

There are only two sacraments whose origin we can with any confidence ascribe to Jesus Christ himself, and they are consequently sometimes called Dominical sacraments. These are baptism and the eucharist. Even in the case of baptism the direct Dominical institution is by no means securely established. The command of Jesus at the very end of the First Gospel (Matt. 28: 19), immensely effective though it is as an ending to the gospel, cannot be regarded as the actual words of Jesus. The Synoptic evangelists record that Jesus was baptized. John's Gospel is curiously confused on the subject, describing Jesus as baptizing, but at one point (4: 2) declaring in parenthesis that Jesus did not baptize but that his disciples did. There can be no doubt, however, that Jesus actually was baptized by John the Baptist. The embarrassment which it causes the evangelist (Matt. 3: 13–17) is sufficient assurance of that. It is quite possible that Jesus did command his disciples to baptize, but even if he did not, the example which he gave by allowing himself to be baptized by John would have been sufficient for Christians to adopt baptism as the rite of initiation to their number. It seems to us unwise to conclude that baptism was originally meant to be either an imitation of the baptism which Jews practised for Gentile converts to their faith or a substitute for circumcision. The earliest Christian males would all have been circumcised and could hardly have envisaged themselves as proselytes. Baptism is evidenced too early for it to have arisen as a Christian alternative to circumcision for Gentiles.

From the earliest moment, witnessed equally in the narratives of Acts and the Letters of Paul, baptism was the ceremony of initiation into the Christian Church. In Acts people invariably believe first and are then baptized into Christ for the 'remission of sins'. In Paul the relationship of faith and baptism is subtler and closer. In the classical passages (Rom. 6: 1–14; 1 Cor. 12: 12, 13; Gal. 3: 23–29) there is no question of baptism being a public declaration or demonstration of what faith has already accomplished in fact. It is rather that baptism is the outer and faith the inner side of the same act, or that baptism represents God's handling of man and faith man's response to God's act. Baptism represents God in Christ reaching man and man by faith at the same moment committing himself to God. Baptism involves the whole man; not merely his mind, not merely his spirit, but his whole existence. 'If anyone is in Christ, he is a new creation' (2 Cor. 5: 17), and it is in baptism that he achieves the state of being 'in Christ'. Paul of course assumes that baptism applies to adults capable of faith. Though the New Testament envisages faith before baptism and faith at baptism nowhere does it clearly envisage the state of affairs which applies to the vast majority of baptized Christians today, baptism before faith.

The relation of the Holy Spirit to baptism in Acts is quite uncertain, even fluid. There are instances of people receiving the Holy Spirit and then being baptized (Acts 2: 1–12, 41; 10: 44–48), and other instances of people being baptized and later receiving the Holy Spirit (8: 9–24). Usually however in Acts baptism and reception of the Spirit are closely associated. In Paul, and indeed elsewhere in the New Testament, baptism in water and reception of the Holy Spirit are simultaneous or at least inseparable. Indeed Paul's doctrine of the Spirit and of the Church demands this.

The New Testament doctrine of baptism is, as might be expected, conditioned by the 'overlap' of the present age and the Age to Come. It is a baptism into Christ's death, a dying with Christ and a crucifying of the old man, and in this sense it looks back to the crucifixion. But it is also an immersion in the Spirit, an encounter with the new, heavenly world and age which the Spirit brings with him, a proleptic sharing of the joys of redemption, a foretaste of resurrection (1 Peter 3: 21). It is an interim rite for entry into the company of those who are waiting for the full unfolding of God's strategy for mankind. It fits into that pattern of the overlap of two ages, the new glorious age of the Messiah and the old evil age that is on its way out, which characterizes and explains much of the thought of the New Testament, not least that of Paul.

One of the implications of this view of baptism is that we must reject either too spiritualising or too materialistic a view of baptism. On the one hand, baptism is not inoculation. We are not vaccinating people with grace when we baptize them, and to conduct baptismal practice in such a way as to give this impression is a disgraceful misuse of the sacrament. Baptism is neither automatic nor magical. On the other hand we do not initiate ourselves into Christ by our own religious experience. Baptism is not an acted parable of a reality which faith has already accomplished. Dr. Beasley-Murray, much the most convincing of modern Baptist writers upon the subject, while maintaining the case for believers' baptism with arguments that are not easy to answer, admits candidly that baptism is sacramental, i.e. it conveys grace, it does not merely symbolize grace given elsewhere. Baptism means entry to the Church. We do not invent the Church; we do not spin it out of the depths of our unconscious. Baptism in one sense is the Church reaching us from outside ourselves; there is an objectivity about it quite distinct from our subjective selves. It is thereby also what Article XXV of the XXXIX Articles calls a badge or token, and the Catechism in the Book of Common Prayer a pledge. It is an objective reassurance to our minds, which are easily deceived by our imagination, that God has received us in Christ, that we belong to his people, his flock, his Body. And, as is the function of sacraments, baptism conveys that which it signifies, it is an 'effectual sign' of God actually justifying us and living in us. But, like all God's gifts, it is a double-edged mercy, a dynamic calling and enabling by which if we do not respond we are judged. Baptism demands faith, as in this life all access to God demands faith. In order to be saved we must indeed believe; but we do not manufacture that salvation in our own consciousness. It reaches us in the sacrament of baptism.

The Catholic Church has held from at least the second century onwards that baptism is essential for salvation, perhaps influenced by Mark 16: 16 (part of a passage which did not form an original element in Mark's Gospel, but was written probably about AD 120). Today educated Christians cannot be expected to hold this belief literally. In fact the Church has always been ready to make certain exceptions: if, for example, someone desires baptism but is arrested and put to death before he can receive it, he would certainly be regarded as having received 'the baptism of desire'. We must however be more liberal than this: we must not condemn to damnation millions of people who have never heard of Christ. Nor must we arbitrarily deny the possibility of salvation to those Christians, such as members of the Society of Friends and of the Salvation Army, who conscientiously refuse to practise baptism.

But, though baptism is not essential for the Christian individual's salvation, it is essential for the continued existence of the Church on earth. Those who have lived in a wholly non-Christian culture soon realize that if in such circumstances the Church does not baptize its new members, it runs a grave risk of being completely absorbed by the surrounding culture and losing its identity. In a Europe which is gradually losing its originally Christian culture, this factor is likely to play an increasing role in the future. We conclude therefore that baptism is entirely necessary for the historical continuance of the Church.

Today for the great majority of Christians in the West baptism means infant baptism: but in New Testament times on the contrary baptism meant adult baptism. It is a much debated question whether there is any evidence for the baptism of infants in the New Testament, and it certainly cannot be described as having been decided either way. Infant baptism as a universal practice only dates from the time when all of Western Europe became nominally Christian. By this time Augustine's teaching on infant baptism had become orthodox doctrine. He taught that infants dying unbaptized went to hell. The fact that he envisaged a rather milder sort of hell than that prepared for adults did little to mitigate the harshness of this sentence. Baptism as soon as possible after birth became the universal practice. Various institutions, such as the provision of godparents and the occurrence of confirmation by the bishop in later years, were devised in order to remedy the unsatisfactory situation whereby what had been in New Testament times a rite in which an adult conscientiously confessed his faith had developed into something performed over helpless infants.

We today inherit this situation, with the added complication that still a great many parents who bring their children to be baptized in this country do not intend to bring them up in a Christian environment in any but the vaguest and most nominal sense. What are we to make of this? Three courses are possible. We can just go on as we are, pathetically hoping that baptism not followed by Christian nurture may do *something* for the child. In other words, we can resignedly accept the fact that we are in a position where we have no choice but to misuse the sacrament of baptism. Secondly, we can go to the other extreme: we can refuse to baptize infants, as members of the Baptist Church do. But this is not satisfactory either; baptism is the rite by which one enters the Christian Church. Are we to say that children cannot be Christians? Though infant baptism is often misused, it can be a meaningful rite: where the parents are committed Christians, where there is a Christian environment to receive the child, where confirmation is seen as the renewal of baptism, the acceptance of the promises made on behalf of the child, where one's baptism day is kept as one's birthday in Christ. We are not justified in abolishing infant baptism.

But we can take a third course: we can discourage baptism for the children of nominal Christians. It is much more satisfactory not to ask people to make promises which they have no intention of keeping. In some parts of the Anglican Communion, and perhaps in other denominations as well, adult baptisms are increasing, and in some infant baptisms are decreasing. This is a hopeful sign. An adult baptism should be a solemn and splendid event, like the eucharist. It is high time that we effected for the sacrament of baptism the same invigorating revival that all Christians have brought about for the eucharist during the last half century. If this makes fewer infant baptisms, and more unbaptized children, that does not matter at all. We do not now hold that those who die unbaptized are destined for eternal punishment. Baptism is the glorious rite by which we enter Christ's Church, not the obol which we pay to Charon in order to cross the Styx. Let us hope that the next half century will see fewer infant baptisms and far more baptisms of adults.

The origins of the rite of confirmation are obscure and its history varied. Some Anglican writers (A. J. Mason, Gregory Dix) have tried to detect its presence in the pages of the New Testament, in such passages as Acts 8: 14–17; 19: 6 and Hebrews 6: 2. And the Confirmation Service in the Book of Common Prayer (1662) appears in places to endorse this view. Those who have thought that the rite was practised by the apostles have usually claimed that it was from the beginning part and parcel of the whole rite of Christian initiation, an indispensable appendix to baptism by water. Usually people who have taken this view have argued that water-baptism conferred forgiveness of sins whereas confirmation conveyed reception of the Holy Spirit.

These theories are, however, impossible to sustain. The evidence in the New Testament is scrappy and this interpretation of it depends too largely on an argument from silence. Few, if any, responsible scholars would defend such views today. It is only Anglicans who have ever maintained that confirmation is a sacrament generally necessary to salvation, and not many even among Anglicans have seriously put forward this theory. The consequences of such theories if they were true would be startling. They would mean that millions of Christians ever since the Middle Ages (when bishops did not always find time or opportunity for confirming) had not received the Holy Spirit, including (for instance) thousands of Anglicans in America during the seventeenth and eighteenth centuries. This kind of doctrinaire theory refutes itself.

It is evident to historians of the ancient Church that by about the year 200 a number of additional rites and ceremonies had become attached to the sacrament of baptism. They varied in form and in the order in which they were performed in relation to baptism. They consisted of such things as anointing with oil or with chrism by a presbyter or by the bishop or the laying-on of hands or a hand by presbyter or bishop; the ceremonies varied from place to place. There were also other ceremonies more or less widespread such as giving the candidates milk and honey to eat, and clothing them after baptism in a white garment. Out of this medley of ceremonies arose the practice of confirmation, that is to say the custom that after baptism and before the candidates joined in the eucharist the bishop should either anoint them with chrism or lay his hands on their heads. A number of ancient authors, such as Cyprian, write as if this rite conferred the Holy Spirit, but this erroneous idea was not widespread in the early Church. Indefiniteness about the meaning of confirmation was encouraged by the fact that the vast majority of Christians in the first few centuries were initiated in a single long rite including baptism, confirmation and first eucharist, usually on Easter Eve.

As the Church grew and dioceses became larger, it became impossible for the bishop to baptize or to confirm every single member of his flock. And by about the year 600 infant baptism had become general in both the Eastern and the Western Church. The consequence was that the custom was widely adopted of the bishop consecrating oil for the parishes of his diocese every so often and distributing it to the clergy. The parish clergy would then at baptisms anoint the infant with the consecrated oil after he had been baptized with water. This custom is still maintained universally throughout the Eastern Orthodox Church, which also observes the practice of communicating infants. In the West, however, during the general reformation of church life which took place during the reign of the Emperor Charlemagne in the eighth and ninth centuries, bishops as a sign of pastoral zeal, and apparently inspired by the example of the apostles as described in the eighth chapter of Acts, began the practice of travelling round their dioceses and laying hands on children of maturer age than infants, regarding this ceremony as a sacrament of strengthening for the full undertaking of the Christian life. It is from this way of administering confirmation that the Anglican Reformers in the sixteenth century took their cue. They abolished the ceremony of anointing with oil in the baptismal rite, but retained and enhanced the ceremony of confirmation by laying-on of hands as a preparation for adult Christian life and as a necessary preliminary to receiving Holy Communion.

Such is the pedigree of the modern Anglican rite of confirmation. It is clear that it can claim institution neither by Christ nor by the apostles. But that does not deprive it of significance nor of usefulness. At the moment among the Roman Catholics it is administered to children, not infants, at quite a young age independently of their being admitted to Holy Communion. Among Anglicans it is used for two purposes, both as a strengthening or preparatory rite for children or adults before they are admitted to receive Holy Communion, and as a ceremony of admission to the Anglican Church of people who are becoming Anglicans after being members of non-episcopal communions. The significant element in both uses of this rite is the presence of the bishop. He represents on both occasions the universal Church in a manner in which the parish priest cannot; he is a reminder that membership of the Anglican communion is membership of the Catholic Church. Much is often made at confirmation of the presence of the Holy Spirit, and not least in both the old (1662) and new rites of confirmation in the Anglican communion. This is understandable and proper, but it should not reach the point of suggesting that the candidates have not received the Holy Spirit already at baptism nor that they now receive a kind of new and maturer version of the Spirit. It is difficult for a bishop administering confirmation who is both knowledgeable and honest to say to the candidates precisely what is happening to them. Baptism admits to full membership of the Church, but full membership cannot be exercised until the Christian has become a communicant. Confirmation as at present administered in the Anglican Communion might be regarded as a rite of admission to effective full membership, which has been potentially possessed since baptism. The idea that confirmation is ordination for the laity is fanciful and likely to introduce unnecessary confusion both of thought and language. On the other hand, confirmation might be regarded as a kind of handing on of the Christian tradition by the older to the younger generation in the Church; the service lends itself well to this interpretation, which could perhaps be more widely used.

Confirmation is also, in the Anglican use of it at least, a renewal by the individual of the vows taken for him when he was baptized as an infant. In this aspect it is a kind of remedy for the deficiencies of infant baptism, and as such has great importance as long as infant baptism remains the prevailing custom in the Church. The difficulties facing the administration of confirmation today arise out of the tension caused in contemporary Western society between confirmation as a renewal of baptismal vows and confirmation as a rite of admission to the eucharist. There is much to be said for the admission of children to Holy Communion at an early age, say 10 or 11. But the freedom which we give to young people in Western society means that just at or just after the period when they are confirmed they are very likely to react against many inherited beliefs and practices and to insist upon acting and thinking for themselves, however crudely. If they are to be asked to renew baptismal vows it would be more realistic to invite them to do this between the ages of 17 and 21, when their period of reaction, confusion and finding of identity is likely to be over, or to be producing less turmoil. A recent report (the *Ely Report*) presented to the General Synod of the Church of England has made the suggestion that admission to Holy

Communion be separated from confirmation, and that confirmation might be postponed until the candidates are older than they usually are at present, and regarded primarily as a renewal of vows and acceptance of responsibility as active members of the Church by those who are mature enough to make this decision. There is much to be said for this view.

Confirmation is therefore a rite caught between the old 'Volks-kirche' idea of the Church as co-terminous with the nation, which still lingers obstinately in the vestigial form of the demand for infant baptism, and the more recent idea of the Church as a voluntary association of those who in a pluralist society opt for the Christian faith. The fact, already alluded to in this book (see above, p. 227), that statistics for infant baptism are slowly dropping, added to the fact that statistics (still very small) for adult confirmations are climbing, may point to a more satisfactory use of this potentially fruitful rite in the future.

It should be noted finally that the precise action of laying-on of hands must not be insisted upon rigorously. Not only mediaeval bishops, but Anglican bishops in the early nineteenth century frequently for reasons of convenience confirmed by blessing at a distance. This only serves to underline how unsatisfactory it is to try to align the rite of confirmation with six other 'sacraments', all as far as possible regarded as similar modes of God's activity.

b. The Eucharist

There are at least four, or (if we count Luke's text as in effect providing us with two) perhaps five accounts of the institution of the eucharist by Jesus, of which Paul's (1 Cor. 11:23–26) is the earliest. A careful reading of the eleventh chapter of 1 Corinthians must convince the reader that Paul is not there assuming that the Corinthian Christians had heard the narrative of the institution repeated at the celebration of the eucharist, but is reminding them of something which they ought to know; Paul's account therefore represents the early Christian tradition which he had received when he was converted and had passed on to his converts, and is very valuable indeed. The tenth and eleventh chapters of this Letter represent almost all the comment upon the eucharist to be found in the New Testament apart from the Gospels. But it is clear that the eucharist possesses the same eschatological character as baptism. It is an ordinance for those who live between the cross and the End. It looks back to what Jesus did and said 'on the night when he was betrayed' (1 Cor. 11:23) and recalls his death on behalf of all men. But it also looks forward to the *Parousia*. Paul comments on it, 'For

231

as often as you eat this bread and drink the cup, you proclaim the Lord's death *until he comes*' (1 Cor. 11:26). It is also an expression of the unity and solidarity of Christians in Christ (1 Cor. 10:14–17), and (as we have seen above p. 221) is closely connected in Paul's mind with his doctrine of the Body of Christ. The early eucharist as witnessed to in the New Testament is therefore likely to have that dynamism which colours almost all the thought of the primitive Church. It will speak of action, of movement, of response, of drama, of event, rather than of static presence, status, or substance.

Controversy has raged round the eucharist in the Church of the West more fiercely than round any other doctrine. It was not without controversy that there was established in the heyday of the Middle Ages (1215) the doctrine of transubstantiation, the dogma that when the bread and wine are consecrated by the priest during the Mass the substance of the bread and wine disappears, its place being taken by the body and blood of Christ and only the accidents, (such things as smell and colour, feel and taste) remain. Though all the Reformed traditions of the sixteenth century repudiated the late mediaeval view of the Mass (or at least what they took to be that view), the Reformers could not agree upon an alternative doctrine. It is ironical to witness Luther and Zwingli earnestly contending about the meaning of the words *Hoc est corpus meum* (this is my body), each insisting firmly upon his own interpretation of the word 'is', apparently unaware that behind the Greek (which they knew to be behind the Latin) was the Aramaic which was certainly the language used by Jesus at the Last Supper, and that Aramaic has no word for 'is'. They were therefore fighting fiercely about a word which Jesus did not use. Calvin's eucharistic doctrine was quite different from that of Luther and of Zwingli. And Cranmer's? What was the doctrine of the eucharist held by that subtle, pliant, and indecisive mind? It would take a very well qualified scholar to answer that question, but whatever it was, Cranmer's doctrine is totally unsuitable to form the norm of doctrine for any Christian communion thereafter. If Anglicans were reduced to appealling to Cranmer's doctrine of the eucharist as their exemplar and criterion they would be in a very unhappy position.

The eucharist is certainly not an unusually effective means of nagging at God. It is not – what it was degraded to by the mediaeval practice of celebrating private masses – a method of manipulating the Deity for the benefit of the celebrant or of those who are paying him. It is not simply a means of producing the body and blood of Christ on the altar to be viewed and adored by the faithful. All these interpretations of the sacrament are distortions into a different key of the original rhythm of the eucharist, which was communal, dynamic, and concerned with an event rather than a thing. As the book *Modern Eucharistic Agreement* (1973) shows, recent conversations between Anglicans and Roman Catholics, between Roman Catholics and Lutherans, between Roman Catholics and French Protestants, and between a number of other religious traditions represented on the World Council of Churches, have discovered a remarkable amount of common ground on the subject of eucharistic doctrine, based largely on an appreciation of the significance of the New Testament witness. 'All the statements agree that the body and blood of Christ are really given in the eucharistic sacrament, that they are received by the faithful believer but are present in some sense independently of his faith.' (*Critique of Eucharistic Agreement*, (1975) p. 27). And all agree that a spatial or natural manner of presence of Christ in the elements must be rejected. Transubstantiation tends to be relegated to a footnote, and it is agreed that this doctrine 'affirms the fact of Christ's presence but does not explain how the change in the elements takes place' (ibid., p. 27). So greatly has the theological amosphere changed since the sixteenth century. Modern liturgies, both in the Anglican and Roman Catholic Churches, have been composed and are everywhere used expressing in word and in ceremony this new understanding of the eucharist which is also a very old one.

If we are to probe further and ask what we mean when we say that in the sacrament of the eucharist the body and blood of Christ are received, we cannot mean that it is Christ's physical body that is here received. Christ did not rise from the dead unchanged. 'Flesh and blood', said Paul, 'cannot inherit the Kingdom of God, nor does the perishable inherit the imperishable' (1 Cor. 15: 50). To revert to *Critique of Eucharistic Agreement*:

the whole tradition of Hebraic thought suggests that words such as 'body' and 'blood' used in solemn religious formulae are most unlikely to be literal in their meaning, any more than they are likely to be purely arbitrary symbols. Biblical language lends itself neither to the mediaeval tendency to turn images into metaphysics nor to the literalist desire to take them as scientific statements. In speaking of Christ's body and blood as present in the eucharist we are using the highly symbolic, highly equivocal language of imagery, and it is only a matter of common sense to tread carefully and delicately here; we are taking one further step in semantic complexity when we say that the consecrated bread and wine are or become Christ's body and blood . . . on the whole it has been the Anglican tradition not to take this further step, i.e. not to say that the bread and wine are not Christ's body and blood, but not to say that they are. The Anglican doctrine upon this subject since the end of the sixteenth century at latest has consistently been that the consecrated elements convey, are the vehicles of, Christ's body and blood, in such a way that he who partakes in faith receives Christ's body and blood. And if challenged further as to what receiving Christ's body and blood means, the great majority of Anglican theologians and of Anglican communicants would say that it means being made sharers in Christ's life. (pp. 28, 29).

In accordance with this dynamic rather than static view of the eucharist, we shall see this sacrament as the place where, the occasion on which, the circumstances whereby, men and women are brought into the redeeming activity of Christ. This is where all that Christ has done for them is focused, gathered and applied to them anew. It is consequently, as the name 'eucharist' implies, supremely an act of thanksgiving and return of God's people in the Holy Spirit. The communicants recall what Christ has accomplished for them with gratitude, commemorating not only the Last Supper and the death of Christ but the whole redemptive strategy of God, Creation, and redemption, through Christ's life, death and resurrection. They offer to God the bread and wine to be blessed by him and by means of eating the consecrated bread and wine they are united again in Christ's life.

But we still must face the question of Christ's presence in the eucharist. It should be noted that what Jesus singled out for attention at the Last Supper was bread and wine, associating them with his body and blood. This selection has unmistakable reference to his sacrificial death. Perhaps because of the tendency observable since the High Middle Ages in the West to withhold the cup at the eucharist from the laity, an unbalanced emphasis has been laid on the word 'body'; that 'blood' was mentioned equally with it has been forgotten. In consequence the subject of Christ's presence in the eucharist has usually been discussed by attempting to answer the question, 'How does Christ's body appear in the eucharist?' The result has been the long history of the formation of the doctrine of transubstantiation, the criticism of this doctrine at the time of the Reformation, its defence by the Counter-Reformation, its revival by some Anglicans in the nineteenth and its reassessment by some Catholics in the twentieth centuries, and so on. A recent able and critically aware restatement of the traditional doctrine (G. Martelet, *The Risen Christ and the Eucharistic World*, E. T. London, 1976 of original French, Paris 1972), for instance, argues that Christ's risen body is a transformation of his earthly body; in the resurrection appearances it was presented in a temporary form, halfway between the former earthly and the later sacramental form, and in the eucharist it has ever since the first eucharist been available and present to the faithful in a sacramental form. The faithful cannot see or feel it but in faith they accept the consecrated elements to be, not equivalent to the body nor a symbol of the body, but the actual identical reality of the body itself.

We cannot agree with this kind of interpretation. In the first place, it is difficult to see the point aimed at. Why should we want to hold in our hands or our mouths Christ's body which is admittedly not present in any spatial way nor in any way capable of apprehension by the senses? The symbolism of bread/wine corresponding to body/blood is not of a reduplication of Christ for us but signifies our involvement in his redeeming self-giving. What needs to be reduplicated is our part in his act, not his presence in consecrated bread and wine. When Paul at I Corinthians 11: 29 says that certain people do not 'discern the body', he is referring to our relationship to Christ, not to some hypothetical body of Christ discernible in one or other of the consecrated elements. In the second place, the concept of Christ's physical body being reproduced after two transformations in the eucharistic elements faces grave, indeed in our view insurmountable, difficulties. The most serious is not any of the arguments against transubstantiation which have by now been worn thin with repetition, but the question of where Christ's human personality comes into this scheme. To have Christ's body sacramentally present in the forms of bread and wine without his personality would seem utterly absurd, indeed to believe that it was so present would be almost blasphemous. But how are we to conceive of the human personality of Christ being repeated millions of times over thousands of years as every eucharist is celebrated? Quite apart from every other consideration, we do not know in any sort of detail what Christ's human personality was like, though we may confidently infer much about his character. As soon therefore as we begin asking ourselves what is meant by the presence of Christ's body at or in the eucharist with any sort of rigour, we find ourselves in difficulties from which it seems impossible to extricate ourselves. It is likely that the reason for this is that in asking 'How is Christ's body present in the eucharist?', we are asking the wrong question.

If we return to the point that it was his body *and his blood* of which Jesus spoke at the Last Supper, we may find a more satisfactory line of thought to pursue. We cannot be far wrong in taking these two together to represent the life of Jesus regarded as given in sacrifice for our sakes. What the consecrated elements represent, then, is his life given for us and, as they are sacraments, 'outward and visible

235

signs of an inward and spiritual grace, the means whereby we receive the same and a pledge to assure us thereof', so they convey that which they signify. They are Christ's gift of his life to us, the gift of life in God-in-Christ. Of course they are only so to those who approach the sacrament in faith. Catholics and Protestants are in agreement here. And they exist as gifts of God independently of our faith in the sense that faith does not create them; we do not conjure them into existence by the power of our vivid imagination nor by our capacity for exalted religious experience. They are gifts of God in the Church and from the Church, even though, like all gifts of God in Christ, they are only available to faith.

We must add to these considerations two points especially emphasized by Fr. Martelet. Whatever happens in the eucharist is not to be thought of as a miracle but as a mystery. It is just as miraculous, if we want to think in terms of miracle, that the consecrated bread and wine should become the gift of Christ's life as that they should become the body of Christ (whatever may be meant by that). It is not because it appears to demand a miracle that we reject the latter alternative. But we should not think of the sacrament in terms of miracle but in terms of mystery, that is to say of an act of God which we may believe in as true but which we cannot fully understand because it concerns God and God's world, and not only us and our world. Fr. Martelet's second point comes in here. In the eucharist Christ introduces us to a new, redeemed world, the world of the risen Jesus Christ, so that the eucharist is a pledge of the renewed universe of which his resurrection is a sign and a pledge. Like baptism, the eucharist looks forward as well as backward. In advance we take part in a redeemed community, foretaste of a redeemed world. Another way of stating this would be to say that everything done, given, and received in the eucharist is done, given, and received in the Holy Spirit. The Holy Spirit is Lord of time and is also the earnest (first instalment) of our resurrection and the arrival and the presence in our midst of heaven. It is peculiarly appropriate to recall that it is only because we are in the Holy Spirit that the eucharist is not an empty formula, a piece of play-acting. This rite is not just a memorial service for a good man. It is full of dangerous possibility. In it we are liable to meet God himself.

We may well ask whether, granted that what is said above is accepted as true of the eucharist, we ought to ask for anything more, 'a higher gift than grace'. But there is no higher gift than grace, and we should not wish for a higher. We do not think that if the believer will confine himself to the view of the relation of the eucharist to Christ's presence expounded here he can seriously be charged with holding doctrine which is either non-Catholic or non-Scriptural.

Finally, if we are faithful to the subject of this section, we must ask 'is this rite a sacrifice?'. This is a subject which is exercising many theologians today and is calling for a new examination.

That Christ is here offered by the celebrating priest, or by the people, as a sacrifice in a manner comparable to the sacrifices offered by the priests of the Old Testament cult we emphatically deny. We have no right nor authority to offer Christ, and if we have priests they are not priests whose function and status are defined in terms of the cult (see below pp. 254–6). These ideas represent developments of doctrine visible from the third century onward and greatly enlarged in the mediaeval Church which are justified neither by Scripture nor by tradition. We do not control Christ, through a priest or by any other means. It is not even satisfactory to say that we plead Christ or plead in his name. As has been indicated above (see p. 109) it is not the Christian's business to nag anxiously at God, and least of all in a rite which should be marked by confident gratitude on our part. In the eucharist we offer ourselves, our prayers, our thanks, our hearts, to God, and we do so only in Christ and through Christ, and in it too we receive the benefits of Christ's Passion. But a calculation of the exact advantages received here is inconsistent with the spiritual intention of the service. Here we may be unprofitable servants, but we are not unjust stewards.

c. Other Sacraments

i. Marriage

Marriage is called by the old Book of Common Prayer 'an honourable estate, instituted by God in the time of man's innocency'. As a social institution it long pre-dates either Judaism or Christianity. It was of course a respected institution in the society in which Christianity grew up. For about a thousand years Christians were content to leave matrimony more or less as they found it, celebrated according to local custom, whether this was the custom reflected in the Parable of the Ten Virgins or the elaborate ancient Roman rite. Christians naturally liked to associate their marriages with the blessing of the Church, either by bringing it into connection with the eucharist, or by asking a Christian priest to bless the partners at some point during the rite. But no such practice was thought to affect the significance of the marriage.

Marriage was always in the Christian view considered to be a state of affairs administered by the parties themselves. It was essentially a public taking of vows of faithfulness to each other by a man and a woman. It was necessary that there should be witnesses, otherwise the marriage would not be public, and in this the State was understandably concerned. That the Church should have a representative present at the ceremony was not at first thought necessary, though it was considered suitable. Gradually however it came to be accepted that a priest not merely might or should but must be present and that the ceremony must take place in church. The mediaevals did not find it easy to determine what was the matter of this sacrament. The vow, or even the ring? But everybody allowed that the marriage could not be regarded as a true or real marriage until it had been consummated in physical union. To ask what was the matter of the sacrament here was indeed a delicate question; and it demanded a great deal of subtlety, not to say sophistry, to envisage marriage as a sacrament comparable to baptism and the eucharist. Christ had attended a marriage in Cana, and Paul had compared the union of Christ with the believer to the union of husband and wife, but these things could hardly be thought constitutive of Christian marriage. They were not much more than good advertisements for it.

On the effect of marriage, however, as distinct from the manner of it, theology could expatiate. It had here good ground in the prohibition of divorce by Jesus (Mark 10: 2–12; Matt. 5: 31f; 19: 3–9; Luke 16: 18), though the Matthaean modification ('except on the ground of unchastity', 5: 32) always caused difficulty and confusion. The mediaeval doctrine of marriage was that the marriage when properly celebrated and consummated created between the husband and wife an indissoluble metaphysical bond. The bond had been created by God and therefore could in theory under no circumstances be broken. The Church from the beginning had disliked divorce, and had tried to avoid its occurring when possible, but it had in the early centuries never regarded divorce as metaphysically impossible, as simply something that could not happen, like a man growing younger instead of older. The indissolubility of marriage is indeed a relatively late doctrine, as the fact that it is unknown in the Eastern Church witnesses. The English government from the Reformation onward took on itself to make divorce available, though only at great trouble and expense, by statute law, and this state of affairs was more or less accepted by the Church of England until the middle of the nineteenth century.

The Oxford Movement, however, which affected the whole Anglican Communion in the nineteenth century, revived in the breasts of many churchmen the conviction that marriage created an indissoluble bond between the husband and the wife. This was, if anything, strengthened by the advance of criticism of the Gospels, which suggested that the 'Matthaean exception' was a later addition to the Gospel and that therefore Jesus had forbidden divorce with no qualification at all. During the nineteenth and early twentieth centuries the Roman Catholic Church developed the (distinctly innovatory) doctrine that marriage, *for Catholics*, was not securely valid or authentic unless it was celebrated in the presence of a Catholic priest, though it was allowed that the marriage of Protestants to Protestants was valid. Even Anglo-Catholic Anglicans could not accept this kind of doctrine and allowed that marriages celebrated in register offices with no benefit of clergy were as binding and valid as marriages in church. On the other hand, Church of England clergy who were not of the Anglo-Catholic persuasion were sometimes ready to accept the law of the land as binding, to recognize the reality of divorce, and to marry divorced people in church to a second spouse while the first was living. As the twentieth century went on, a series of divorce laws carried by the Westminster Parliament made divorce simpler and more accessible by stages until at the present moment divorce by consent (and in certain circumstances by the consent of only one party) can be said to be now virtually available.

The situation of the Church of England as regards divorce has consequently become very much confused. In other Anglican provinces, such as the USA and Canada, ecclesiastical machinery exists for dealing with the cases of divorced people who wish to be remarried in church, and for deciding each case on its merits. In Britain never has divorce been so accessible and widespread; never has the Church of England been more formally intransigent in maintaining the indissolubility of the marriage bond. The Roman Catholic Church in recent years, while formally maintaining that marriage is indissoluble, has stretched the concept of nullity to cover so many possibilities that to the outsider it looks as if that Church might as well recognize the possibility of a marriage ceasing to exist as perpetuate the fiction that no marriage can ever cease to exist while discovering all sorts of new reasons for deciding that marriages have in fact never taken place.

A new approach to the theology of marriage, which has recently been suggested in different forms by theologians of both Protestant and Catholic traditions, could deliver Anglicans from the present highly unsatisfactory situation. This consists in regarding marriage not as a kind of metaphysical trap into which God shuts husband and wife, from which no efforts of their own can deliver them, but primarily as a covenant. The concept of a covenant between man and man and between God and men has good precedent in the thought of both the Old and the New Testaments. If marriage is considered to be a solemn and lifelong covenant between a man and a woman taken, if the marriage is celebrated in church, in the presence of God and invoking his name and blessing, but in any circumstances a covenant responsibly entered into, then much of the, as it were, dogmatic oppression is removed from the whole subject. Covenants involving lifelong vows are serious matters and should not be lightly broken, nor, if broken lightly, lightly re-made with others. But covenants *can* be broken; it is possible to recognize situations where they have been broken and cannot be renewed between the same partners. And it is possible to imagine cases where those who have broken one matrimonial covenant, or who have experienced the breaking of it by their partner, could be permitted and even encouraged to make another responsible covenant with another partner. The objection that Jesus specifically forbade the dissolution of marriage (as he certainly appears to have done) can be met by pointing out that he either himself modified this prohibition by adding the words 'except on the ground of unchastity' (Matt. 5:32), or the early Church thought itself authorized to make this modification. In either case, the words of Jesus at Mark 10:2–12 cease to be regarded as constituting immutable law. The whole policy of envisaging the utterances of Jesus as directly constituting divine law for the Church to stand unchanged and unqualified for eternity is full of difficulty anyway. It should perhaps be noticed that at one point (1 Cor. 7:15) Paul seems to envisage the possibility of circumstances arising in which a marriage could be dissolved.

This kind of theology of marriage is still in its infancy and is not yet widely known, far less accepted, in the Anglican (any more than in the Roman) communion. Further, if it were adopted it would inevitably entail the setting up of bodies within the Church of England capable of dealing with cases of matrimony, and it can hardly be said that such bodies yet exist. Indeed, even in churches of the Anglican communion outside the Church of England, which have sometimes been compelled by circumstances to develop institutions for dealing with such cases, these institutions have mostly reached no more than a rudimentary form, and this new theology of marriage can hardly be said to have been accepted. But this alternative theology of marriage, while it does not alter, and is not meant to alter, the character of Christian marriage as in intention binding and binding for life, offers a hopeful possibility of an understanding of marriage which is not contrary to Scripture nor tradition and does not merely oppose contemporary permissiveness by an unrealistic rigorism.

ii. Holy Orders

The origin and development of the Christian ministry are dealt with elsewhere in this book (see below, pp. 249–56). Here it is sufficient to consider whether we can properly speak of a 'sacrament of orders'. Those who, during the Middle Ages, developed such a concept held two assumptions which it is impossible for us today to share, that all existing major orders in the Church were directly instituted by Jesus himself or his apostles, and that priesthood is properly defined in terms of the priest's cultic activity, that is his capacity by blessing the bread and wine in the eucharist to cause them to become the body and blood of Christ, and to offer Christ's body, thus present, as a sacrifice to God. Building on these convictions, mediaeval theologians had made a sacrificing priesthood central to their doctrine of the ministry, regarding the deacon as one training for the priesthood, and the bishop as no more than a priest with enlarged powers. From these premises they deduced that the priest had an 'indelible character' and a 'capacity'. The 'capacity' (*potestas*) was the power to consecrate the eucharistic elements, and the 'character' was a special impression implanted in his soul which made him irretrievably a priest who could (though he should not) exercise his 'capacity' even apart from any association with the rest of the Church. These were, of course, powers and faculties given him directly by Christ (through the hand of the ordaining bishop) independently of the rest of the Church. They sufficed indeed to set up in the Church nothing less than a sacerdotal caste.

At the Reformation the Anglican Church disavowed much of this doctrine. It refused (as we shall see) to define the priest in terms of his cultic powers even though it retained for him the exclusive right of celebrating the eucharist, and it suppressed all thought of his offering Christ as a sacrifice or possessing a capacity for consecrating bread and wine to be the body and blood of Christ, though it retained in some of its formulae some vestiges of the doctrine of 'indelible character'. If we are to judge by the Ordinal in the Book of Common Prayer, it thought of priesthood mainly in terms of authority or commission. As well as calling the presbyter a priest, and emphasizing his authority to forgive sins, it spoke of him as a 'messenger', a 'watchman', a 'steward', and a 'shepherd', all images drawn directly from the Bible.

On the subject of the significance of the ministry, therefore, the Anglican Reformation was unusually explicit, perhaps more in what it deliberately omitted than in what it positively said, but still explicit enough. It is now not only undesirable but impossible to return to the mediaeval, or Counter-Reformation, or Anglo-Catholic position on the subject of priesthood; no Anglican Ordinal has ever defined the priest in terms of his cultic functions, nor is ever likely to do so. The Anglican priest receives authority from Christ in the Church through the bishop to perform those functions which are listed as priestly. Among them is that of celebrating the eucharist, and as he celebrates he is most appropriately and effectively a priest, but his priesthood is not to be defined by that activity exclusively. He can be quite confident of his authority, and it is fitting and right that a priest should lead a life of peculiar devotion to his office, in the words of the Prayer Book, 'drawing all his studies that way'. But this is not to say that he has imprinted on his soul an 'indelible character' in the mediaeval sense of that term.

Is it right then to call Orders a 'sacrament'? We do not think that anything is gained by using the term in this context. In the first place, the concept of the 'threefold ministry' of bishop, priest and deacon is unreal and schematic. The deacon as used by Roman Catholics, Orthodox and Anglicans cannot be compared as an office to those of priest and bishop; he is an apprentice priest. The difference between a deacon and a full-time lay worker who can preach and baptize is minimal. To say that the deacon has Holy Orders whereas the other has not is almost meaningless. They both have virtually the same authority. The fact is that in almost all churches in the Western world the dividing line between clergy and laity is becoming blurred. There is nothing whatever wrong with this as long as the authority of Christ in his Church is properly preserved and administered.

We do not wish to deny in what we say here that in both matrimony and the conferring of Orders God gives his grace. On the contrary, we think it important to realize that he does give his grace on these occasions. What we deprecate is the attempt to assimilate all these occasions into a single scheme of the conferment of sacramental grace, entailing an attempt to find the matter, the form and so on in each case, so that the determination to turn each into a sacrament comparable with the others obscures their actual diversity and often their real significance also.

iii Others

We do not intend to deal here at length with any other sacraments or ordinances or rites of the Church. This is not because we wish to disparage them, but because we do not think that they are strictly comparable with the two Dominical sacraments. The practice that grew up in the Middle Ages of classing a number of ceremonies or rites (finally seven) together and attempting to find a theological lowest common denominator for them was unsatisfactory. It was based on an inadequate understanding of their origins and significance and assumed quite wrongly that they had all been either instituted or approved by the Lord or his apostles.

The so-called 'sacrament of penance' is the continuation of the practice of auricular confession to a priest which grew up first in the Irish Church from about the sixth century onward, itself a transposition into a private and individual form of the custom of public confession of sins to the local church, which had existed since the earliest days of the faith. To say that James 5: 16 witnesses to the institution of the sacrament by the apostle James is ridiculous. This is not to deny that the practice of a Christian having a 'soul-friend' (clerical or lay) with whom he discusses his spiritual state is an excellent one, which should be more widely practised in the Anglican communion than it is; nor should we disparage the similar but not quite identical practice of an individual confessing his sins to a priest and asking for forgiveness. But it adds little or nothing to these customs to call them a sacrament.

The 'sacrament of extreme unction' is the continuation in an atrophied form, restricted to the individual's last moments, of the practice of praying over the sick and anointing them with oil which is witnessed to in James 5: 13 (but is not thereby exalted to the status of a sacrament instituted by an apostle). The custom of laying hands on the sick, with or without anointing with oil, with prayer for their recovery has in recent years been rightly emancipated from its restriction to the dying (who ironically were *not* going to recover) and it is at the moment widely used in many religious traditions with, by and large, fruitful results manifestly blessed by God. It is precisely by not treating this practice as a 'sacrament of extreme unction' that it has been so usefully and successfully extended in its use.

15 The Reformation is Over

In our generation an event has taken place which future historians of the Church will regard as an outstanding landmark. This is the Second Vatican Council of 1962–3. It is now plain that what happened at that council was this: the Roman Catholic Church decided to come to terms with reality. For more than a hundred years its leaders had been engaged in a struggle to keep out from their church the questions which modern thought was insistently pressing upon Christian theologians: questions about the origin of man, about the nature of historical enquiry, about the history and authenticity of the documents which the Bible contains. The official apologists for the Church had either ignored these questions, or given answers to them which no informed person regarded as satisfactory. At the same time they had pursued with unrelenting hostility anyone in their own ranks who expressed any sympathy with doubt or criticism or attempted to give different answers to those provided officially.

At Vatican II it became obvious that this attempt at keeping out the questions the outside world was asking could no longer be maintained. Too many Roman Catholic scholars knew that the questions had to be faced, not run away from. The consequence is that now the great majority of informed Roman Catholics freely admit that the Christian faith is under question from modern thought, and that, if the challenge of modern thought is to be met, the faith must undergo a drastic reassessment. Of course this had been realized and admitted by Protestant and Anglican scholars long before this, but the Roman Catholic Church up till Vatican II had officially regarded the efforts of other Christians to meet the challenge of modern thought as an exhibition of rankest heresy and had preened herself on maintaining her orthodoxy intact.

Today we hear much less about the proud record of orthodoxy of the Roman Catholic Church. Roman Catholic scholars admit that the faith needs to find new forms of expression. Books and articles by Roman Catholics that even thirty or forty years ago would have earned instant censorship and perhaps excommunication for their authors now appear without any expressions of disapproval from the Vatican. It is generally admitted among thinking Roman Catholics that they have much to learn from Protestants in the spheres of both biblical scholarship and theology. Study and research in a wide range of subjects is now undertaken by Roman Catholics and Protestants jointly. In other words, informed Roman Catholics now freely admit that we are all in the same boat, all facing the same intellectual problems, subject to the same pressures, encountering the same crises. Nobody has a talisman that will enable him to give guaranteed correct answers to our problems. We must all wrestle with them, and we will do so more successfully if we do it together.

'But', exclaim some doubters among the Protestants, 'is there not bound to be a reaction inside the Roman Catholic Church? Indeed, is a reaction not already perceptible? What about the movement headed by Monsignor Lefebvre?' Yes, of course there had to be a reaction. Even in so apparently monolithic and autocratic a church as was the Roman Catholic Church between 1870 and 1962 you cannot say 'About turn!' and expect everyone to obey immediately. The astonishing and heartening thing is that so many have obeyed, suggesting as it does that the former policy of exclusivism and triumphalism was not really popular. There will naturally be plenty of people who will prefer the old ways. To take an example from one area only, you cannot turn overnight from regarding Protestants as miserable heretics and schismatics, hardly distinguishable from pagans, to regarding them as beloved brethren only separated by the accidents of history. The encouraging factor is that the Lefebvre movement has not been a great deal more successful. In fact the only place where it has had very much response seems to be France, where it is associated with a particularly unsavoury type of right-wing politics.

But the reaction will not succeed in putting the clock back. There are certain features of the pre-Vatican II Roman Catholic Church that we will not see again, not at least for many generations, if ever. What we will not have again is:

(a) A Pope whose mere dictum all Catholics will obey. This was made plain by the reception of the Encyclical *Humanae Vitae*. It was indeed accepted by the majority of Catholics, but a substantial minority, perhaps as much as a third, have shown that they are not willing to accept it, and they have not been disciplined. Future Popes will know that their authority henceforth must be backed up by knowledge and genuine argument. The naked fiat will not run.

(b) A church claiming to know the answers to all the important questions simply from its own tradition or *magisterium*. This attitude was surely brought to the point of absurdity by the Biblical Commission which Leo XIII set up in the year 1902 in order to answer difficult questions concerning the Bible. It answered the questions with great alacrity and assurance, but anybody who had any training in the subject knew that the answers were almost invariably wrong. In future any guidance given by any church on matters of biblical or theological scholarship will have to commend itself by its own intrinsic merit, not by any claim to special inspiration.

(c) A church which proudly isolates itself and denies the churchly status of other Christians. It is true indeed that the Roman Catholic Church does not yet recognize other churches as full and proper parts of the Catholic Church: but the old exclusive spirit has gone. Co-operation at many levels and friendliness now prevails. Deep friendship between Catholics and Protestants in many and varied situations have been formed. These bonds will not be repudiated.

But this movement, which its inaugurator Pope John XXIII called an *aggiornamento*, a bringing up to date, has very wide implications for all Christians. The great Catholic-Protestant divide, which has immensely affected European history for four hundred and fifty years, is rapidly coming to an end. Catholics are becoming more like Protestants: they are studying the Bible, preaching the word of God, taking part in evangelical campaigns, sharing in the charismatic movement, holding prayer meetings at home. And Protestants are becoming more like Catholics. This is clearest in the area of eucharistic worship, where there is very wide agreement indeed among Christians of all traditions as to what shape a eucharistic service should take. But Protestants are also losing their traditional fear of symbolism: crosses and candles and pictures appear in Protestant churches. A Methodist minister has recently written a book commending the use of the rosary. A very successful monastic order has been founded in Taizé in France by Lutheran and Reformed Christians. Catholics and Protestants have discovered that what they have in common is far more important than what divides them.

Curiously enough, most non-Roman Catholics have not really woken up to the fact that the Reformation is over. The Church of England in particular does not seem yet to have realized that its four-hundred-and-fifty-year isolation from the Church on the continent has ended. The truth is that Rome's reorientation has disorientated us all. We have lost our way. This is indicated by some extreme Protestant sects who seem to be unwilling to accept the fact of Rome's reorientation precisely because it has removed their *raison d'être*, to be a protest against Rome. In a very similar way one meets some old-fashioned Anglo-Catholic clergy whose theology really is more ultramontane than the Pope's. They have been left behind by the march of events. But we cannot go back to square one. We are all now living in a Church which is both Catholic and Protestant and which is one whether we like it or not. Theological and biblical research has long ago abandoned the Catholic-Protestant divide. The only area in the British Isles where it has hitherto been impossible to study theology at university level on an ecumenical basis is Ireland, where religion has occupied the minds of Christians rather than theology, and not always for the better. The great divide within the Church is henceforward no longer between Catholic and Protestant but between East and West, and perhaps between conservative and liberal.

The Orthodox Church, however, presents us with an entirely different subject. The first point to understand is that this historic communion embracing millions of believers is *there*. It will not disappear just because we ignore it, as Newman seemed to think it would in his *Development of Christian Doctrine*. On the contrary, this Church gives every sign of continuing and increasing in numbers, even in those countries which are behind the Iron Curtain. We must resist the temptation to treat it as if it was a slightly different version of the Roman Catholic Church. There are some things which Anglicans have in common with the Orthodox, such as a tendency to recoil from authoritarian ecclesiastical government, a readiness to trust the laity and give them a prominent part in the work of the Church, and the habit of expressing doctrine in worship rather than in creeds or formal dogmas. But if we are to be realistic we must recognize that the Anglican communion has far more in common with the Roman Catholic Church than with the Orthodox. Anglicans come from a Latin 'Western Tradition'; we have Augustine and Anselm and Thomas Aquinas as our ancestors, not Photius, the stormy petrel of ninth-century controversy between Rome and Byzantium; nor Gregory Palamas, the fourteenth century theologian and exponent of mystical prayer. We cannot emancipate ourselves from that heritage; indeed we ought not to want to do so.

The Orthodox are conservative in a way which is quite different from the conservatism of Rome. The Roman system is in one sense extremely 'modernist' in that the reigning Pope can always overrule or reinterpret all his predecessors, always on the understanding that his successors may overrule or reinterpret him. A Pope can pre-cipitate the whole church into a revolution, as John XXIII did. But conservatism appears to be built into the Orthodox Church; the view of this church appears to be that in matters of doctrine or practice whatever is new must be wrong because it is new. So far it seems to have shown little desire to adapt itself to the intellectual and cultural conditions and demands of the Western world in the twentieth century. In accordance with this, though the rules of the Orthodox about relations with other denominations are flexible and to an extent liberal, the attitude of that Church to reunion with others is much more intransigent than that of the Church of Rome. It declares that it knows its own Church to have the true faith and order and discipline which are in no serious need of change or improvement, and though it does not pronounce others to be non-Christian, nor to be outside the true Church, it does not know that they are within the true Church.

At the same time we must recall that the Orthodox have taken part in the ecumenical movement, to its great benefit, and are members of the World Council of Churches, thereby manifesting their serious desire for unity more effectively than the Roman Catholics. As we find it difficult to understand and judge this mysterious Eastern church with its inherited attitudes and customs which are so different from ours, so we must realize that we are only just beginning to explore it, as the Orthodox are only just beginning to find out about us. One of the outstanding characteristics of the Orthodox communion is its emphasis upon the Holy Spirit, an emphasis which we would do well to learn from them. We should trust that the Holy Spirit will, answering the prayers of both communions, lead both into greater understanding of and sympathy for each other's idiosyncrasies.

16 Ministry

a. Ministry in the New Testament

The New Testament is greatly interested in ministry, far more than it is in the ministers. Ministry in the New Testament springs from that of Jesus Christ. The key text is Mark 10:45; 'For the Son of Man came also not to be served but to serve, and to give his life as a ransom for many'. The Church inherits this ministry to the world, which the New Testament calls *diakonia*, and it is primarily the Church that exercises this ministry. Christ is in a very similar vein described as a high priest throughout the Epistle to the Hebrews, and in several parts of the New Testament the Church as a whole, and Christians as members of it, are spoken of in priestly terms; see Romans 12:1–2; I Peter 2:5; Revelation 1:6; but individual ministers are never called priests. From this it follows, not that there should not be an ordained priesthood in the Church, but that this priesthood must be seen as coming from Christ through the Church, and not as having authority direct from Christ over against the Church.

Paul has plenty to say about *diakonia*. In several places he describes his ministry and that of his colleagues in mission, but always with the implication that the church to which he is writing ought to take the duty of ministry upon themselves; (see I Cor. 4:9–13; 2 Cor. 4:1–15; 6:1–10). The author of the Epistle to the Ephesians expresses it with beautiful clarity when he writes in 4:11–12 that God has given various gifts and ministries to the Church 'in order to equip the saints for the work of ministry.' The Second Edition of the RSV has this rendering; the First Edition, by inserting a comma after 'saints', seriously misrepresented the writer's meaning. Here 'the saints' means of course all Christians; it is all Christians who are to be equipped for the work of ministry. If therefore we are to have a doctrine of the ministry that is faithful to the New Testament, we must begin by acknowledging that ministry is the function of the whole Church, both the whole Church universal and the whole local church.

From a very early period Christians have professed to find the particular form of ministry which commended itself to them authenticated, and usually authenticated exclusively, in the New Testament. Cyprian serenely read into the Gospels and Acts the episcopal ministry of his own day, the third century; later when the

Pope began to make claims for his office he thought them to be endorsed by the words of the Lord to Peter. At the Reformation, and since then, every diverse form of ministry exhibited by every denomination has been confidently read into the New Testament – Presbyterianism, Congregationalism, the Methodist ministry, the Baptist ministry, and the Society of Friends has even found in the New Testament support for having no ministry at all. In particular Roman Catholics, Orthodox and some Anglicans have purported to find in the New Testament evidence that our Lord founded a Christian priesthood, and have appealed in making their case to what they call 'apostolic succession'.

The surest way to ruin any form of ministry is to make excessive claims for it; history in the end takes its revenge for such claims. The history of the Papacy should convince anybody of that. Rigorous examination of the evidence shows that none of these claims can be sustained and that any attempt to claim biblical authority for the form of ministry known today in those Christian bodies which have a ministry is doomed to failure.

The earliest documents of the Christian faith are the Letters of Paul; they reflect the state of the Christian Church during the period, roughly, between AD 45 and AD 60. It must be made clear that among the letters actually written by Paul we do not number the First and Second Letter to Timothy and the Letter to Titus. These are usually called the Pastoral Epistles; a considerable weight of scholarly opinion believes these to have been written much later than Paul's day, at earliest at the end of the first century but more probably in the second. The words of Paul concerning ministry if carefully considered must be seen to exclude the possibility of the existence in his day of an official ministry such as we know today, that is a number of ministers or clergy who are thought of as occupying a permanent office to which they succeed and to which they are appointed by ordination, in such a way as to make a distinction between clergy and laity. The most important passages for this purpose are I Corinthians 12 and Romans 12 (and we might add Ephesians 4), where lists of what look like ministers, but are in fact ministries, are given. The vital clue is provided by Romans 12: 6–8 in which there are included in the list of ministries 'he who contributes' and 'he who does acts of mercy', and I Corinthians 12: 8–11 and 28–31 in which similar lists include faith, speaking with tongues and the interpretation of tongues. By no conceivable means could these be construed as equivalent to ministry or to the official work of ministers in our modern sense of those words. In fact these two chapters make it quite clear that for Paul (and we may assume therefore for the early Christian Church) ministry is a matter of what the Holy Spirit calls the individual to do within the community. There is no hard-and-fast distinction between clergy and laity; there are only those who respond to the Spirit's vocation to do what they have a power or skill to do – speak with tongues, interpret, show an example of faith, give liberally of their substance, organize, teach, utter prophetic words, administer, interpret the Scriptures, and so on. We can find no fixed ranks nor a single rank of ministers here; neither the 'apostles, prophets and teachers' of 1 Corinthians 12:29 (where the 'first . . . second . . . third' suggest an order of evangelizing in beginning a new church), nor even the 'apostles, prophets, evangelists' of Ephesians 4:11, offer promising ground for such a theory. It is true that Philippians 1:1 mentions 'bishops and deacons' and that in one place (Acts 14:23) Paul and Barnabas are represented as setting up presbyters in newly-evangelized churches, and that the evidence seems clear that the church in Jerusalem had presbyters from the very beginning. But there is no evidence that presbyters (which in this context may mean no more than 'older men') were a uniform and original feature in every church; quite the contrary, for Paul never mentions them. And if the church at Philippi chose to have inspectors and helpers (which is all the Greek probably means), it does not follow that other churches had them, nor that they were regarded as more than the particular callings given by the Spirit to individuals in that church. The reference to Paul and Barnabas setting up elders is unique. Luke does not otherwise speak of elders in churches outside Judaea; elders were an already known feature in Jewish synagogues. It is likely, in view of Paul's silence about presbyters, that Luke is here reading into the evangelizing activity of Paul and Barnabas a later practice.

But what about apostles? Surely the eleven apostles were constituted ministers of the infant Church of Christ and saw to it that their ministry was continued? Here again we must answer in the negative. The eleven apostles were indeed in a genuine sense the founders of the Church, as they are symbolically represented to be in Revelation 21:14. They were the first proclaimers of the gospel and the first planters and fosterers of the Churches in Palestine. This was inevitably their role as they were those who had known Jesus in the flesh and had witnessed his resurrection. But there is no satisfactory evidence that they founded a ministry nor that they attempted to institute apostolic officials in their place. In one important sense they could have no successors. They were witnesses of what had happened at the beginning. Officials can have successors, but witnesses cannot. There is much truth in the traditional Reformation observation that

251

the real successor of the apostles is the New Testament. The word 'apostle' in fact is used in the New Testament not only for the twelve and for the eleven but also for anyone who has seen the risen Lord and received a command to evangelize (1 Cor. 15:7–9) or who has planted a church in a place where it did not exist before, like Apollos (1 Cor. 4:1–13), Barnabas (Acts 4:4,14) and probably Andronicus and Junias (Rom. 16:7). This too is a function in which there can be no successors.

Ministry in our modern sense of it, then, is a development. There were no ministers, as we rate ministers, in the beginning. The first appearance of successors to the twelve is not in Acts (which shows no interest in the subject) but in the late Pastoral Epistles, which are invaluable witness for what was happening about AD 100 or later but not for the primitive Church. The evidence of Paul is decisive. A permanent ministry, a 'clergy', is a development, as the creed and the Canon of the New Testament were developments. This does not mean that they were not right, good, healthy, and proper developments. They certainly were. Circumstances, the pressures of history, the continuous existence of the Church as an institution, made it imperatively necessary that a permanent ministry in our modern sense should develop, and within a little more than a century after the resurrection a uniform permanent ministry of inspectors, older men, and assistants had developed. We can catch glimpses of the process as we read early Christian literature. We have deliberately called bishops, presbyters, and deacons by these synonyms in order to emphasize that the names given by the Church to its first officials were not those hallowed by long use in the Old Testament nor of particular theological significance, but simply words representing precisely the functions which the Church found it convenient and necessary to perform. Later ages were of course to find all sorts of theological significance in them as they became stereotyped and hallowed by history. However, it would be quite wrong to deny that the emergence of a permanent ministry was a development in the life and structure of the Church led by the Holy Spirit and produced as an entirely necessary response to circumstances, and that that necessity still operates today. If all denominations suddenly abolished all their ministries tomorrow, within fifty years the great majority of them would be operating again under different names.

This account of the emergence of a permanent ministry, however, demands the sacrifice of two ideas which are dear to the hearts of many. The first is that of apostolic succession. The second is that of a scriptural ministry. The recent Anglican-Methodist Reunion Scheme was wrecked by a combination of two bodies of opinion within the

Church of England each respectively obsessed with one of these illusions. The apostles did not appoint successors. In Acts the organ of continuity in the Church is the Holy Spirit, not any official. Any appeal to the succession of ministers going back in unbroken succession to Jesus or his apostles is built on sand. This appeal began to be made in the second century (Pastoral Epistles, Clement, Hegesippius, but *not* Ignatius), and was further developed by the production of succession-lists of bishops in the principal sees, which are interesting historically but cannot be taken *au pied de la lettre*. It was a factor of the second-century Church's gradual realization that it was an institution in history with both a past and a future, not merely a body of the saved waiting for the *Parousia* to manifest itself in the very near future. But even so this apostolic succession was a succession of officials teaching in the same place and in the same tradition (comparable to contemporary Greek philosophers), not a succession of officials linked by ordination, as in the much later concept of apostolic succession. This drastic conclusion does not of course mean that the Church has no right to call itself apostolic, nor even that the clergy have no right to do so. The mission and ministering begun by the apostles of Christ have always existed and always will. But the ministry has no right to claim apostolic succession in the conventional sense. It is equally clear that the concept of a 'scriptural ministry' has very little content. If it means a ministry whose form is authorized, exclusively or not, as uniform and originally designed for the Church in Scripture, there is no such thing. If it means anything else, the concept is scarcely worth entertaining. The New Testament in this, as much as anything else, gives us a picture of a development. At the beginning there is no official ministry at all. Gradually, piecemeal, in response to circumstances, a rudimentary official ministry can be seen emerging. By the end of the New Testament period the ministries of bishops, presbyter and deacon which are eventually to establish themselves as stereotyped and permanent can be seen to be present, though certainly not yet as exclusive major ministries. To describe this as either an example of apostolic succession or of a scriptural ministry is to empty those terms of meaning.

The emergence of a Christian priesthood was an even later phenomenon. In the New Testament there are no Christian priests, except Christ himself. There are pagan priests and Jewish priests, some of whom become Christian without functioning as priests in a Christian ministry. But the only individual Christian priest is Christ himself, as expounded above all in Hebrews, though not in Hebrews alone. In correspondence with Christ's priesthood, as has already been mentioned (see above, p. 249) the whole body of Christians constitute a single priesthood. The clearest texts showing this are 1 Peter 2: 5 and Revelation 1: 6; 5: 10 and 20: 6, but the consciousness of Christians that they are collectively the medium or *locus* of God's self-communication of Christ pervades the whole New Testament and is visible clearly in much early Christian literature. This is one of the signs of what might be called the collectivity, or solidarity of the early Christian Church; it is the Church as a collective, so to speak, that represents Christ and that acts in the name of Christ, that possesses authority, exercises it, and delegates it.

Until about AD 200 nobody speaks of Christian officials as priests. Then in the West Tertullian and Hippolytus begin attaching the word 'priest' or 'high priest' (*sacerdos* or *summus sacerdos* Latin, *hiereus* or *archiereus* Greek) to the bishop, and, very occasionally, to the presbyter. The reasons for this, as far as can be ascertained, have nothing to do with his function in celebrating the eucharist. The only priestly function which they, or any other source until the middle of the third century, attribute to him is that of forgiving sins. Two main causes probably account for this new development, the desire to claim for the Christian bishop the not inconsiderable prestige attached in pagan cults to the title of *sacerdos* or *archiereus,* and the conviction that as the bishop is representative of Christ so he should be representative of Christ as the high priest. There is a certain logic in this development once it is granted that a permanent ministry has emerged to embody and implement the ministry of the Church.

It is not till the middle of the third century, in the West, and considerably later in the East, that the next important step in the development of a Christian priesthood is taken. It was Cyprian, bishop of Carthage from 249 to 258, who took it. He directly likened the Christian bishop to the sacrificing priest of the Old Testament cult, attributing to him the power, privilege and sacrosanctity of the priests of the old dispensation, and even going as far as to say that as the Old Testament priest offered animals in sacrifice so the Christian bishop when he celebrates the eucharist offers Christ as a sacrifice. He imitates Christ in this rite. As Christ at the Last Supper offered himself as a sacrifice to God, so the celebrant offers Christ at every celebration. That is his sacrifice. The mediaeval doctrine of a Christian priesthood offering sacrifices on behalf of the living and the dead has here a broad foundation. It should be noted that in this theory it is the bishop who is the priest *par excellence* and the presbyter only by delegation from him. The later mediaeval and present Roman Catholic doctrine that the bishop is only a priest with rather enlarged powers is very poorly supported in the historical sources.

This doctrine of priesthood is a development indeed, but it is not to be condemned outright simply because it is a development. The question is, is this a proper and healthy development? We need not hesitate long in deciding this question in the negative. The gradual turning of the ministry into a sacerdotal caste controlling exclusively the means of grace, marked off from the laity by the possession of supernatural powers, and the practice (or at least the formal practice) of celibacy, occurred very largely because of the Cyprianic doctrine of Christian priesthood. Its chief defect is that *it defines the priest in terms of the cult*, thereby apparently tending to reintroduce a Jewish form of priesthood. It dangerously impairs the scriptural doctrine that Christ has offered the final and perfect sacrifice. It entirely obscures, indeed it contradicts, the New Testament doctrine of the priesthood of all believers. It has traditionally always rested on the illusory assumption that Christ instituted a priesthood independently of the priesthood of all believers. It has been the parent of many errors and many superstitions.

One of the clearest and most unmistakable moves of the Anglican Church (by which we mean not merely the Church of England but those Churches in communion with it in Ireland, Wales and Scotland) at the Reformation was to disown this cultic interpretation of priesthood and yet deliberately to retain the title and function of the priesthood. Its ordinal went back to the earlier and better priestly function of the forgiveness of sins. It dissociated the definition of a priest from his function in celebrating the eucharist, but it still (appropriately and rightly) retained for him this function, where indeed he is seen most clearly in his priestly activity, of representing man to God and God to man.

This is indeed a perfectly good doctrine of priesthood. The priest represents and implements the priesthood of all believers, which is the earthly expression of Christ's priesthood, even though he does not necessarily do this in an exclusive nor monopolistic way. In all his work in countless ways he stands for man to God and for God to man. The Anglican laity certainly regard their clergy as doing this. But he does not behave like an Old Testament sacrificing priest. He does not offer any sacrifice, except the sacrifice of himself and his people, and that in Christ. He does not offer Christ. Christ does not need to be offered in the eucharist. The priest is not an agent of the Church as the minister of that anxious nagging at God which has so often been deprecated in this work. When Pope Leo XIII pointed out in his Bull *Apostolicae Curae* (1896) that the Anglican Church when it ordained priests had no intention of ordaining people to offer the sacrifice of Christ on behalf of the living and the dead, he was quite correct. But when he drew from that fact the conclusion that Anglican orders were absolutely null and utterly void he condemned his own church. There is no evidence whatever that early ordination services expressed or were intended to express this intention for at least the first three hundred years of the Church's existence.

This then is the true understanding of priesthood. It is one of the clearest doctrines and most precious inheritances of the Anglican Church. There are even some signs that the concept of a priesthood not defined in cultic terms is attracting a few theologians in the Roman Catholic Church. This doctrine is not vulnerable when historical research is applied to it. It does not rest on the assumption that Christ directly instituted a priesthood and therefore avoids the curious arguments which are currently being brought forward against the priesthood of women on the score of Jesus Christ being a man and not a woman. This doctrine rests the priesthood of the priest on the priesthood of all believers, and this priesthood is not usually thought to exclude female believers. The Anglican Reformers were led astray by late mediaeval doctrine so that they could not rightly evaluate the relation of the bishop to the presbyter in priesthood. But there is no reason why we today should do this. Indeed the doctrine of priesthood outlined in these pages, far from being exclusive, is, in our opinion, capable of being extended to identify the ministerial activity of clergy in other, non-episcopal, communions as at least potentially a priestly activity. And we would like to see this principle seriously discussed and considered among leaders of churches beyond the bounds of the Anglican communion.

b. Authentication and Authority

Every Christian denomination wishes to authenticate its ordained ministry both as it actually functions in history and by the standard of the New Testament. Ever since the Reformation however there have been two distinct ways of doing this, a Catholic way and a Protestant way. The Catholic way can be called *lineal* authentication; it makes the claim that the Catholic ordained ministry can show an unbroken line of succession by ordination right back to the apostles and that this proves the regularity, authenticity, and sole right to function of the Catholic ministry. This claim is not confined to Roman Catholics; it is also made by the Eastern Orthodox Churches and would be put forward on behalf of the Anglican ministry by many Anglo-Catholics. The other way of authenticating the ministry could be called *doctrinal*: Protestants on the whole tend to justify the authenticity of their ordained ministry by claiming that their ministers preach pure doctrine according to the standard of the New Testament, and that it is this, and not any line of succession, that authenticates the ministry.

Both claims encounter considerable difficulties in practice. There are two drawbacks to the Catholic claim: the first is that the claim that their ministry goes back in an unbroken line to the apostles is historically very dubious, as we have seen. It breaks down just at the point where it is essential that it should hold firm, the period between the apostles and the Church of the early second century. The other objection is that mere lineal descent does not necessarily preserve the ministry from a corruption so far-reaching as to annul any claims to authenticity. The *reductio ad absurdum* of this view is that a church which had preserved unbroken lineal descent, but whose ministry had become so corrupt, worldly, and obscured by historical accidents as to be hardly recognizable as a Christian ministry could still be a true Church, while, let us say, the Presbyterian church would not be judged a true Church at all. Lineal descent alone will not authenticate a ministry. The difficulty about the Protestant claim is that it assumes that everyone knows what New Testament standards of doctrinal purity are: but this is not the case. In order to decide what is and what is not true doctrine, we have to appeal to the rule of faith or tradition of the Church: but which Church? We are back again where we started, for the whole question is about the authority of the Church. Again, if the authority of the ministry is solely constituted by the purity of its doctrine, does it lose that authority when it strays from that doctrine? There have been periods in the history of all the Churches of the Reformation when their clergy have been gravely affected by gross doctrinal error (e.g. during the Enlightenment of the eighteenth century). Did the Protestant Churches during that period simply cease to have an effective ministry? The Protestant criterion proves to be too subjective.

The essential task of the ordained ministry is to exercise Christ's churchly authority at certain vital points in the life of the Church: but it is a ministry of the Church; it does not operate independently of the Church as a clerical caste or an ecclesiastical order of brahmins. Hence the authenticity of the ministry comes from Christ through the contemporary Church: but that Church is divided, hence the authority of the ordained ministry is divided and to that extent ineffective and irregular. This is a great insight of that fine theologian of the inter-war period, Oliver Chase Quick. We must firmly repudiate the notion which caused such anguish to our nineteenth-century forebears, the idea that we must choose among the existing churches in order to find the 'right' one, the only one that God really approves. The Church is a broken plate, broken into several unequal pieces, not a whole plate slightly chipped, the chips being the Churches of the Reformation. The authority of the ministry properly belongs to the whole Church, which exists in a divided condition, so the authority of all our ministries is to that extent impaired.

One of the notions which has introduced much confusion into the discussion of the authority of the ministry is that of 'validity'. It is a term used in Catholic theology. According to this way of thinking, only the Catholic ministry is valid, i.e. can celebrate the sacraments, declare absolution and excommunication etc., in such a way that God honours it. Thus only a eucharist celebrated by a Catholic priest is valid. The extreme version of this view takes the form of saying that a eucharist celebrated by a minister whose orders are not valid is an empty show, a mere masquerade at which Christ is not present sacramentally. This is to take a very peculiar view of God: even when a group of Christians assembles in perfectly good faith, under the impression that they have a true ministry, and attempt to celebrate the eucharist, he will not (or cannot?) be present as he is present at Catholic altars. In the modern ecumenical climate this extreme version is rarely heard, but a more moderate version involves just as great difficulties: 'we do not say that nothing happens when Protestants celebrate the eucharist, but Christ is not present in the same way as he is at our eucharist:' Well, how is he present at Protestant eucharists? The game becomes absurd, as if there was a first-class guaranteed eucharistic grace for Catholics, and an inferior utility brand for Protestants. It is better in our opinion to abandon the notion of validity altogether: our understanding of God in Christ excludes the possibility that he will refuse to be present at the eucharistic assembly of any Christians who approach him in faith.

'But what about the unjustified schism? What about the layman who, without any justification, quarrels with the Church, sets up his own conventicle, and ordains himself? Are we to recognize the authority of his orders?' No, not necessarily: in the first place, he will have very little authority indeed, only the authority of a tiny dissenting sect. Secondly, the authority of the Church is not, as we have already seen, the only criterion by which we must judge the ordained ministry. The Protestants are right in saying that pure doctrine must be *a* criterion, not the only one, but one certainly. Luther thought he was justified in breaking away from the ministry of the Church of his day specifically on doctrinal grounds. We cannot judge the rights and wrongs of that controversy, but Luther had a case, as many fair-minded Roman Catholics today would admit. There must come a point when doctrinal aberration affects the authority of a church, and therefore of its ministry. For example, the Church of the Latterday Saints, though very numerous in some parts of America, does not have the authority of God in Christ, because it has hopelessly corrupted the teaching of the New Testament.

To sum up: we do not need, and should not attempt, to unchurch any body of Christians. The question must arise in the case of some who claim to be Christian whether they are so. Obviously difficult decisions may have to be made, but we may suggest that not only Mormons, but also Jehovah's Witnesses and the Christian Scientists have forfeited the right to be regarded as Christians by the rest of the Church because they have deviated so far from the tradition of the Church and the teaching of the New Testament by claiming new revelation through individuals. Next, we must strive to unify the ministries of the divided Church: this will bring benefit to all in the shape of a more fully authorized ministry. And lastly, there are circumstances in which we should refuse to recognize a man's (or woman's) orders, in order to emphasize the wrongness of arbitrary schism: but this does not mean that God in Christ will not be present at the prayers or eucharist of the misguided group. As the devil remarks somewhere in C. S. Lewis' *Screwtape Letters*, God has no proper sense of his own dignity. Indeed we might have guessed that long before C. S. Lewis' day if we had understood the significance of the cross.

The doctrine of the ministry which we have outlined here carries the implication that the essential continuity of the Church through the ages is provided by the body of the faithful, not primarily by the succession of the ordained ministry. Hence we may not unchurch any group of Christians solely on the grounds that they cannot claim unbroken ministerial succession; but this does not mean that ministerial succession can be ignored. In fact the vast majority of existing denominations take great care to safeguard succession in the ministry, whatever their historical antecedents. We may therefore claim that ministerial succession is a sign of the continuity of the Church, though not a sacrament of it. As such, succession in the ministry is not to be discarded lightly.

c. Episcopacy

It is no longer possible for conscientious scholars to defend episcopacy on the grounds that it was the form of Church government instituted by Our Lord, nor that it can be traced back in unbroken succession to the apostles, nor that it is the only form of Church government which can guarantee a valid ministry. This does not mean, however, that episcopacy is simply one of a number of equally satisfactory methods of governing the Church. Much can be said in defence of episcopacy without indulging in indefensible claims for it.

In the first place, it is undoubtedly the oldest method. Mon-episcopacy (government of the local church by one bishop and a group of presbyters) goes back to a time very early indeed in the second century. It must be said however that the bishop of the second to the fourth century was a rather different functionary from the figure we associate with the name 'bishop' today. He would correspond more closely to the vicar of the parish church in a town which had only one outstanding parish church. The huge sees to which we are accustomed nowadays had not yet emerged. However, bishops there certainly were in most churches very early in the second century. This means that episcopacy is older than any Catholic creed, older than the Canon of the New Testament, older than any liturgy known to us. The institution has therefore a great weight of tradition on its side.

There is another reason why episcopacy may well be the best form of government for the Church. Christianity is a religion much concerned with persons and the personal. It preaches a personal God, who uniquely revealed himself in a person, Jesus Christ: but episcopacy, when rightly used, is a very personal form of ministry. The bishop represents his diocese to the rest of the Church and the rest of the Church to his diocese. This representational office is carried out not, as in some other forms of Church government, by a commission or committee, but a person. The bishop is expected to have a personal, spiritual, paternal, relationship towards all his clergy and most of the laity in his diocese. Episcopacy properly exercised is a very personal work. The average lay person ought to see in the bishop the presence of the Church in person.

Undoubtedly many bishops succeed in exercising this personal ministry very well: but, just because episcopacy is perhaps potentially the best method of governing the Church, its corruption produces the worst evils: a tyrannical, petty-minded, weak, or ambitious bishop can do more harm in his diocese and elsewhere than the most ineffective kirk session or ministers' committee. A personal ministry exercised by an unworthy, ineffective, or conceited person is worse than no ministry at all.

d. The Papacy

One of the earlier reactions of the Church of England at the Reformation was to draw up a new Litany and in that Litany to place one prayer:

> From the bishop of Rome and all his detestable enormities:
> Good Lord, deliver us!

It is significant that this petition was omitted from the Elizabethan Prayer Book. Anglicanism has never finally, irreversibly and unforgivably repudiated the Pope, as other religious traditions appear to have done. One reason for this is that Anglican churches have always had a strong sense of continuity. In England this continuity is emphasized by the Church's possession of the mediaeval churches and cathedrals; in Ireland it is emphasized by the insistence of parishes on retaining their old Irish names which date to periods long before the Reformation. A consciousness of continuity with the past cannot fail to recall that there were many centuries when the Pope was not a *persona non grata* in the English Church, when on the contrary both the person and the institution were respected and welcomed.

Nobody who is acquainted with the history of the early mediaeval Church can doubt either that the supremacy of the Pope as it developed during that period was accepted *ex animo* by the vast majority of Christians in the West, and not least in England, nor that there were occasions when the Pope was genuinely a champion of freedom and justice and truth against those who were their enemies. The Western Church undoubtedly accepted the Papal leadership at least till the outbreak of the Investiture Contest in the eleventh century and felt that it was in the interest of the whole Church to see that the institution of the Papacy did not suffer either by corruption from within or by assault from without, and even after the Investiture Contest it readily accepted Papal leadership during the early Crusades. The Western Church was quite ready to allow the Pope to rule as arbiter, as supreme court of appeal in ecclesiastical causes and as moral leader of Europe.

Later history drastically changed the character and destiny of the Papacy as it changed the attitude of the nations of Europe to it. Perhaps it was when the Pope was a relatively distant figure that he was at his most popular and useful. The more he made himself felt in the ordinary affairs of the local church the more his popularity waned. When in the sixteenth century, under the influence of the continental Reformation and domestic needs, the Church of England repudiated the authority of the Pope, he had reached his lowest point of unpopularity. And when in the nineteenth century under the pressure of various historical circumstances the Roman Catholic Church pursued a policy of centralization round the office of Papacy whose most dramatic moment was a declaration of the Pope's infallibility in 1870, the gulf between Anglicans and the Papacy was wider than ever. It only needed the Bull of Leo XIII in 1896 condemning Anglican Orders as invalid to make the gulf seem impassable.

But the Roman Church of 1980 is very different from that of 1896. In the ecumenical atmosphere of today it is the duty of Anglicans to think seriously and unpolemically about their attitude to the Papacy. They cannot agree that this institution exists as of divine right if this means that it was directly founded by Jesus Christ. The arguments about the Church and ministry in many parts of this book will have made clear why this is so. The connection of the see of Rome with words which the Lord may or may not have said to Peter is tenuous in the extreme and a quite inadequate basis upon which to build any doctrine of papal authority. But if the Pope were to rest his claim for authority over Western Christians upon history, i.e. tradition, and not upon Scripture, merely maintaining that the claim is not inconsistent with Scripture, he would have a much stronger case to which Anglicans would be bound to listen. The days of a despotic Papacy are over, even for Roman Catholics. The Pope, having been forced reluctantly to give up his claim to temporal power in the nineteenth century, has gained greatly in moral authority. As long as, in the words of George Salmon, he insisted upon his right to misgovern a few thousand Italians, his deeds so loudly belied his words that they could not be heard. But now the case is different. If a future Pope were to approach the Anglican communion, wholly disavowing any desire to exercise jurisdiction over them, but asking them to recognize him as honorary Primate of the Western Church wielding moral, not legal, authority and leadership, and showing himself ready to consult them instead of condemning or excommunicating them, they would find it hard to reject such an offer. Anglicans need an international Papacy to safeguard them against one of their chief temptations, insularity, or, to put the matter more plainly, the tendency to think that what matters is not Catholicity but Englishness. In the proper circumstances they could probably be induced to recollect their past happy relations with the Pope and to re-enter his fold.

But the shepherd of that fold would have to make it quite clear that he was a different shepherd from most of his immediate predecessors, one who had learnt from history, and perhaps was even ready to learn from the toleration of scholarly opinion and comprehensiveness which today are among the best features of Anglicanism. If Anglicans are morally bound to reconsider their attitude to the Papacy, the Pope himself should look at his own position in the ecumenical scene. Is a single bishop justified in holding up the reunion of Christendom because of claims made about himself and his see? Can these claims seriously be regarded as touching the very nature and life of the Church? It is difficult, perhaps it is impossible, for Orthodox, Free Churchmen and Anglicans to answer these questions in the affirmative.

Epilogue

An epilogue to a work like this one should serve the purpose of justifying certain leading features in the work itself, and of attempting to set the reader on the path of continuing the theological task which has been undertaken in the work.

Two features of this book might seem to require some justification: the first is the proportion of space which we have allotted to the various areas of Christian belief. We have in fact concentrated our main attention on belief in God and on belief in Christ, both the person of Christ and the work of Christ. The topics of Church, Sacraments and Ministry have been given relatively less attention. This is because belief in God and belief in Christ are areas of Christian belief about which there is most debate among theologians at the present time, and which therefore call for closer attention. Had we been writing in the last century, perhaps we might have given more attention to the doctrine of the Church, since this is a topic on which many thoughtful people were then deeply divided and which they regarded as of literally eternal significance. Today the progress of the ecumenical movement has taught us both to be less certain that we know the exact limits of the Church, and to be less convinced that it matters that we should know them. On the other hand there has been during the last fifteen years a radical reappraisal of the Christian doctrine of God, and a sharp challenge to the traditional doctrine of the person of Christ. We decided therefore that we must give most attention to those areas of the battlefield of faith where the conflict rages most strongly.

The other point that might seem to call for some defence is the attention we give to contemporary thought. Not that we invariably walk according to the *Zeitgeist*, but that we try to be aware of what the *Zeitgeist* is saying about the topics which we discuss. We wish to be in dialogue with the *Zeitgeist*, as far as this is practicable. The reason for this is probably that when we were students we experienced the effect of two quite distinct movements of thought among Christians, both of which were based on the principle that contemporary thought should be ignored by Christian theologians. Catholics seemed to be held in thrall by a form of Integralism which maintained that all saving truth was already securely within the grasp of the Catholic Church, and that attempts to come to terms with modern knowledge, whether in the form of cosmology or of biblical criticism, were merely a sign of weakness and lack of faith. Among Protestants on the other hand the Barthian thesis was most influential, to the effect that Christian thinkers should never attempt to harmonize their theology with contemporary (or indeed more ancient) philosophy, and that all efforts on the part of man to understand anything of God apart from revelation were sinful and bound to mislead. The consequence of these two movements was that the Catholic Church found itself unable to put forward any account of Christianity that could be seriously considered by well-educated unbelievers; and that non-Christian philosophers came to regard theology as nothing more than a form of learned nonsense. With these two terrible warnings before us, we could not fail to aspire that our theology should always be written with the challenges and criticism of contemporary thought in mind.

We hope that the book itself adequately illustrates what we conceive to be the task of an Anglican theologian: Christian belief must be justified in terms of the witness of the Bible, of the history of Christian tradition (i.e. the theology which Christians have written since New Testament times up till the present day), and of what our own reason can tell us. None of these three elements must be regarded as infallible or in itself decisive, but none can safely be ignored.

We have, perhaps arrogantly, claimed that this is a characteristically Anglican approach. But if it is regarded as an *exclusively* Anglican approach it will have failed in its objective. Our hope is that this will become increasingly the ecumenical way of writing theology. Indeed the main (perhaps the only ultimate) justification for Anglicanism is that is has perhaps been appointed by God for a certain period to hold the ring until the rest of the Christian tradition can join it in the same task. To Anglicanism surely can be appropriately applied that sentence that is the motto of the Irish School of Ecumenics: *floreat ut pereat* (may it flourish in order to perish). We only wish to continue calling ourselves Anglicans (itself a restrictive name – the whole Church can never be Anglican any more than it can be Roman) until the time comes when all Christian theologians can write as Catholic Christians, not Roman Catholic or Anglo-Catholic, not even as Protestant or Evangelical, but merely as Catholics who, just because they are Catholic, are also evangelical. That aim today seems a great deal more capable of realization than it did even as recently as twenty years ago. We look forward in faith and hope to the time when a survey of Christian belief can be written no longer from the point of view of one tradition, but from the point of view of the ecumenical Church. We pray that this book may in some measure serve to hasten that day.

Books recommended for Reading

Books marked with an asterisk are more advanced.

Introduction
*Karl Barth, *Church Dogmatics* (8vols. Eng. tr. Edinburgh, 1936–1962)
*Paul Tillich, *Systematic Theology* (3 vols. London, 1978)
*Karl Rahner, *Foundations of Christian Faith* (Eng. tr. London, 1978)
*Hans Küng, *On Being a Christian* (Eng. tr. London, 1977)
*J. Macquarrie, *Principles of Christian Theology* (London, 1979)

Barth's vast work is a classical monument of neo-orthodox systematic theology, written with great verve and no little wit, and will lead the reader into deep waters. Tillich's trilogy is rather less demanding: he is still a favourite theologian among Anglicans, perhaps because he does not eschew calling upon the aid of philosophy. Rahner's *Foundations* represents the work of a Catholic theologian who has drunk deeply at the well of Protestant Existentialism. Küng's *On Being a Christian* is an outstanding piece of writing, at once comprehensive, compact, and brilliant, and wholly devoid of inhibition or prejudice.

I.1
H. D. Lewis, *Our Experience of God* (London, 1959)
H. P. Owen, *The Christian Knowledge of God* (London, 1969)
N. Smart, *The Religious Experience of Mankind* (London, 1971)
*I. T. Ramsay, *Religious Language* (London, 1957)
*W. Pannenberg, *Theology and the Philosophy of Science* (Eng. tr. London, 1976)
R. Garaudy, *The Alternative Future* (Eng. tr. London, 1976)
*E. L. Mascall, *The Openness of Being* (London, 1971)
*P. Teilhard de Chardin, *The Phenomenon of Man* (Eng. tr. London, 1959)
B. Lovell, *The Centre of Immensities* (London, 1979)
Ian Barbour, *Issues in Science and Religion* (London, 1966)
T. F. Torrance, *Space, Time, and Incarnation* (Oxford, 1978)
    Theological Science (Oxford, 1978)
*R. C. Neville, *God the Creator* (London, 1978)
P. Homans, *Theology after Freud* (Indianapolis, 1970)
G. Zilbodeg, *Psychoanalysis and Religion* (London, 1967)
*J. Moltmann, *The Crucified God*, Cap. 7 (Eng. tr. London, 1976)

H. D. Lewis' book is an excellent philosophic defence of religious experience, in terms of regarding God as the limit of our knowledge. R. Garaudy's book is the third in a series in which he describes how he came to Christian faith by means of his reflections on man's relation to nature and history. Mascall's *The Openness of Being* is a skilful defence of a neo-Thomist position. Teilhard de Chardin's work is his *magnum opus*, difficult but well worth attempting.

I.2

James Barr, *The Bible in the Modern World* (London, 1977)
James Bright, *The Authority of the Old Testament* (London, 1967)
*J. H. Newman, *The Grammar of Assent* (Penguin ed., Harmondsworth, 1964)
*S. Kierkegaard, *Concluding Unscientific Postscript* (Eng. tr. London, 1945)
G. Ebeling, *The Nature of Faith* (Eng. tr. London, 1961)
R. P. C. Hanson, *The Attractiveness of God* (London, 1973)
A. V. Harvey, *The Historian and the Believer* (New York, 1966)
John Baillie, *The Idea of Revelation in Recent Thought* (London, 1956)

Newman's *Grammar of Assent* sets out at length his original theory about the mechanics of belief. Kierkegaard's *Concluding Unscientific Postscript* is generally reckoned to be the climax of his theological and philosophical work, dense, difficult, but most rewarding for those who are ready to wrestle with him. Ebeling's book on faith is a lucid and persuasive presentation of Luther's concept of faith.

I.3

James Barr, *Old and New in Interpretation* (London, 1966)
    Fundamentalism (London, 1977)
S. Neill, *The Interpretation of the New Testament 1891–1961* (London, 1966)
A. Richardson, *The Bible in an Age of Science* (London, 1961)
D. Nineham, *The Use and Abuse of the Bible* (London, 1976)
D. H. Kelsey, *The Uses of Scripture in Recent Theology* (London, 1976)
G. H. Tavard, *Holy Writ and Holy Church* (London, 1959)

Barr's *Fundamentalism* is a recent and rare book on the subject. Neill's *The Interpretation of the New Testament* is an able and moderate account of New Testament criticism since the mid-nineteenth century. Nineham and Kelsey represent the school of thought which decries or denies the possibility of our using the Bible as a norm of faith.

I.4

N. Smart, *A Dialogue of Religions* (London, 1961)
    World Religions – A Dialogue (London, 1966)
E. J. Sharpe, *Not to Destroy but to Fulfil* (Lund, 1965)
H. Kraemer, *The Christian Message in a non-Christian World* (Eng. tr. London, 1938)
L. W. Gillet, *Communion in the Messiah* (London, 1942)
K. Cragg, *The Christian and Other Religions* (London, 1977)
    The Call of the Minaret (Oxford, 1956)
R. Pannikar, *The Unknown Christ of Hinduism* (London, 1965)
K. Klostermaier, *Hindu and Christian in Vrindaban* (London, 1968)
Wm. Johnston, *Silent Music* (London, 1976)

E. J. Sharpe describes the work of a pioneer in the field of positive relations between Christianity and Hinduism. K. Kraemer boldly defends a Barthian position of discontinuity between Christianity and other religions. K. Cragg is a sympathetic and well-informed exponent of Islam. Both R. Pannikar and K. Klostermaier write from extensive knowledge of Hinduism from the inside. Wm. Johnston has great acquaintance with Japanese Buddhism. L. W. Gillet's book is about common ground between Christians and Jews.

II.5

D. M. Baillie, *God was in Christ* (London, 1956)
N. J. Pittenger, *The Incarnate Word* (London, 1959)
A. T. Hanson, *Grace and Truth* (London, 1975)
H. E. W. Turner, *Jesus the Christ* (London, 1976)
G. Vermes, *Jesus the Jew* (London, 1976)
C. F. D. Moule, *The Origin of Christology* (Cambridge, 1977)
*W. Pannenberg, *Jesus: God and Man* (Eng. tr. London, 1970)
*A. Grillmeier, *Christ in Christian Tradition* (Eng. tr. London, 1975)
J. N. D. Kelly, *Early Christian Doctrines* (London, 1977)
M. Hengel, *The Son of God* (Eng. tr. London, 1976)
*Karl Rahner, *Theological Investigations* Vol. I (Eng. tr. London, 1966)
J. A. T. Robinson, *The Human Face of God* (London, 1974)
*W. Kasper, *Jesus the Christ* (Eng. tr. London, 1976)
*H. Oppenheimer, *Incarnation and Immanence* (London, 1973)
R. H. Fuller, *The Formation of the Resurrection Narratives* (London, 1972)
W. Marxsen, *The Resurrection of Jesus of Nazareth* (Eng. tr. London, 1970)
S. Sykes and R. Clayton, *Christ, Faith, and History* (Cambridge, 1972)
M. Wiles, *The Making of Christian Doctrine* (Cambridge, 1975)
   The Remaking of Christian Doctrine (London, 1975)

D. M. Baillie's work was a seminal one when it was published. It is completed and continued by N. J. Pittenger; both advocate what could be called a neo-Nestorian approach to the doctrine of the incarnation. H. E. W. Turner's little book is chiefly valuable for its account of the doctrine of the incarnation in the Fathers. G. Vermes, writing as a Jew, shows remarkable insight in his handling of the historical life of Jesus. W. Pannenberg is interesting as one who, coming out of the school of Bultmann, works out a full doctrine of incarnation. K. Rahner's essay is not at all easy, but (as always with this author) very rewarding for those who persevere. R. H. Fuller gives a critical but not wholly reductionist account of the resurrection (in contrast with Marxsen). M. Wiles is illuminating in his first book, and rather disappointing in the sequel: very little Christian doctrine remains when he has finished with it.

II.6

St. Anselm, *Cur Deus Homo*
J. McLeod Campbell, *The Nature of the Atonement* (mod. ed. London, 1959)
R. C. Moberly, *Atonement and Personality* (London, 1901)
E. Brunner, *The Mediator* (Eng. tr. London, 1967)
J. Moltmann, *The Crucified God* (Eng. tr. London, 1976)
H. A. Hodges, *The Pattern of Atonement* (London, 1959)

F. W. Dillistone, *The Christian Understanding of the Atonement* (London, 1968)
*Martin Luther, *Commentary on Galatians* (ed. and tr. P. Watson, London, 1953)
*S. Kierkegaard, *The Sickness unto Death* (Eng. tr. Princeton, 1946)
G. Rupp, *The Righteousness of God* (London, 1953)
P. Watson, *Let God Be God* (London, 1948)
*F. Dostoevsky, *The Brothers Karamazov*
*Reinhold Niebuhr, *The Nature and Destiny of Man* (2 vols, London, 1941)
Blaise Pascal, *Pensées* (Eng. tr. London, 1979)
    Provincial Letters (Eng. tr. London, 1967)
N. Berdyaev, *The Destiny of Man* (Eng. tr. London, 1937)
    Freedom and the Spirit (Eng. tr. London, 1938)
J. W. Oman, *Grace and Personality* (Cambridge, 1925)
Karl Barth, *The Humanity of God* (Eng. tr. London, 1961)

Anselm's seminal work, published in 1096, set the current for the theology of the atonement until the Reformation. McLeod Campbell's book is written in a dreadfully clumsy style, but was the first blast of the trumpet against the hitherto dominant Calvinist doctrine of the atonement. Brunner's *The Mediator* reflects the full flood of neo-orthodox reaction against Liberal Protestantism. Dillistone's work is a particularly useful and full account of the different approaches to the atonement to be found throughout Christian history. Rupp and Watson supply able and sympathetic accounts of Luther's atonement doctrine. Reinhold Niebuhr's book is now a classic. It is the work of an American liberal theologian of great ability, captivated by the light that Augustine throws on morality, politics and human existence. Oman's *Grace and Personality* is a Modernist polemic against Augustine's doctrine of grace. Pascal's two works show a French Catholic genius working on the age-old problem of God's grace and man's free will.

III.8

*G. W. H. Lampe, *God as Spirit* (Oxford, 1977)
J. D. G. Dunn, *Baptism in the Holy Spirit* (London, 1970)
    Jesus and the Spirit (London, 1975)
Michael Green, *I Believe in the Holy Spirit* (London, 1975)
V. Lossky, *Mystical Theology in the Eastern Church* (London, 1957)
J. V. Taylor, *The Go-Between God* (London, 1975)

Dunn's *Baptism in the Holy Spirit* is a persuasive and well-documented argument for the relevance of charismatic Christianity. Michael Green's work is a moderate and wise presentation of Anglican doctrine by an Evangelical theologian. Lossky's book is a well-known vindication of Orthodox theology, perhaps a little too good to be true.

IV.9

C. Welch, *The Trinity in Contemporary Theology* (London, 1953)
*Karl Rahner, *The Trinity* (Eng. tr. London 1975)

L. Hodgson, *The Doctrine of the Trinity* (London, 1963)
*G. C. Stead, *Divine Substance* (Oxford, 1977)

C. Welch has written a lively account of the doctrine of the Trinity from a Barthian point of view. Leonard Hodgson's work on the Trinity adopts a position which veers much too far in the direction of tritheism, but it is one which is typical of much recent Anglican writing on the subject. G. C. Stead in *Divine Substance*, giving a full account of the meaning of the word *ousia* in Greek thought, shows how far the term had changed its meaning between Plato and Athanasius.

V.10

*J. H. Newman, *Essay on the Development of Christian Doctrine* (Penguin, Harmondsworth, 1974)
George Salmon, *The Infallibility of the Church* (2nd ed. London, 1880)
Y. Congar, *Tradition and Traditions* (London, 1966)
 Tradition and the Life of the Church (Eng. tr. London, 1964)
F. F. Bruce, *Tradition Old and New* (London, 1970)
*R. P. C. Hanson, *Tradition in the Early Church* (London, 1962)
*E. J. Meijering, *God Being History* (Amsterdam, 1975)
J. Pelikan, *The Development of Christian Doctrine* (New Haven, 1969)

Newman's essay is indispensable for understanding the subject. Salmon's *Infallibility* is a sparkling, hard-hitting reply which only partly succeeds in answering Newman. Congar from the viewpoint of a liberal Catholic, and Pelikan from that of a liberal Lutheran, give weighty and useful accounts of the subject.

V.11

A. Richardson, *History, Sacred and Profane* (London, 1964)
*W. Pannenberg, *Basic Questions in Theology*, Vol. I (Eng. tr. London, 1970), Vol. II (1973)
 Revelation as History (Eng. tr. London, 1979)
R. Garaudy, *Marxism in the Twentieth Century* (Eng. tr. London, 1970)
J. Hick, *Evil and the God of Love* (London, 1977)
A. Farrer, *Love Almighty and Ills Unlimited* (London, 1962)
Klaus Koch, *The Rediscovery of Apocalyptic* (Eng. tr. London, 1972)
*R. Bultmann, *History and Eschatology* (Eng. tr. Edinburgh, 1957)
John Baillie, *And the Life Everlasting* (8th imp. London, 1960)

History, Sacred and Profane is a typically Anglican work in its moderation and good sense. Hick's and Farrer's books complement each other as outstanding works by two theologians of very different traditions. Bultmann's book illustrates the possibilities of a non-futurist use of eschatology.

VI. 13

E. Mersch, *The Whole Christ* (Eng. tr. London, 1949)
L. S. Thornton, *The Common Life in the Body of Christ* (London, 1942)
E. Best, *One Body in Christ* (London, 1955)

L. Newbigin, *The Reunion of the Church* (London, 1948)
The Household of God (London, 1953)
Hans Küng, *Structures of the Church* (Eng. tr. London, 1965)
The Church (Eng. tr. London, 1969)
A. T. Hanson, *Church, Sacraments and Ministry* (London, 1975)

Mersch's book as a very full account of ecclesiology written before the reconciling event of Vatican II. L.S.Thornton's work is a splendid piece of biblical exegesis. Both of L. Newbigin's books are obligatory reading because they come from a most competent theologian in the Reformed tradition, and also because they reflect experience in the one place where there has been a breakthrough in church unity, the Indian sub-continent. H. Küng should be read as a Roman Catholic theologian deeply influenced by the ecumenical movement.

VI.14

G. R. Beasley-Murray, *Baptism in the New Testament* (London, 1962)
G. Wainwright, *Christian Initiation* (London, 1969)
J. D. C. Fisher, *Christian Initiation: Baptism in the Mediaeval West* (London, 1970)
Modern Eucharistic Agreement (London, 1973)
A Critique of Eucharistic Agreement (London, 1975)
H. Martelet, *The Risen Christ in Eucharistic History* (Eng. tr. London, 1976)
O. C. Quick, *The Christian Sacraments* (London, 1929)
D. M. Baillie, *The Theology of the Sacraments* (London, 1957)
E. Schillebeeckx, *Christ: The Sacrament of the Encounter with God* (Eng. tr. London, 1975)
The Eucharist (Eng. tr. London, 1977)
R. J. Daly *The Origins of the Christian Doctrine of Sacrifice* (Philadelphia, 1978)

G. Wainwright gives a most competent account of the doctrine of baptism from what might be called a Methodist-ecumenical point of view. H. Martelet is worth reading because as a Roman Catholic starting from a rather conservative biblical position he shows a remarkable willingness to reassess the way in which we should express the nature of Christ's presence in the eucharist. O. C. Quick and D. M. Baillie give excellent and well-balanced accounts of the Sacraments; one is an Anglican, the other a Church of Scotland theologian; their agreement at so many points is impressive. The book by the Jesuit father R. J. Daly, the fruit of massive research, describes Christian sacrifice as moral and practical and not ritual; it is likely to make a considerable impression.

VI.15

Hans Küng, *Justification* (Eng. tr. London, 1966)
Küng's book is an attempt to show that the doctrine of the Counter-Reformation Council of Trent on justification is in fact the same in substance as that of Luther and Calvin. In a preface to the book Karl Barth suggests that if Küng is right, the Reformation is over.

VI. 16

A. T. Hanson, *The Pioneer Ministry* (2nd ed. London, 1975)

A. von Campenhausen, *Ecclesiastical Authority and Spiritual Power in the Church of the First Three Centuries* (Eng. tr. London, 1969)

E. Schweizer, *Church Order in the New Testament* (Eng. tr. London, 1961)

R. C. Moberly, *Ministerial Priesthood* (ed. with intro. by A. T. Hanson, London, 1969)

R. P. C. Hanson, *Christian Priesthood Examined* (London, 1979)

N. Lash, *Voices of Authority* (London, 1976)

J. W. Oman, *Authority and Religion* (London, 1902)

B. C. Butler, *The Church and Infallibility* (London, 1969)

S. Sykes, *The Integrity of Anglicanism* (London, 1978)

S. Neill, *Anglicanism* (Oxford, 1978)

W. Telfer, *The Office of a Bishop* (London, 1962)

J. J. Hughes, *Absolutely Null and Utterly Void* (London, 1968)

Stewards of the Lord (London, 1970)

P. J. McCord (ed.), *A Pope for all Christians* (London, 1976)

R. C. Moberly's work is the classic Anglican exposition of the doctrine of the ministry, basing it ultimately on Mark 10:45 rather than on the eucharistic sacrifice. Von Campenhausen has written a magisterial treatment of the origins of the ministry, showing how impossible it is to claim that Jesus initiated an 'apostolical succession' in the conventional sense of the term. E. Schweizer tells us what can, and what cannot, be claimed about the ministry if we are to treat the New Testament evidence honestly. W. Telfer gives some valuable insights on the evolution of episcopacy during the first four centuries. J. J. Hughes' book gives an amusing and illuminating history of the event that led up to Pope Leo XIII's condemnation of Anglican orders in 1896.

Index of Bible References

Index of Names